D0787049

Dramaturgy: A Revolution in Theatre

Dramaturgy: A Revolution in Theatre is the first substantial history of the origins
of dramaturgs and literary managers. It frames the recent explosion of professional
appointments in England within a wider continental map reaching back to the
Enlightenment and eighteenth-century Germany, examining the work of the major
theorists and practitioners of dramaturgy, from Granville Barker and Gotthold
Lessing to Brecht and Tynan. This study is the first to position Brecht's model of
dramaturgy as central to the world-wide revolution in theatre-making practices,
and is also the first work to make a substantial argument for Granville Barker's
and Tynan's contributions to the development of literary management today.
With the territories of play- and performance-making being increasingly
hotly contested, and the public's appetite for new plays showing no sign of
diminishing, Mary Luckhurst investigates the dramaturg as a cultural and
political phenomenon.

MARY LUCKHURST is Senior Lecturer in Drama at the University of York.
Her publications include *On Directing, On Acting* and *The Drama Handbook*
(with John Lennard), and she has co-edited *Theatre and Celebrity in Britain
1660–2000*. Her current projects include editing *Blackwell's Companion to
Modern British and Irish Drama* and *Blackwell's Companion to Contemporary
Drama*, and writing a book on Caryl Churchill. She has written numerous
articles on contemporary theatre for journals such as *Contemporary Theatre
Review*. In addition to her academic research, Mary Luckhurst is also a
playwright, dramaturg and director, and has most recently directed Caryl
Churchill's *Far Away* at the York Theatre Royal.

CAMBRIDGE STUDIES IN MODERN THEATRE

Series editor
David Bradby, *Royal Holloway, University of London*

Advisory board
Martin Banham, *University of Leeds*
Jacky Bratton, *Royal Holloway, University of London*
Tracy Davis, *Northwestern University*
Sir Richard Eyre
Michael Robinson, *University of East Anglia*
Sheila Stowell, *University of Birmingham*

Volumes for Cambridge Studies in Modern Theatre explore the political, social and cultural functions of theatre while also paying careful attention to detailed performance analysis. The focus of the series is on political approaches to the modern theatre with attention also being paid to theatres of earlier periods and their influence on contemporary drama. Topics in the series are chosen to investigate this relationship and include both playwrights (their aims and intentions set against the effects of their work) and process (with emphasis on rehearsal and production methods, the political structure within theatre companies and their choice of audiences or performance venues). Further topics will include devised theatre, agitprop, community theatre, para-theatre and performance art. In all cases the series will be alive to the special cultural and political factors operating in the theatres examined.

Books published
Maria DiCenzo, *The Politics of Alternative Theatre in Britain, 1968–1990: the Case of 7:84 (Scotland)*
Jo Riley, *Chinese Theatre and the Actor in Performance*
Jonathan Kalb, *The Theatre of Heiner Müller*
Richard Boon and Jane Plastow, eds., *Theatre Matters: Performance and Culture on the World Stage*
Claude Schumacher, ed., *Staging the Holocaust: the Shoah in Drama and Performance*

Philip Roberts, *The Royal Court Theatre and the Modern Stage*

Nicholas Grene, *The Politics of Irish Drama: Plays in Context from Boucicault to Friel*

Anatoly Smeliansky, *The Russian Theatre after Stalin*

Clive Barker and Maggie B. Gale, eds., *British Theatre between the Wars, 1918–1939*

Michael Patterson, *Strategies of Political Theatre: Post-War British Playwrights*

Elaine Aston, *Feminist Views on the English Stage: Women Playwrights, 1990–2000*

Gabriele Griffin, *Contemporary Black and Asian Women Playwrights in Britain*

Loren Kruger, *Post-Imperial Brecht: Politics and Performance, East and South*

David Barnett, *Rainer Werner Fassbinder and the German Theatre*

792.023
L964

WITHDRAWN

Dramaturgy

A Revolution in Theatre

Mary Luckhurst
University of York

CAMBRIDGE
UNIVERSITY PRESS

CAMBRIDGE UNIVERSITY PRESS

Cambridge, New York, Melbourne, Madrid, Cape Town, Singapore, São Paulo

Cambridge University Press

The Edinburgh Building, Cambridge CB2 8RU, UK

Published in the United States of America by Cambridge University Press, New York

www.cambridge.org
Information on this title: www.cambridge.org/9780521849630

© Mary Luckhurst 2006

This publication is in copyright. Subject to statutory exception
and to the provisions of relevant collective licensing agreements,
no reproduction of any part may take place without
the written permission of Cambridge University Press.

First published 2006
Reprinted 2007

Printed in the United Kingdom at the University Press, Cambridge

A catalogue record for this publication is available from the British Library

ISBN-13 978-0-521-84963-0 hardback

Cambridge University Press has no responsibility for
the persistence or accuracy of URLs for external or
third-party internet websites referred to in this book,
and does not guarantee that any content on such
websites is, or will remain, accurate or appropriate.

For John Lennard

C H A P. XX.

A manager's difficulty arifing from the offer of new plays and farces --- Reafons affigned for refufing them ---- Colley Cibber's behaviour to authors ---- Mr. Garrick puts a negative on Douglas ---- Cleone and the Orphan of China ---- Agrees to refer the merit of the latter to the arbitration of Mr. Whitehead --- Manœuvres of the author and manager --- Obliged to act it.

THE moft difficult and irkfome tafk which a manager of a theatre can, perhaps, undergo, arifes from his connection with authors. To accept, or refufe a play, is a matter of more confequence than the world in general imagines.

Thomas Davies, *Memoirs of the Life of David Garrick* (2 vols., London: [n.p.] 1780), I, 207. By permission of the Syndics of Cambridge University Library.

Contents

List of illustrations   x
Acknowledgements   xi
List of abbreviations   xiii

1   Introduction   *1*
2   Gotthold Lessing and the *Hamburg Dramaturgy*   24
3   Dramaturgy in nineteenth-century England   *45*
4   William Archer and Harley Granville Barker:
    constructions of the literary manager   *78*
5   Bertolt Brecht: the theory and practice of the
    dramaturg   *109*
6   Kenneth Tynan and the National Theatre   *152*
7   Dramaturgy and literary management in England
    today   *200*
8   Conclusion   *263*

Select bibliography   *268*
Index   *286*

Illustrations

Figure 1.1   Michael Maslin, 'Is there a doctor of literature in
the house?' Reproduced with permission from the
New Yorker   3

Figure 1.2   Joseph Farris, 'Is there a spin doctor in the house?'
Reproduced with permission from the *New
Yorker*   4

Figure 7.1   Model for context of value judgements. Diagram
by Graham Whybrow, Royal Court Theatre,
London.   *217*

Acknowledgements

This book was born of my curiosity as a playwright, dramaturg and theatre historian. All playwrights wonder about the readers of their plays, and in England dramaturgs encounter mystified questions about their work. I simply began with the question of why so little appeared to be known about the history and practice of literary management in England.

I could not have undertaken this research without funding. The Harold Hyam Wingate Foundation and the AHRB were my principal backers. The Society for Theatre Research financed my survey work, the F. R. Leavis Fund paid for illustrations, and Corpus Christi College provided further support. To all I am deeply grateful.

I have been privileged to have distinguished scholars reading my work throughout. Anne Barton, John Barton, Jean Chothia, Mike Cordner, Peter Holland, Dennis Kennedy, Adrian Poole and Richard Rowland encouraged my work and I owe them much. Marion Kant's feedback on Lessing and particularly Brecht was inspirational, and with her help I was able to interview the *eminences grises* of the Berliner Ensemble. John Lennard was indefatigable in his support, never tired of listening to me, and taught me much about academic rigour. Dominic Shellard and Chloe Veltman gave useful insights, and students at the Central School of Speech and Drama, the University of Birmingham, RADA, the University of York and St Margaret's College, Edinburgh, stoked me with provocative questions.

I have spoken to numerous theatre practitioners in the course of my work, especially playwrights, literary managers, directors and dramaturgs, and it is impossible to name them all. David Edgar has enabled my work in ways which I have found humbling. Francis Alexander, Alan Ayckbourn, Barbara Bell, Suzanne Bell, Volker Braun, Ian Brown, Colin Chambers, Sarah Dickinson, Laura Harvey, Ben Jancovich, Edward Kemp, Jonathan Meth, Louise Mulvey, Julia Pascal, Michael Raab (everybody's dream dramaturg), Simon Reade, Esther Richardson, Paul Sirett, Max Stafford-Clark and Steve Waters dedicated time and thought to my questions. Discussions with Graham Whybrow and Maja Zade, Jack Bradley, Ben Payne and Lloyd Trott were very enlightening.

I have consulted many libraries and theatre archives, and would especially like to thank the Secretary to the Board and Gavin Clarke at the NT, the staff at the Bertolt Brecht Archives, Sally Brown at the British Library, the BBC, the RSC and librarians at the Churchill Archive. Lloyd Trott generously made his personal collections available. Readers' reports were a great help, and Victoria Cooper was an enthusiastic and supportive editor.

Finally, I am grateful to my father for all his support over the years; to my brother Roger for trying to find theatre 'interesting'; to Mike Cordner for his passion and genius; to Richard Rowland for his boundless generosity and musical tastes; and to John Lennard, whose devotion to me and my ideas is at once extraordinary and baffling.

Abbreviations

AD	Artistic Director
BBA	Bertolt Brecht Archive
BBC	British Broadcasting Corporation
BL, UTM	British Library, unbound Tynan manuscripts
CA	Churchill Archive
DNB	*Dictionary of National Biography*
GDR	German Democratic Republic
HWA	Helene Weigel Archive
NPT	New Playwrights Trust (Writernet)
NT	National Theatre
NTA	National Theatre Archive
OED	*Oxford English Dictionary* (2nd edition)
PA	personal assistant
RNT	Royal National Theatre
RSC	Royal Shakespeare Company
RST	Royal Shakespeare Theatre
SED	Sozialistische Einheitspartei Deutschlands
SJT	Stephen Joseph Theatre
ZK	Zentralkommittee

1 Introduction

In Germany, Eastern Europe, Scandinavia and the Netherlands dramaturgs and literary managers are a lynchpin of mainstream, state-funded theatre, and have been officially employed for well over two centuries. Playreaders, advisers on repertoire and textual, critical and practical experts working in partnerships with directors and/or writers are accepted as an integral part of theatre-making. Similarly, though the history is much more recent, advances in American theory and practice since the 1960s mean that dramaturgy and literary management are now embedded both in subsidised theatre and as recognised disciplines in academic curricula at over forty universities.[1] The latest edition of Brockett's standard theatre history contains significant new sections on both fields, seeking to define differences while acknowledging that the concept of the dramaturg is still not widely understood.[2] England is now belatedly following in the wake of continental and US practice, and its dramaturgical cultures have undergone an extraordinary transformation, particularly in the last decade – a pace of change still so great that it is difficult to keep abreast of developments. Though literary managers became official only in 1963 with the arrival of Tynan at the National Theatre, and professionalisation was at first slow, it quickened exponentially in the 1990s and the number of appointments continues to rise. Literary managers are now key figures in the artistic running of many theatres, and the deployment of dramaturgs, who in England most commonly develop new plays, has become widespread.

This book explores the origins and causes of this recent and revolutionary sea change in English theatre culture: the professionalisation of literary management and dramaturgy. It is a grand narrative

I

that traces and analyses the transmission of a set of ideas and practices from eighteenth-century Germany to twenty-first-century England, setting English reception history against the larger map of dramaturgical proliferation in continental Europe and the English-speaking West. Historically, the major intellects are Gotthold Lessing, the world's first officially appointed dramaturg, Harley Granville Barker, Bertolt Brecht and Kenneth Tynan – all of whom get chapters to themselves earned by their radical contributions to the troublesome theory and painful practice of dramaturgy, and all of whom have been under-appreciated.

Dramaturgs have traditionally brought contention and the general history of dramaturgy is fraught, full of local battles, accidents of circumstance, and sometimes deliberate attempts to ensure the continued invisibility of the numerous unofficial but vital figures in theatres who acted as playreaders, play-doctors, literary advisers and critical thinkers. Theatrical cultures would have been much impoverished without these functionaries, yet their working lives were conducted out of the limelight and their significance has been overlooked. In many ways, therefore, this book reveals secret histories and seeks to make visible what has been rendered invisible. In the English-speaking West the history of dramaturgy exposes persistent struggles over the control of creative territories and profound cultural resistances to the idea that play-making processes, dramatic literature and repertoire can be objects of intellectual enquiry; it also highlights a deep-rooted suspicion of working models that insist on a dynamic relationship between critical reflection and artistic practice. Even so, the invisibility of playreaders, literary advisers and literary managers in English theatre history is a real curiosity. If the dramatic canon is formed largely on the basis of who and what gets performed (as opposed to published), as it certainly seems to be, then there can be little that is more political than the selection of plays for a repertoire. But who is involved in the selection? Why do they choose certain plays and not others? What is the agenda of the theatre concerned? What underlying state agenda might affect the choices made?

In 1990 an issue of *New Theatre Quarterly* tellingly led with Jan Kott's 'The Dramaturg', an idiosyncratic two-page piece on his experience at the Burgtheater in Vienna: it played perfectly into common

"Is there a doctor of literature in the house?"

Figure 1.1   Michael Maslin, *New Yorker*, 21–8 June 1999 and 9 November 1992.

English prejudices about the dramaturg's essential foreignness and redundancy.[3] Even more revealingly, there was no serious attempt to balance this Kafkaesque account with any description of the tasks of any other working dramaturgs, but merely an assumption that the dramaturg was self-evidently a 'mysterious creature'.[4] Fifteen years later the situation has changed, though not beyond recognition. There is continuing and powerful resistance to the very word *dramaturg*, which can still be met by English theatre practitioners with incomprehension and a belief that self-reflexive dramaturgical processes and the dramaturg's functions must be 'other' to indigenous theatre practices. Nevertheless, dramaturgs have gained greater public attention in the US and England. Their representation in cartoons is a clear sign that they have become part of a popular consciousness in the US (see figures 1.1 and 1.2), and in both countries it is increasingly common to see dramaturgs named in the credits of

3

"Is there a spin doctor in the house?"

Figure 1.2   Joseph Farris, *New Yorker*, 21–8 June 1999 and 9 November 1992.

new plays (a rare occurrence even five years ago in England) – publicity that highlights their rising visibility and the nature of the changes taking place in new play-making cultures.[5]

More controversially, dramaturgy has been the subject of a high-profile litigation case. In 2003 a US court ruled against dramaturg Lynn Thomson, who had filed a claim for a share of the royalties due to the late Jonathan Larsen, author of the smash-hit musical *Rent*. The prosecution was overturned on the basis that no contract between author and dramaturg had been drawn up, though the judge found that Thomson had played a part in 'the radical transformation of *Rent* from an unproducible work in development into a critically and commercially viable play'.[6] Thomson pursued an appeal and the case was eventually settled out of court.[7] In another very public incident, writer, director and RSC veteran John Barton and director Peter Hall fell out rancorously over Hall's decision to appoint a dramaturg to make substantial cuts in Barton's epic cycle of plays *Tantalus*. Barton eventually dissociated himself from the production, refusing to recognise the script as his own.[8] These examples attest to the ways in which dramaturgs both challenge traditional play-making processes and alter the balance of conventional power structures in theatre. Thomson's willingness to take the Larsen estate to court also indicates a new assertiveness in demanding financial recognition for her pains, and in her desire to be named as an author. Debates about collaboration and credit are likely to intensify as the status of the dramaturg rises in the US and in England, but they also underline the contested ambiguity of the rôle in these cultures.

Definitions and functions

The meanings of the words *dramaturg* and *dramaturgy* are unstable, sometimes bitterly so – 'Few terms in contemporary theater practice have consistently occasioned more perplexity'[9] – yet both words can be traced back to classical antiquity. In Liddell and Scott's *Greek Lexicon* the noun δραματουργια, *dramatourgia* , is a subentry under *dramatourg-eo*, a verb meaning 'to write a text in dramatic form', used by Josephus in his *Jewish War* (75–9 CE).[10] *Dramatourg-eo* is related to *dramatopoi-eo*, 'to put into dramatic form'; *dramatopoia*, 'dramatic composition'; and *dramato-poios*, 'dramatic poet'. Both verbs are active, *dramatourg-eo* containing the idea of working on drama, and *dramatopoi-eo* the idea of 'making' or 'doing', from *poien*. A work attributed to the Pseudo-Lucian *dramatopoiou* literally invokes a 'drama-maker',[11] a creator of plays who can imaginatively compose a drama and realise it on stage.

The earliest reference to *dramatourgia* cited by Liddell and Scott is *The Geography of Strabo*. *Dramatourgia* is translated in the Loeb edition as 'structure of the play', and in this sense describes the organisation of formal elements in a tragedy, the structural composition of action into a dramatically cohesive work.[12] Lucian (*c*. 120–*c*. 180 CE) used *dramatourgia* in *De Saltatione*, 'The Dance', written *c*. 162–5 CE, denoting the 'doing' or 'practice of tragedy'.[13] In this sense, *dramatourgia* is external, the activity of a performance, specifically tragic, in contrast with Strabo's use of the word to denote inner dramatic action. For *dramatourgos* Liddell and Scott give one reference, again to Josephus's *Jewish War*: Eurycles is the *dramatourgos* of a deplorable plot to betray King Alexander. Loeb renders the word as 'stage-manager';[14] Liddell and Scott prefer 'contriver'. While the subject matter is not directly connected with theatre the passage stresses Eurycles as a worker of drama in the context of his treacherous planning and orchestration of a plot, as well as his own duplicitous rôle-play within it: like the dramatist he has fabricated his story, like the actor he realises it, like the director he manipulates those around him to play their part in his invented world. The *dramatourgos* Eurycles was a man of considerable skills, though it is interesting to note that the word is used in a derogatory sense.

Definitions of dramaturgy as a collection of writings that theorise drama, and as the activity of the dramaturg in the staging of a play, common today, are conceptually linked to another word, διδασκαλια, *didascalia* (Gotthold Lessing's working title for the *Hamburgische Dramaturgie*). The *OED*, citing the Latin *didascalicus* and the Greek διδασκαλικοσ, *didaskalikos*, records *didascalic* as 'Of the nature of a teacher or of instruction; didactic; pertaining to a teacher', mentioning διδασκαλοσ, *didaskalos*, 'teacher', and διδασκειν, *didaskein*, 'to teach'. In the twentieth century Brecht certainly emphasised the pedagogical import of his redefinition of the dramaturg, and the association of dramaturgs with pedagogy is still powerful: Shannon Jackson opens her book *Professing Performance* with an intellectually unflattering representation of a dramaturg, described as 'the in-house academic of the theatre profession'.[15] An *OED* entry for *didascaly* cites διδασκαλια, *didascalia*, in the singular 'instruction, teaching' and in the plural 'The Catalogues of the ancient Greek Dramas, with their writers, dates, etc., such as were compiled by Aristotle and others.'[16] This allusion refers to Aristotle's lost *Didascaliai*, on which he worked from c. 334 BCE until his death and in which he seems to have recorded details of dithyrambic, tragic and comic performances.[17] Aristotle's lost but reported work and the whole notion of cataloguing performances and recording the author, actors and time and place of performance greatly influenced theatre chroniclers, particularly Leone Allacci, who titled his eighteenth-century catalogue of

Italian productions in Europe *La Drammaturgia*. Allacci, in turn, was an influence on Lessing's dramaturgical writings.

The *OED* records *dramaturge*, a 'composer of drama', as derived proximately from French (in 1787) and radically from Greek *drama*, 'deed' plus *ergon*, 'work'. Parallels with *thaumaturge* and *thaumaturgy*, respectively 'A conjuror; worker of wonders or marvels' and 'the art of working miracles', suggest a dramaturg as a conjuror of drama; one practised in 'secret' arts of theatre. An 1859 entry from *The Times* is the earliest citation: 'Schiller was starving on a salary of 200 dollars per annum, which he received ... for his services as "dramaturg" or literary manager.' The supposed equivalence with 'literary manager' occurs in many German–English dictionaries, contributing to the confusion. The adjective *dramaturgic* (subhead *dramaturgical*) is defined as 'Pertaining to dramaturgy; dramatic, histrionic, theatrical'; while *dramaturgy* is a separate headword defined as '1. Dramatic composition; the dramatic art ... 2. Dramatic or theatrical acting.' Again the proximate etymology is deemed French, this time with a seventeenth-century tag; but the earliest quotations (supporting sense 1), from the *Monthly Magazine* in 1801 and 1805, name Lessing's *Hamburgische Dramaturgie*. A French connection is borne out only by an 1837 quotation from Carlyle. Thus indications are that *dramaturgy* and *dramaturg(e)* entered English between 1755 (Johnson records neither) and 1801 from Lessing's *Hamburgische Dramaturgie*.

Yet until very recently *dramaturgy* and *dramaturg(e)* have been notable absentees in most specialist English dictionaries. In 1966 the *Penguin Dictionary of the Theatre* offered a rare entry:

> *Dramaturg*: German term which resists determined attempts at acclimatisation, despite its usefulness. A dramaturg is a sort of reader-cum-literary editor to a permanent theatrical company; his primary responsibility is the selection of plays for production, working with authors (where necessary) on the revision and adaptation of their texts, and writing programme notes, etc., for the company. The National Theatre appointed Kenneth Tynan to just such a position in 1963, giving him the title 'Literary Manager'.[18]

The term is identified as German, but equivalence with 'literary manager' is preserved, and though more helpful than the *OED* this remained a limited definition, pointing as much to difficulties as to positive senses. Dictionaries in French, German and Italian commonly included both dramaturg and dramaturgy,[19] and comparison with American dictionaries was also unfavourable to English lexicography: *Webster's Third New International Dictionary* (1971) offered a far more specific sequence of definitions:

> *dramaturge*: a person skilled in the writing or revision of plays; also a functionary of certain European theatres who is resp. esp. for selecting and arranging the repertoire and often cooperates with and advises the producer in the course of rehearsal.
> *dramaturgic, – al*: relating to dramaturgy esp. to the technical aspects of play construction.
> *dramaturgy*: Gk. *dramatourgia*, dramatic composition, action of the play. See G. E. Lessing's *Hamburgische Dramaturgie*.
> 1. The art or technique of writing drama.
> 2. The technical devices that are used in writing drama and that tend to distinguish it from other literary forms.

The *OED*'s generalising is replaced by attention to process ('writing or revision') and a distinction between a general meaning and specific contemporary European use. Specialist theatre dictionaries published since 2000 now include the term 'dramaturg': the *Continuum Companion to Twentieth-Century Theatre* suggests that many English companies use the 'alternative term "literary manager"'.[20] The *Drama Handbook* contains a brief historical overview of dramaturgy in Europe and gives recent terminology.[21] The *Oxford Encyclopaedia to Theatre and the Performing Arts* goes into welcome detail and again suggests that labels overlap:

> A dramaturg is a person with a knowledge of the history, theory, and practice of theatre, who helps a director, designer, playwright, or actor realise their intentions in a production. The dramaturg – sometimes called a literary manager, is an in-house artistic consultant cognisant of an institution's mission,

a playwright's passion, or a director's vision, and who helps bring them all to life in a theatrically compelling manner. This goal can be accomplished in myriad ways and the dramaturg's rôle often shifts according to context and is always fluid. As there is no one way to create theatre, there is no single model of the dramaturg.[22]

Overall, the entry is carefully composed, but while the functions of the dramaturg are context-specific, there are theoretical and practical models that have been drawn on – namely, Lessing and Brecht.

Since Lessing, German theatre has dominated critical thinking about dramaturgy and strategically positioned different functions of the dramaturg at the centre of mainstream theatre. The two most prominent German playwrights of the twentieth century, Brecht and Heiner Müller, worked and in part identified themselves as dramaturgs; and it is common German practice to employ at least one dramaturg in a theatre building. In larger theatres the *Chef* or head *dramaturg* reads new plays, assumes a prominent advisory rôle in selecting the repertoire and acts as primary thinker about the political and social objectives of the theatre – what John Rouse calls the 'literary conscience' of the theatre.[23] The *Chefdramaturg* and the rest of the team also work on individual productions as researchers, sounding boards and textual consultants to the director. In the Brechtian model the dramaturg has principal responsibility for research and philological work on the text and historical context, as well as its author; he or she has additional responsibility for editorial work on the text, any necessary translation or retranslation, rewriting or restructuring. Often the dramaturg for a production takes responsibilty for the programme, a task deemed central to educating the public about the play and its directorial concept. In this way the dramaturg is part of an interpretational team that includes the director, designer and actors, *and* is a bridging mechanism to the audience. Volker Canaris has stated:

> The dramaturg became the director's most important theoretical collaborator. Dramaturgy in Brecht's sense comprises the

entire conceptual preparation of a production from its
inception to its realisation. Accordingly it is the task of
dramaturgy to clarify the political and historical, as well as
the aesthetic and formal aspects of a play.[24]

This model of what is known as the 'production dramaturg' has spread,
with variations, across Middle and Eastern Europe and North
America, whilst director–dramaturg partnerships, if not always the
norm in all continental countries, are visible and articulated.

The search for viable definitions of dramaturgical praxis and a
dramaturg's functions have been a particular preoccupation with continental theoreticians and practitioners since Brecht, and have been of
increasing concern to North Americans since the 1960s. Recent work
targeted at students on dramaturgy courses in the US, such as
Dramaturgy in American Theater: A Source Book, offers a plethora of
contrary positions, and rightly argues that only individual case histories
can be taken into account because a dramaturg's or literary manager's
functions vary according to the economic and political conditions of
production. The vested ideologies, both right-wing and left-wing, behind
many of those positions are sometimes overt, sometimes obscured, and
the desire of many of the contributors for a rigid definition is striking, but
the book does not seek to eliminate contradictions in subject matter, nor
proffer sound-bite interpretations.[25] If anything, the over-enthusiasm of
some of the contributors to define themselves as dramaturgs and jump on
the bandwagon is something of a drawback and blurs an already very
complicated picture. Thus *dramaturgy* has acquired a wide range of
meanings, from theorisation of the dramatic structure and internal
logic of play or performance (it 'is frequently used as a synonym for the
theory of drama and theatre'),[26] to the work of a dramaturg who (on the
Continent) is usually based in a theatre but (in England) may work freelance. To summarise, one of the two common senses of *dramaturgy*
relates to the internal structures of a play text and is concerned with
the arrangement of formal elements by the playwright – plot, construction of narrative, character, time-frame and stage action. Conversely,
dramaturgy can also refer to external elements relating to staging, the
overall artistic concept behind the staging, the politics of performance,

and the calculated manipulation of audience response (hence the associations with deceit). This second sense marks interpretation of the text by persons like those now known as directors, the underlying reading and manipulation of a text into multidimensional theatre. Clearly, this interpretative act encompasses the creation of a performance aesthetic and as such can underpin a theoretical framework for any number of plays. There are significant political implications in imposing a rigid theory of dramaturgy on to any play text – Brecht was not immune from criticism at the Berliner Ensemble – but the key to both senses of the word is concern with the business of creation, the actual construction of text and theatre at their most practical level. Both senses also signal the articulation of process, which may explain why the meaning of *dramaturgy* is so (bitterly) contested. The term *dramaturg* does not have a single meaning, even when it is accepted as the proper designation. *Literary manager* seems more transparent, and has until now been preferred in England, but no two literary managers can agree on an exact job description for *literary management* because no two institutional cultures and artistic policies are identical.

All four terms accrete, mutate and dissolve meanings over time and place, and today have multiple but often incompatible definitions, so that there are no specific meanings independent of specific contexts. 'Definition' is from the Latin *definire*, to limit, and rigid definition of *dramaturg* and *literary manager* may usefully corral some material aspects of theatre-making, but necessarily excludes others. Scholarship which promulgates universal definition merely layers confusion upon confusion. This book therefore offers no fixed definitions, but instead examines certain functions of professional theatre-making which from Shakespeare to the present persistently fall within the (overlapping) spheres of dramaturgy and literary management. Any public performance of a play by a company necessitates the accomplishment of these functions: the play must have been read and selected; unless perfectly crafted (rare indeed), it must also have been made stageworthy by cutting and/or rewriting; been cast; and, in some measure, rehearsed. Furthermore, if performed more than once, or subsequently revived, judgement about its artistic, ideological, popular and/or commercial appeals must have been exercised.

It is across this span of functions that the terms *dramaturgy* and *literary management* play, running through a line of cohering concerns that begin with play selection and end with the critique of a play's effect on audiences. These functions pre-exist the actor-manager and modern-day director, and long pre-exist the official appointment of dramaturgs and literary managers. Some overlap with what may be regarded as the rôles of the writer or of the critic; others now fall more obviously within the remit of the assistant director, director, or Artistic Director. In these pages readers will meet many individuals who would claim these rôles and titles or who were (and are) professionally defined by them, but whatever the titles, and irrespective of whether an individual would acknowledge this or that definition of dramaturgy, it is with the theory and practice of these functions that I am concerned. When a historically or culturally specific meaning must be understood, or seems helpful, it is established and analysed, but from chapter to chapter, *mutatis mutandis*, it is functions not labels that define my investigation.

Dramaturgical functions and functionaries 1576–1800

The most obvious point of reference to begin any history of dramaturgy is the appointment of Lessing at the Hamburg Theatre in 1767. But the functions of play-reading, literary advising and critical reflection on practice have clearly existed since the beginning of professional theatre. In considering the English case, it pays, therefore, to give a brief overview of the situation there before 1800.

Theatre records between 1576 and 1642 are sparse, and the history, structure and organisation of the first professional theatre companies and custom-built playhouses well-rehearsed elsewhere.[27] Professional theatre in England was *ab initio* commercial, and companies funded through capital investment and box-office sales. The functions of play-reading, selecting and planning repertoire, casting, and preparing and amending play texts were obviously being carried out; and although indistinct disciplines, often occurring in haphazard ways under considerable duress, and in their nature difficult to penetrate, they can be glimpsed from time to time.

Today's system of literary management at a theatre, a private, silent reading of a play by someone other than the author, was not the norm, and evidently not regarded as an obvious or useful practice. Apart from the work entailed in fair-copying manuscripts, very real fears of piracy, and authors' desires to safeguard work, the playwright's reading was regarded as the most effective way to judge the merits of a play for performance (not least because critical dialogue could take place without delay).[28] Playreading, therefore, was not the responsibility of a single, designated person, and may have involved two stages: an initial private reading to an official of importance at the theatre – a leading actor, actor-sharer, or manager, followed by a reading to the assembled company of actors.[29] Commanding the individual attention of a sharer or grandee of a company was no mean feat, and indicates that playwrights who reached this first stage were, in all probability, either attached to the company, known in the trade, or had been recommended by influential persons; and as Bentley points out, actor-dramatists such as Thomas Heywood, Samuel and William Rowley, and Shakespeare had advantageous insider knowledge of what appealed to leading actors.[30] It is unlikely that scripts by inexperienced and unknown playwrights got far without a significant patron, and it is not surprising that many came to playwriting through their success in other careers or aspects of the theatre world.

The Elizabethan appetite for new plays was at its height from the late 1580s to 1612, and, as Gurr notes, unlike the repertoire for touring theatre companies, which could be repeated numerous times, regular attendances at permanent, purpose-built theatres 'required the impresarios to offer a constant supply of novelty'.[31] Competition and demand for new plays during this period meant that it was in every company member's interest to be alert to potential talent. As a rule the idea for a play derived from the playwright, but there is evidence that writers also developed ideas given to them: Dekker claimed that *Keep the Widow Waking* was based on a suggestion by Ralph Savage, book-keeper to the King's Men, and in some cases playwrights worked from plot outlines or sequences of scenes.[32]

There seems little doubt that the leading players in a company usually made the ultimate decision of rejecting or accepting a play, and were in the best position to know the strengths of the text, the actors to match, and the tastes and expectations of the audience. There are records of scripts being rejected by players after the most cursory attention: John Jones wrote of his *Adrasta; or the Woman's Spleen and Love* that the players rejected it 'upon a slight and a half view of it',[33] though his account may be coloured by resentment. Richard Brome found the 'scornful and reproachful speeches' of the actors in response to a new play a mere prelude to the cessation of his wages and the attempt to hound him out of the theatre.[34] Players and company playwrights were also passionate defenders of plays, though the truth of Rowe's appealing account of Shakespeare's advocacy for Jonson is moot:

> Mr *Johnson* ... had offer'd one of his Plays to the Players, in order to have it Acted; and the Persons into whose hands it was put, after having turned it carelessly and superciliously over, were just upon returning it to him with an ill-natur'd Answer, that it would be of no service to their Company, when *Shakespear* luckily cast his Eye upon it, and found something so well in it as to engage him first to read through, and afterwards to recommend Mr *Johnson* and his Writings to the Publick.[35]

During the Interregnum unofficial productions occurred but did not amount to the re-establishment of professional theatre. In contrast to some continental troupes, English theatre companies had no state subsidy and relied on monies from investors as well as box-office takings – commercial success was therefore vital. After the initial turbulence and competitive schemings of the early Restoration, managers increasingly followed Davenant's example of planning and selecting repertoire and from Colley Cibber's time at Drury Lane (1708–33) it appears to have become their province entirely.[36] Throughout the eighteenth century there was bitter castigation of managers by writers and theatre commentators for their poor choices of new plays and slack reading services, and Cibber, John Rich (Lincoln's Inn Fields, 1714–32; Covent Garden, 1732–61), Garrick (Drury Lane, 1747–76) and Sheridan (Drury Lane, 1776–1809) were regularly targeted for vilification.[37] Expectant of managers' inefficiency in reading plays, many authors sought the intervention of influential literati.[38] In 1735 the editors of *The Prompter* claimed that Rich had: 'declared that *no new play will* (according to the usual phrase) *do*, and is from that principle inclined to reject all plays whatsoever that are offered to him'.[39] Furthermore, they expressed their disgust that there were 'new plays lying *unread*, or *ungiven to read*' at his house.[40] Stories abounded, including Rich's alleged habit of inviting authors who had come to reclaim scripts to look in his drawer, saying that 'if they could not see their own there, they would find several better, to any of which they were welcome'.[41] Cibber was notoriously brutal in rejecting plays, apparently referred to his mortification of young playwrights as 'the choaking of singing birds', and according to Davies 'deserved ... keen reproaches and bitter sarcasms'.[42] Garrick was circumspect, all too aware that 'the refusal of a play was almost universally treated as the deadliest of insults', and employed Poet Laureate William Whitehead as his 'sifter' of plays, habitually reading plays himself on the journey between his home in Hampton and London,[43] and frequently reading plays to friends.[44] Garrick was excessively polite to authors, often avoiding direct negatives as a strategy to eschew public embarrassment (which could backfire),[45] but nonetheless tended to view playwrights with all the warmth due to potential assassins, stalking him relentlessly:

> who with a Play, like pistol cock'd, in hand,
> Bid Managers to stand.[46]

Garrick's trepidation is not surprising, for he was ceaselessly importuned by the rich and famous; his letters reveal many hours dutifully spent critiquing plays which did not merit his scrutiny,[47] though Whitehead (poet, critic and playwright) was no doubt employed to lend critical status and credibility to reading procedures and to filter the flow of new plays. Garrick also relied on his business partner Willoughby Lacy to screen him from stubbornly persistent writers.[48]

The practice of authors reading their plays to assembled companies once the manager or leading player approved it was generally valued in the immediate Restoration period,[49] but the influence of the playwright had diminished so much by the end of the eighteenth century that in 1775 Francis Gentleman described it as a 'ridiculous custom' that gave authors 'a false consequence'.[50] Similarly, writers were gradually excluded from casting decisions. Attached playwrights (such as Dryden[51]), commissioned writers and leading actors (notably Betterton) often advised on casting from 1660 to 1710,[52] but from c. 1710 managers increasingly took sole responsibility for casting, and attachments became rarer in the eighteenth century as managers took a central rôle in rewriting and adapting texts, steadily marginalising playwrights from production processes.

One feature of the eighteenth century was power struggles between managers and playwrights. The Interregnum meant dramatists had been unable to refine skills through regular practice, and unless already established as writers they had to struggle hard to gain the attention of managers. Managers not surprisingly looked to stocks of old plays, though new plays were weapons in times of competition.[53] Further, the patents granted to William Davenant and Thomas Killigrew brought about a monopoly that no other theatre was able successfully to challenge on a commercial basis, and the smaller theatres founded in the 1730s were stifled by the 1737 Licensing Act. Competition was therefore disabled and playing spaces drastically limited. To complicate matters, (very free) adaptations of existing plays were increasingly regarded as 'new' material, were popular, and could be relied on as business ventures.

From 1660 to 1710 playwrights, actors and managers revised scripts much as before 1642. Dryden was commissioned to write and adapt plays as well as to write additions such as prologues;[54] the actor Betterton consulted playwrights on his rewrites and revisions,[55] and Davenant, with origins in playwriting, chose as a manager to focus on bold adaptations of Shakespeare, with great success. The provinces of adaptation and revision were markedly colonised by managers from Cibber's time onwards, and became different disciplines in their extent and audacity, blurring distinctions between playwrights and managers and problematising the whole notion of authorship – particularly in the case of Garrick, whose adaptations (and restoration) of Shakespeare's plays are in a category of their own.[56] Playwrights felt increasingly threatened by what they saw as an incursion into their territory and hostilities mounted, Garrick preferring on occasions to go as far as concealing his identity as author.

> I have so many Enemies among Writers on Account of my refusing so many of their Performances Every Year, that I am oblig'd to conceal Myself in order to avoid the Torrent of abuse that their Malice would pour upon Me.[57]

Managers also steadily took it upon themselves to revise or rewrite new plays, and playwrights who wished for productive relations accepted and complimented their 'benefactor', knowing there was little use protesting. Those who found this intolerable accused managers of 'castrating, curtailing and defacing' works through 'an act of the most arbitrary power ... and in its consequences of a most pernicious tendency to poetry itself'.[58] The wrath of a spurned author such as Tobias Smollett could be vehement and prolonged; after ten years hawking his play *The Regicide* to various managers and literary patrons, he published it in 1749 with a preface detailing his 'mortifications', 'his labour and chagrin' *etcetera*, listing the sins of managers (and other critics) and masking his fury with the justification that

> the usage I have met with will be as a beacon to caution other inexperienced authors against the insincerity of managers, to which they might otherwise become egregious dupes; and after a cajoling dream of good fortune, wake in all the aggravation of disappointment.[59]

The possibility that his play might have been politically uncomfortable material for managers to handle, or not good, never seemed to occur to Smollett.

The prompter's rôle rose in status throughout the period, and as early as the King's Company he is named as the manager's official agent.[60] By the time of William Chetwood (d. 1766), who gained a reputation in his own right at Drury Lane from 1722 to 1740, the prompter's functions had multiplied beyond safe-keeping and maintaining promptbooks, corresponding with the Lord Chamberlain and correcting scripts, to include drafting playbills, conducting routine rehearsals, and undertaking tasks associated with modern-day stage management. Also a dramatist and bookseller, Chetwood was entrusted with specialist literary functions such as cutting, and his name lent credibility to certain printed plays merchandised as corrected from the promptbook.[61] In many ways Chetwood deputised for his manager, and the proliferation of functions marked a shift into a more managerial rôle.

There was a rising critical consciousness after 1660 (first evident in Sidney's *Defence of Poesy* (1595) and Francis Meres's *Palladis Tamia* (1598)[62]) that a body of literature, including Shakespeare's plays, had been written which could politically constitute a national corpus to compare with the Roman and Greek classics. Critical awareness of theatre grew from simple personal accounts of performances by, for example, Simon Forman in 1611,[63] and the impressions which Samuel Pepys recorded in his diary in the 1660s, to formal and systematic journalistic criticism. Gray has examined how Richard Steele first introduced periodical criticism of drama, and traced how the practice of regular theatre reviewing became established in London during the eighteenth century.[64] Newspaper and periodical coverage provided publicity opportunities that theatre managers were eager to exploit, and 'open' rehearsals for critics were instituted at some theatres.[65] The notion of a theatre's critical relationship with its audiences did therefore develop to a limited degree, but as Davies wrote in 1780, most Englishmen looked upon theatre as 'a place of amusement', and it became 'a place of instruction by chance, not by choice'.[66] Thirty years before, one might have said as much in Germany, but by the time Davies wrote a gulf had begun to open between English and German practice that has never subsequently closed.

Notes

1. The Yale School of Dramaturgy is perhaps the most prestigious.
2. Oscar G. Brockett, *The Essential Theatre* (8th edn, Fort Worth: Harcourt Brace, 2004), pp. 306–13.
3. Jan Kott, 'The Dramaturg', *New Theatre Quarterly* 6.21 (February 1990): 3–4.
4. *Ibid.*, p. 3.

5. See, for example, Katie Douglas, *Fly* (London: Josef Weinberger, 2004), and Tony Green, *The Kindness of Strangers* (London: Oberon, 2004), where Suzanne Bell is credited as dramaturg.

6. Brockett, *Essential Theatre*, p. 308.

7. See www. dramaturgy.net/RENT/.

8. The dramaturg was Colin Teevan. *Tantalus* premièred in Denver in 2000.

9. See Susan Jonas, Geoff Proehl and Michael Lupu, eds., *Dramaturgy in American Theater* (New York: Harcourt Brace, 1997), p. vii.

10. Josephus, *Bellum Judaicum*, trans. H. St.J. Thackeray (London: William Heinemann, 1927) [Loeb Classical Library], II, 1.24.1, lines 222–3. The verb recurs in the second or third century CE and is translated as to 'bring out' a play; see Alciphron, *Letters of Courtesans*, trans. A. R. Benner and F. H. Fobes (London: William Heinemann, 1949) [Loeb Classical Library], IV, 17, letter 18, 2, lines 322–3.

11. Pseudo-Lucian, *The Patriot*, trans. M. D. Macleod (London: William Heinemann, 1979) [Loeb Classical Library], VIII, 438.

12. Strabo, *The Geography of Strabo*, trans. Horace Leonard Jones (London: William Heinemann, 1917) [Loeb Classical Library], p. 122. Generally agreed to have been written *c.* 7 BCE.

13. Lucian, *The Dance*, trans. A. H. Harmon (London: William Heinemann, 1936) [Loeb Classical Library], V, p. 271.

14. Josephus, *Bellum Judaicum*, 1.26.4, lines 532–3.

15. Shannon Jackson, *Professing Performance: Theatre in the Academy from Philology to Performativity* (Cambridge: Cambridge University Press, 2004), p. 1.

16. Didascaliai were amongst the earliest known theatre records. Pickard-Cambridge makes it clear that in the City Dionysia Festival, which took place in Athens in the fifth and fourth centuries BCE, dramatists or their professionally trained representatives were required to function as teachers of the chorus and actors, and that this function was called 'didascalia'. The word was also used for the collective works of a dramatist. See A. Pickard-Cambridge, *The Dramatic Festivals of Athens*, 2nd edn, rev. John Gould and D. M. Lewis (Oxford: Clarendon Press, 1988), pp. 70–3.

17. Pickard-Cambridge's estimates, *ibid.*, p. 70.
18. J. R. Taylor, *The Penguin Dictionary of the Theatre* (Harmondsworth: Penguin, 1966), p. 90.
19. See, for example, Patrice Pavis's intellectually rigorous entries in his *Dictionary of the Theatre: Terms, Concepts, and Analysis* (Paris: Dunod, 1996; trans. Christine Schantz, Toronto: University of Toronto Press, 1998), pp. 122–6.
20. Colin Chambers, ed., *The Continuum Companion to Twentieth-Century Theatre* (London: Continuum, 2002), p. 227.
21. John Lennard and Mary Luckhurst, *The Drama Handbook: A Guide to Reading Plays* (Oxford: Oxford University Press, 2002), pp. 186–92.
22. Dennis Kennedy, ed., *The Oxford Encyclopaedia to Theatre and the Performing Arts* (Oxford: Oxford University Press, 2004), p. 387.
23. John Rouse, *Brecht and the West German Theatre* (Ann Arbor: UMI Research Press, 1989) [Theatre and Dramatic Studies, no. 62], p. 3.
24. Volker Canaris, 'Style and the Director', trans. Claudia Rosoux, in *The German Theatre*, ed. Ronald Hayman (London: Oswald Wolf, 1975), pp. 250–1.
25. The same cannot be said of Bert Cardullo, ed., *What is Dramaturgy?* (New York: Peter Lang, 1995) [American University Studies, series 26, vol. 20], which does not answer the question with particular clarity.
26. Rouse, *Brecht and the West German Theatre*, p. 3.
27. See Andrew Gurr, *Playgoing in Shakespeare's London* (1987; 2nd edn, Cambridge: Cambridge University Press, 1996); Andrew Gurr, *The Shakespearean Stage 1574–1642* (1970; 3rd edn, Cambridge: Cambridge University Press, 1994); Andrew Gurr, *The Shakespearian Playing Companies* (Oxford: Clarendon Press, 1996); G. E. Bentley, *The Profession of Player in Shakespeare's Time* (Princeton: Princeton University Press, 1984); T. W. Baldwin, *The Organisation and Personnel of the Shakespearean Company* (New York: Russell and Russell, 1961). The founding year of the first effective purpose-built theatre in London, the Theatre, was 1576.

28. G. E. Bentley, *The Profession of Dramatist in Shakespeare's Time 1590–1642* (New Jersey: Princeton University Press, 1971), p. 76: 'A normal part of the dramatist's preparation of his play for the acting troupe was the reading of his manuscript to them for their approval.'

29. See Tiffany Stern, 'A History of Rehearsal in the British Professional Theatre from the Sixteenth to the Eighteenth Century' (unpublished dissertation, Cambridge University, 1997), pp. 41–2.

30. Bentley, *Profession of Dramatist*, p. 76.

31. Gurr, *Playgoing*, p. 119. For the repertory system see Gurr, *Playing Companies*, pp. 100–2.

32. Cited in Neil Carson, *A Companion to Henslowe's Diary* (Cambridge: Cambridge University Press, 1988), p. 55.

33. *Ibid.*, p. 80.

34. *Ibid.*, p. 82.

35. Cited in S. Schoenbaum, *Shakespeare's Lives* (Oxford: Clarendon Press, 1991), p. 57.

36. See Robert D. Hume, ed., *The London Theatre World 1660–1800* (Carbondale: Southern Illinois University Press, 1980), p. 192; Judith D. Milhous and Robert D. Hume, *Producible Interpretation* (Carbondale: Southern Illinois University Press, 1985), pp. 43–4.

37. See Thomas Davies, *Memoirs of the Life of David Garrick*, 2 vols. (London: [n.p.] 1780), I., 208.

38. Milhous and Hume, *Producible Interpretation*, p. 43.

39. Aaron Hill and William Popple, *The Prompter*, ed. William W. Appleton and Kalman A. Burnim (New York: Benjamin Bloom, 1966), p. 97.

40. *Ibid.*, p. 97.

41. Mrs Clement Parsons, *Garrick and his Circle* (London: Methuen, 1906), p. 97. Smollett referred to Rich as 'the greatest Scoundrel under the Sun'; see *Letters of Tobias Smollett*, ed. Lewis M. Knapp (Oxford: Clarendon Press, 1970), p. 12.

42. Davies, *Life of Garrick*, I, 209, 211.

43. Parsons, *Garrick and his Circle*, pp. 197 and 186. Whitehead (1715–85) became Laureate in 1757, after Cibber's death. There

is no reason to think that Garrick referred to Whitehead as his 'sifter', the belittling term is presumably Parsons's, who underestimates the significance of Whitehead's functions.

44. Garrick, *The Letters of David Garrick*, ed. David M. Little and George M. Kahrl, 3 vols. (Oxford: Oxford University Press, 1963), I, 246.

45. Davies, *Life of Garrick*, I, 211.

46. From Garrick's poem, *The Sick Monkey*, in Parsons, *Garrick and his Circle*, p. 198.

47. For an example see Garrick, *Letters*, I, 244–7.

48. See Lewis Melville, *The Life and Letters of Tobias Smollett* (New York: Kennikat Press, 1966), p. 25.

49. Stern, *History of Rehearsal*, p. 96. Cibber was not impressed with Dryden's reading; see his *An Apology for the Life of Colley Cibber*, ed. B. R. S Fone (Ann Arbor: University of Michigan Press, 1968), p. 67.

50. Francis Gentleman, *The Modish Wife ... to Which is Prefixed a Summary View of the Stage* (1775; New York: Readex Microprints, 1963), p. 22.

51. Contracted to the King's Company in 1668.

52. Many rôles were typecast and there was less need to involve writers in casting. See Peter Holland, *The Ornament of Action* (Cambridge: Cambridge University Press, 1979), ch. 3.

53. See Milhous and Hume, *Producible Interpretation*, pp. 36–40.

54. See Judith Milhous and Robert D. Hume, *A Register of English Theatrical Documents 1660–1737*, 2 vols. (Carbondale: Southern Illinois University Press, 1991), I, 225, no. 1144.

55. Judith Milhous, 'Thomas Betterton's Playwriting', *Bulletin of New York Public Library* 77 (1974): 375–92.

56. See Peter Holland, 'David Garrick: 3rdly, as an Author', *Studies in Eighteenth-Century Culture* 25 (1997): 39–62.

57. See Garrick, *Letters*, I, 301.

58. Hill and Popple, *Prompter*, p. 98.

59. Reprinted in Melville, *Life and Letters of Smollett*, pp. 279–86 (p. 279).

60. Hume, *London Theatre World*, p. 28. See John Downes's description of his work in his *Roscius Anglicanus*, ed. Judith Milhous and Robert D. Hume (London: Society for Theatre Research, 1987), p. 2.

61. Stern, *History of Rehearsal*, pp. 154–6.
62. See E. K. Chambers, *William Shakespeare: A Study of Facts and Problems*, 2 vols. (Oxford: Clarendon Press, 1930), II, 193–5.
63. *Ibid.*, II, 337–41. Forman saw *Macbeth*, *Cymbeline*, *Richard II* and *The Winter's Tale*.
64. Charles Harold Gray, *Theatrical Criticism in London to 1795* (New York: Columbia University Press, 1931).
65. Stern, *History of Rehearsal*, p. 139. See also, Tiffany Stern, *Rehearsal from Shakespeare to Sheridan* (Oxford: Oxford University Press, 2000).
66. Davies, *Life of Garrick*, I, 142–3.

2 Gotthold Lessing and the *Hamburg Dramaturgy*

Lessing: the first official dramaturg

Gotthold Ephraim Lessing (1729–81) was the world's first officially appointed dramaturg. Though his appointment in Hamburg lasted only two years, from 1767 to 1769, and the venture that inspired it sank rather ignominiously, Lessing's experimental work pioneered reforms of practice and theory throughout Germany. His example led rapidly to the centrality of the dramaturg in German-speaking theatres, and to the spread of official positions in Eastern Europe. In the West the implications of Lessing's appointment for the national reform of theatre practice were not fully absorbed until the mid to late nineteenth century, most notably through Harley Granville Barker and William Archer, and in the twentieth century the first official appointments of literary managers in English-speaking western theatres certainly owed a great deal to Lessing's model of the dramaturg. Similarly, the significance of the *Hamburgische Dramaturgie* (the *Hamburg Dramaturgy*),[1] the theatre criticism he published while dramaturg, was not significantly appreciated by western critics until the 1880s and 1890s – yet few would now dispute that these writings rank amongst the most important theoretical documents of eighteenth-century drama. For any student of dramaturgy an understanding of Lessing's work and the cultural background to his appointment is vital.

The National Theatre in Hamburg and Lessing's appointment

There are three important points about the context of Lessing's appointment: his post was created for Germany's first national theatre project; his position was part of a scheme to galvanise a distinctively German dramatic literature; and Lessing, as Germany's foremost man of letters, polemicist, and playwright, was specifically sought out. The founders of the first German National Theatre invited Lessing to Hamburg because they saw in him a man uniquely qualified to help advance an ambitious programme of theatrical reform.

The National Theatre of Hamburg was also inspired by a political agenda. Eighteenth-century 'Germany' was not, like France and England, a single national state, but comprised a loose confederation of over three hundred principalities, each with its own autonomous courts for the regulation of legal and political affairs.[2] Germany lacked its own national literary figures, its own definable traditions and, to some extent, a common literary language. If Shakespeare and Garrick dominated British theatre, Germans pinned their hopes on Lessing as playwright and critic, and on Konrad Ekhof (1720–78) as actor.[3] If German theatre was polarised between popular travelling companies doing low-brow comedy and court theatres steeped in French and Italian traditions, theatre reformists saw a new national theatre as the answer.

As an outspoken critic of Germany's contemporary dramatic literature and a renowned literary controversialist, Lessing's participation in the new venture was conceived as a vital component of a radical pedagogic and aesthetic agenda to lead Germany into a new era of theatrical innovation. Much, therefore, has been made of the theatre's collapse two years after its launch, and of Lessing's own failings in this regard. From the first, Lessing was painfully aware of the difficulties confronting the experimental enterprise and made it his task to anatomise and articulate them in his critical work. His functions at the National Theatre and his writing of the *Hamburgische Dramaturgie* must be seen through the lens of Enlightenment Germany and within the context of progressive desires to challenge theatrical orthodoxy and accelerate cultural change.

The objectives for the National Theatre were laid out in a document entitled 'A Provisional Report on Changes at the Hamburg Theatre effective from Easter 1767'.[4] This report is credited to Johann Friedrich Löwen,[5] then director of the new Hamburg enterprise, and its contents shed light on the rationale for the theatre's reorganisation and on Lessing's appointment there. The report begins:

> We hereby announce to the public the perhaps unexpected hope of raising the German drama in Hamburg to a dignity which it will not attain in any other circumstances. For whilst this most excellent, pleasing and edifying branch of the fine arts remains in the hands of such men, albeit the most upstanding of men, who are forced to turn their art exclusively into a means of earning their crust; whilst mutual encouragement and the noble pride of imitation is lacking amongst actors themselves; whilst we fail to inspire the writers of the nation to compose national dramas; whilst theatrical policy-making fails to pay heed either to the selection of plays or to the morals of actors; whilst all this exists we will never see German drama emerge from its infancy.[6]

Löwen's statement denounces actors, managers and playwrights. In particular, the tradition of a lead actor or *Principal* heading a company is condemned for its tendency to result in crude crowd-pleasing. Actors are castigated for their lack of discipline, professionalism and literary knowledge, as well as for their inattention to a new style of acting developed by Ekhof in the 1750s.[7] Actors, Löwen argues, are interested only in the size of their rôle, and have scant respect for plays as works of literature. Managements are held to account for the absence of a tradition of German dramatic literature, for failing to nurture promising writers, and for showing little interest in educating their audiences. Playwrights are charged with slavishly imitating the French. Löwen's remedy is to provide a stimulating and disciplined working environment in which to train German writers and actors. Changes are promoted from the top down: the National Theatre becomes the first independent theatre in Germany, funded by a consortium of twelve Hamburg businessmen. The position of *Principal* is abolished. Konrad Ekhof is appointed to train the actors. Lessing is employed for both his creative and critical capacities.

Löwen's report envisages the new National Theatre as an 'academy' for actor training, operating as an ensemble with actors paid a salary; as a teaching institution offering lectures covering the entire span of theatre history and theory to date; and as a literary hothouse awarding prizes for the best original tragedies and comedies. The aim of the operation is specified as nothing less than the beginnings of a grand scheme to improve the tastes and moral sensibility of every German citizen.

Negotiations over Lessing's rôle at the National Theatre appear to have lasted some weeks. The ideal appointment was envisioned as a resident dramatist, who could be relied on to produce a substantial supply of challenging plays and to spearhead the campaign for a distinctive German drama. Lessing's multilingual talents, his formidable knowledge of foreign literatures and scholarly approach to translation meant that he was also in a position to advise on and undertake translation work himself if the necessity arose.[8] The attachment of a man of letters to a theatre company did have precedents in Germany: Löwen himself had assumed this rôle under Konrad Ackermann in the period immediately preceding the National Theatre, and another famous actor-manager, Johann Friedrich Schönemann, had established a rich partnership with Johann Krüger. In his last critical article of the *Hamburgische Dramaturgie* Lessing claims that he cannot comprehend how the directorate could possibly have imagined he would be useful to the enterprise.[9] He cites the resident dramatist and reformer of Italian theatre, Goldoni, as his model: 'What Goldoni achieved for Italian theatre by enriching it in a single year with thirteen new plays, I have been unable to do for German theatre.'[10] But reform through practice was Lessing's preferred route, and, though a practising playwright, he argued that he did not possess that 'vital source' (*lebendige Quelle*) in himself that allowed for a spontaneous creative process; instead he worked with slow, painstaking rigour. This provides some insight into why Lessing negotiated for a different primary rôle: he doubted his capacity to produce plays to demand, and did not perceive himself as a dramatist of sufficient stature to act as the pioneer of a new German drama. He refers to his plays as 'experiments' (*Versuche*),[11] argues that any apprehension of himself as a great creative writer is a misjudgement and presents himself categorically as a critic who writes plays.[12] His employers always saw him as excelling at both.

Lessing's background as a scintillating essayist and journalist, editor, translator and polemicist had made him prominent and also the first writer in Germany to earn an independent living. He had been responsible for three theatre journals prior to his appointment in Hamburg: *Contributions to the History and Progress of the Theatre*;[13] the *Theatrical Library*;[14] and *Letters Concerning the most Recent Literature*.[15] The latter work ensured his notoriety: in a scathing attack on Johann Christoph Gottsched's exhortation to German playwrights to emulate the structures and rhythms of French classicism,[16] Lessing implored German dramatists not to shackle themselves to France but to seek their own models, suggesting that Shakespeare was an appropriate example. Lessing's argument went totally against the grain of assumed tastes in Germany, demolished Gottsched's standing, and presented such a radically new agenda that its impetus could not be immediately absorbed – it was the next generation of dramatists, specifically Goethe and Schiller, who grasped the significance of Lessing's proposals and followed his advice. But Lessing was also a trail-blazer in his own practice: one of his plays, *Miß Sara Sampson*, written and performed in 1755, had pioneered domestic tragedy (*bürgerliches Trauerspiel*) and provided a window of opportunity for the evolution of a dramatic phemonenon that Germany might call its own.[17] Lessing, therefore, offered the best of both worlds to his employers at the National Theatre: as critic, he lent prestige and controversial edge; as playwright, he embodied a spirit of progress and offered new agendas.

Whilst Lessing's dissenting voice made him the ideal choice for Hamburg, it also guaranteed him a turbulent tenure. The decision to appoint him as an in-house critic was unprecedented. Lessing was given responsibility for analysing plays and productions at the theatre, and was expected to publish his critiques in a periodical twice a week. He was expected to assess a play from a literary viewpoint – providing background information on the playwrights themselves, the sources of plays and their structural and linguistic merits and demerits – and from the practical viewpoint of production – especially actors' portrayals of character, delivery and technique. By employing Lessing in this rôle the theatre's managers were underlining their commitment not just to making performance processes visible but also to articulating them. Lessing's appointment stressed the importance of a reflective voice at the heart of theatre-making, and at a stroke invented a new form of theatre criticism designed to have a direct, dynamic dialogue with and impact on the theatre company, whilst simultaneously ensuring that play-making itself became a subject of public debate. Above all, Lessing's work was conceived of as an ambitious educational project, designed to set high literary and production standards and to develop new critical vocabularies to enable actors to appraise their performance and managers their policies. The rôle of educator extended most importantly to the public, and in this respect Lessing became the cultural intermediary between the National Theatre and its audiences, critiquing its work both practically and theoretically, an arbiter of artistic quality and managerial decision-making. It was an attempt to teach those in the industry and those outside how to be informed critics. It was an experiment that saw in theatre a potential for broad cultural reform. Most importantly, it was a venture which insisted that theory and practice are not separate disciplines but rather inform one another constantly, and that vital, progressive theatre-making must make room for maximum cross-fertilisation. The enterprise may have failed in the short term, but German theatre practitioners immediately understood the pragmatics of yoking togther theory and practice, and the dramaturg has been an integral part of their theatre-making ever since.

The *Hamburg Dramaturgy*

Lessing's initial idea for the title of his periodical was the *Hamburgische Didaskalien* (the Hamburg Didascalia),[18] which was inspired by Aristotle's didascalia: brief production notes on plays which recorded when, where and how the play was performed, who had written it, and how it was received. Lessing also knew of Leone Allacci's *La Drammaturgia*, published in 1666, which catalogued all known Italian plays performed in Europe, simply giving details of author, date and place of performance and whether they had musical accompaniment. But Lessing felt that the word *didascalia* was too awkward, and that Allacci's precedent could not offer him a useful format.[19] He expressly did not want a rigid form that closed off debate and presented his criticism as hegemonic, but a more fluid form that would allow for first thoughts, incomplete schemata, and the rehearsal of ideas, contradictions, and meditations. The purpose of the *Hamburgische Dramaturgie* was not that of a historical chronicle, as Aristotle's and Allacci's had been, but of an informative, topical collection of running articles intended to provoke. Consequently he structured the periodical in self-contained numbers, *Stücke*, which could vary considerably in length and which proffered a flexible and accessible layout. Lessing began to write on 1 May 1767. Altogether 104 numbers were published. Interest in the experiment was so keen that early issues were pirated and appeared in Leipzig. After the 32nd issue, numbers were massed together as a precaution against piracy and printed irregularly until Easter 1769. At this point the entire work was published in two volumes by J. H. Cramer in Bremen.

Lessing's prologue to the *Hamburgische Dramaturgie* is very cautious.[20] And well it might be. From the first the management's actions failed to meet their stated intentions in important ways, and Lessing sensed that he was in an invidious position. Remarkably, he was excluded from the decision-making process for selecting plays and allowed no influence on the repertoire, a state of affairs which totally undermined his credibility and flew in the face of the theatre's supposed objectives. No doubt the managers feared that Lessing's controversial tastes would expose the theatre to too much financial risk, and economic security, not cultural reform was the priority when the theatre opened. But their exclusionist tactics were extreme and the profound suspicion of Lessing indicative of less than enlightened minds. If the majority of the managers showed no trust in their dramaturg's judgement, Lessing at once dissociated himself from them by making it clear in the prologue that he wished to be exonerated from all charges regarding the mediocrity of the repertoire.[21] From the outset Lessing found himself in the dilemma of being expected to realise programmatic reform without access to the major institutional process by which change might come about. It is clear that infighting between Löwen and the other managers did occur, and that the first few weeks saw frequent disputes. In particular, the chaos over the demarcation of rôles and the squabbles over territory alarmed

Lessing so much that only a month after its inauguration he vented his frustrations to his brother Karl: 'All sorts of things are happening at our theatre (in the strictest confidence!) which I don't care for. There is disagreement amongst the directorate, and no one knows who is cook or waiter.'[22] Despite Löwen's protestations, the management appeared to view Lessing as a good marketing catch and little else. This was a bad enough start, but Lessing had no illusions about the difficulty of promoting and developing a national German drama: this project, Lessing stated pointedly in his prologue, was likely to founder because of misguided notions of taste, institutional structures which reduced art to mere consumption, a climate unreceptive to theatrical reform, and the mediocre dramatic imagination of contemporary German playwrights. He states that the *Dramaturgie* will be 'a critical register of all the plays performed [at the National Theatre] and will follow every step of both the writer's and the actor's art'.[23] This description implies a rigorous interrogation of text and performance. Indeed, Lessing stresses the necessity of a critical eye that can not only distinguish text from *mise-en-scène*, but also understand how differently the two function:

> The drama critic's greatest skill is in knowing, in every case, how to distinguish between the fortune or the misfortune of a play, and in knowing what is to be laid at the writer's and what at the actor's door.[24]

The assessment of an actor's performance is particularly sensitive, he argues, since a performance is in essence transitory, dependent on many unreproducible factors, whilst a play text can also be critiqued on literary terms. The *Dramaturgie* was to be a running critical commentary on *performance* as much as on dramatic literature, and in its conception was the first experiment of its kind.

In fact, the fields of inquiry in the *Hamburgische Dramaturgie* turned out to be predominantly literary, relating to matters such as source and translation, consistency of character and the validity of Aristotle's or French dramatic theories.[25] Lessing touches on audience reception, but never comments on stage-setting or costumes in detail. He promotes a theatre that presents the individual within precise social circumstances, and advocates Shakespeare as the great example for German dramatists. A recurrent theme in the work is his admiration of French neoclassical drama but his dismay at its saturation of the repertoire in Germany.

The reasons for the mainly literary analysis were twofold: in the first place, Lessing did not keep pace with performances from the opening night, and this, with the suspension of serial publication, collapsed any claim of his writings to be a running critique of productions. But the second reason left Lessing with no choice but to refrain from offering critiques of acting at all and was a disaster that he did not anticipate: the performers revolted at Lessing's public dissection of their talents and took up their complaints with the management. The leading actress, Madame Hensel, in particular objected to such scrutiny. Löwen's literary ideals, as had rapidly become clear, held no interest for the actors, and a cardinal feature of the new enterprise, the abolition of the *Principal* was tacitly allowed to lapse. Konrad Ekhof took on the rôle and made the casting and artistic decisions on productions: his concerns were with disciplining and organising his actors and his energies were entirely consumed by his ambitious actor-training programme. Literary concerns were marginalised, hence only one lecture took place and the schemes for recognising and rewarding promising new playwrights were dropped. The actors argued that Lessing was not lauding them as they deserved, and without doubt his interests lay more with literary analysis and historiography. But Lessing also made no secret of what he saw as the surface fripperies of theatre and the poverty of most actors' integrity. He was unequivocal in his belief that an actor's most significant gift was a facility to penetrate the playwright's creativity: in other words, he believed the playwright was more important than the actor.[26] It is not wholly surprising that actors perceived Lessing as an enemy in their camp. After all, his pen could do serious damage to their career; his background in their own practice was negligible, and his judgements on it, in their eyes, highly questionable. It was not only against their interests to support Lessing in his critical function; it went against their knowledge and experience of theatre to entrust their livelihood to a man of letters, as opposed to another actor. The directorate, who in any case regarded Lessing as a force to be controlled, sided with the actors: after issue 25 actors' performances were no longer critiqued. This nullified Lessing's promise to analyse and articulate the actor's art at each step in his writing, and prevented him from carrying out what he saw as a major rôle. After only six months his function as in-house critic had all but broken down.

Towards the end of the *Hamburgische Dramaturgie* Lessing reveals the extent of his disillusion with the quality of acting in Hamburg, indeed in the country:

> I explained what I intended for this work in my prologue; my readers will know what it has actually become. It is not exactly the work I promised: it is something else, but for all that, I think, not a bad piece of work … I soon grew very weary with the latter half [of the *Dramaturgie*]. We have actors, but we have no dramatic art. If we had such an art in ancient times, we no longer have it today: it has been lost and must be invented from scratch.[27]

Perhaps it is a sign of how alienated Lessing had become from his work at the theatre, or an indication that he was not as fundamentally fascinated by acting as he was by writing. Ekhof, as Michael Sosulski has demonstrated, was a pioneer actor-trainer himself and in his lifetime did much to professionalise acting and introduce new techniques.[28] He was one of the outstanding actors in Germany as well as a progressive educator: it is certainly true that he achieved only a limited amount in two years, but Lessing learned much from him and was inspired by his ideals – though clearly was not persuaded that Ekhof could improve acting standards as thoroughly as was necessary. Lessing seemed more absorbed by the lack of critical vocabularies for analysing acting techniques, arguing that had defined standards existed, his rôle as in-house critic would have been acceptable to the actors. Without criteria, Lessing claimed, statements about acting could only be vague and equivocal. This is a moot point. Despite the fact that Lessing had found it virtually impossible to write anything about the actors which had not been construed as an insult, his quandary unquestionably inspired inheritors to develop critical vocabularies – Denis Diderot's

Le Paradoxe sur le comédien, for example, was written between 1770 and 1778.

Lessing cannot escape criticism himself. There is the matter of his writing style for the *Hamburgische Dramaturgie*. If it was not as racy and controversial as its piraters would have liked, it is also difficult to believe that Lessing was not as impatient with his readership as he was with the state of German theatre. He made little attempt to adjust his style of critical writing to the general reader. Throughout he assumed a knowledge and scholarly understanding of theatre and literature equal to his own, and his earnest digressions on the sources of certain plays and analyses of comparative translation were more appropriate for the polymath and historian. His style ranges from the pedantic and circumlocutory to the discursive and sometimes idiosyncratic harangue. There are several moments in the *Dramaturgie* when the author, suddenly reminded of the purpose behind his writing, interrupts himself, apologises for a lengthy diversion, and forces himself back to the task in hand. After spending fourteen consecutive numbers examining the ancient sources for Voltaire's *Merope*, for example, Lessing makes an apology to his readers for failing to meet their expectations.

> Am I still harping on about *Merope*! Truly, I pity the readers
> who had hopes of a theatre newspaper in these pages, one as rich
> and varied, as entertaining and droll as only a theatre newspaper
> could be ... instead they are getting lengthy, serious and
> turgid criticism of old familiar plays; complicated explorations
> of what tragedy may or may not be, and explanations of
> Aristotle to boot.[29]

In his defence, Lessing was always battling to locate and define his rôle as critic at the National Theatre. He clearly felt pressured to be more of a populist communicator than he was inclined to be, but his occasional ironic apologies were also implicit critiques of public attitudes to theatre, and he increasingly came to feel as though he had been called upon to fulfil a task regarded with indifference by the majority. He questioned the artistic and critical sophistication of theatregoers, most of whom, he claimed, were not eager for instruction and moral edification, but went to satisfy social curiosity, stifle boredom and raise a public profile.[30] Lessing was preaching to audiences who were not yet agreed on the significance of theatre at all, let alone its national importance. By the end of the *Hamburgische Dramaturgie*, Lessing has formed the view that the whole venture was doomed from the start because of its historical prematurity. The German nation, he opines bitterly, has not developed a sufficiently advanced moral awareness and has contributed to the downfall of the National Theatre through apathy. Enlightenment crusade aside, he was correct to identify a central contradiction undercutting the very basis of the theatre's foundation and supposed objectives: 'What a well-meaning flash of inspiration it was to create a National Theatre for the Germans, given that we Germans don't even have a nation!'[31]

Lessing perceived that the National Theatre had very little to offer a German repertory. In its brief life the National Theatre offered 308 performances of French plays, against 176 performances of German;[32] Voltaire proved the dominating figure (as he is in the *Dramaturgie*), with ten plays chosen for production. Of the German tragedies, only Lessing's *Miß Sara Sampson* did not sink into obscurity; of the German comedies comprising more than one act, ten playwrights are named, and again only Lessing's reputation has held. This compares with a list of twenty-one French dramatists, including Molière, Diderot, Beaumarchais and Voltaire. The National Theatre was attempting to celebrate German dramatists of stature who did not exist; and its inauguration presupposed a burgeoning dramatic culture, which, as it turned out, did not exist either. The directorate had certainly made the right choice in Lessing as a dramatist: with sixteen performances his comedy *Minna von Barnhelm* was by far the most popular play in the repertoire. The problem was that, besides Lessing, there were no other groundbreaking German dramatists.

There were certainly critics of the time who believed that the *Hamburgische Dramaturgie* had achieved the very opposite of its intentions, indeed, that it had positively harmed the chances of developing a confidence in German theatre and its playwrights:

> Though the evolution of dramatic theory would have lost much, I still almost wish that Lessing had not been responsible for criticism at the Hamburg theatre, but for its management. In my

opinion, our theatre is at far too an early and delicate stage of
its development to bear the regal sceptre of Lessing's
criticism ... Or has the *Dramaturgie* only been written for
our humiliation? ... Art critics are not the public, but they
form it. Now that we have a *Dramaturgie* are we likely to get a
theatre? An original German theatre? I doubt it very much.[33]

Aesthetes may find the *Dramaturgie* a rich source of interest, the
critic continues, but German playwrights will sink into depression.
The learning process has been entirely negative, the message insistent
on absence and lack without a strategy for action. But the critic contra-
dicts himself by pleading for reform by example. Lessing was that
example, but there were no obvious disciples.

The same critic also voices frustration with Lessing's long,
distracting digressions from the substance of the repertoire itself
and his tendency to dwell 'endlessly' on a single play, accuses him
of simply using the *Dramaturgie* to indulge his own aesthetic preoccupations with Aristotle, and questions the appropriateness of the
periodical form, condemning it as 'episodic' and lacking a clear, structured plan. This 'problem' with the form of the *Dramaturgie* dogs
even contemporary criticism: the work is often either condemned
for structural disjunctiveness or appropriated as a systematic political or aesthetic manifesto.[34] Lamport claims that the *Dramaturgie*
'embodies a coherent doctrine', and acknowledges it as 'a critical
work of immense importance'.[35] Whilst Lessing certainly failed
in his intention to create a 'critical register' that followed 'every
step of the writer's and actor's art', he never envisaged a conventional critical form for the work, and given its intended serial publication this is not surprising. The lack of a coherent analytical line
through the *Dramaturgie* cannot be denied; but Lessing was not
seeking one:

> I remind my readers, that this periodical is not intended to form
> a dramatic system. Consequently, I am not obliged to find
> solutions for problems which I raise. My thoughts may seem to
> connect less and less, indeed they may even appear to contradict
> each other: but they are thoughts that give substance to further

musings. I want only for this work to be a *Fermenta cognitionis.*[36]

Whatever its flaws, the *Hamburgische Dramaturgie* was totally original in conception. Though strangled by the contradictions of specific historical and cultural conditions, Lessing still acted as a critical mirror for Germany and articulated the dramatic crisis it faced. His appointment marked the beginning of a recognition of the need for a literary-critical presence in theatre, for self-analysis and public debate, the obstacles and challenges he set out in the *Hamburgische Dramaturgie* serving as an agenda for his intellectual heirs to address. What makes the *Hamburgische Dramaturgie* doubly unique is not just its contents, but the fact that it was written in conditions designed to facilitate the most direct of cultural interventions.

Lessing's legacy

Within two to three decades of its publication the *Hamburgische Dramaturgie* spawned imitators, and the employment of a specialist playwright/critic to reflect on practice began to be seen as desirable. In Austria the *Wienerische Dramaturgie* appeared in 1775, in Germany O. H. von Gemmingen's *Mannheimer Dramaturgie* was published in 1779, followed by J. F. Schink's *Dramaturgische Fragmente* (1781–4), A. von Knigge's *Dramaturgische Blätter* (1788–9), and the *Neue Hamburgische Dramaturgie* (1791) by H. C. Albrecht. An anonymous volume published in Leipzig melded two titles which Lessing had considered, *Didaskalien, oder Streifereyen im Gebiete der Dramaturgie* (Didascalia or Reflections on Dramaturgy) (1796). Lessing's immediate disciples, Friedrich Schiller (1759–1805) and Johann Wolfgang Goethe (1749–1832), found the *Hamburgische Dramaturgie* an inspirational text. Writing to Goethe in June 1799, Schiller described it as 'brilliant and animated'[37] and praised Lessing as the sharpest, most precise and broad-minded critic of his age, lamenting the lack of any German man of letters to equal his critical genius.

Two notable official dramaturgs in Germany in the century after the Hamburg experiment were Schiller and Ludwig Tieck

(1773–1853). Schiller became Dramaturg at the main theatre in Mannheim for twelve months, from 1783 to 1784. Theatre managers expressly modelled their enterprise on Schröder's original plans for Hamburg, and went public with their ambitions to found a national theatre. Earlier, they had even tried to persuade Lessing to resume his work as a dramaturg, though not surprisingly he had turned them down.[38] Fashioning himself after Lessing, and believing strongly that 'if we could have a national stage, we should be a nation',[39] Schiller drew up his own proposal for a *Mannheimer Dramaturgie* a year into his post. It was never written, and Schiller's life developed in a different direction, but his plan reveals the *Hamburgische Dramaturgie's* influence: he proposes to write a history of the Mannheim theatre, an annotated programme of the repertoire, an account of its constitution, actors' biographies and critiques of their performances and general essays on dramatic literature.[40] In a letter to the theatre's director he reveals the extent of his ambitions for the *Mannheimer Dramaturgie*, envisaging it as a means of securing the theatre's national standing.[41]

Schiller's actual work at the Mannheim theatre was mainly that of a house-dramatist, but he felt the strain of committing himself to three plays a year and only managed two; he did advise on repertoire but found, like Lessing, that theatre boards opted for commercial safety and populism rather than the new and unknown.[42] A major difficulty was that Schiller simply did not, at that stage in his career, have the outstanding critical and creative reputation that he later acquired, and could easily be sidelined. His contract was not renewed and he moved on.

In contrast to Lessing and Schiller, Tieck's creative work was not primarily dramatic. He was employed for his prowess at writing journalism and theatre essays, and the most obvious testament to his success as Dramaturg is that he remained in post for sixteen years. A leading theatre critic, distinguished prose writer, translator and ardent promoter of Shakespeare, Tieck became Dramaturg in Dresden in 1825. It meant a post, a salary, and a title for the first time in his life. Specifically, he advised on play selection, trained the younger actors in the art of declamation, and wrote critiques of company productions and plays at Dresden and other theatres in a local newspaper, the *Abend-Zeitung*. Tieck also cherished hopes of nurturing a nationally celebrated theatre and raising acting standards.[43] He was ultimately disappointed in his achievements at Dresden, but though he often found himself 'hemmed in from all sides' he was an authoritative figure with strong backers, and only voluntarily started to withdraw from his duties after 1836, finally leaving in 1841.[44] Like Lessing, he bore the brunt of wounded egos: actors resented his style of teaching,[45] Dresden playwrights his harsh pronouncements on their work, and the management were often wary of him.[46] But although he experienced turbulent times, including a plot to have him thrown out (by popular dramatist Theodor Winkler, who saw his promotion of élite literary tastes as a threat),[47] he was resilient, had a European-wide reputation and was a watchful diplomat. More importantly, whatever the managers' suspicions, they supported the endeavour and were pragmatic about some of its consequences.

Tieck's real impact was on repertoire and criticism. Though he was forced to agree that Winkler should be free to choose comedies at Dresden, Tieck certainly made his mark. Shakespeare was produced more often than ever before in Germany, plays by Lope de Vega and Calderon were staged, and German-speaking playwrights such as Kleist, Goethe, Lenz, Schiller, Solger and Grillparzer were championed. In 1826, only twelve months into his post, he published the *Dramaturgische Blätter*, a collection of essays written over the previous decade, including his *Abend-Zeitung* articles and his famous commentary on the London theatres in 1817. In 1852 Eduard Devrient published two further volumes of Tieck's theatre essays as part of Tieck's *Kritische Schriften*. The *Dramaturgische Blätter* were hailed as outstandingly original and as a very significant step in Germany's evolution of theatre criticism, drawing fulsome praise from Goethe and Heine.[48] A well-travelled theatre critic, Tieck's wide-ranging comparative analyses of the dramatic arts in his homeland and abroad were groundbreaking: he wrote on Spanish, French and Italian theatre arts, and as Zeydel argues, came close to making Shakespeare 'a household word'.[49] Where Lessing had been remorselessly scholarly, Tieck's style was more palatable, and if he thought a play or playwright particularly challenging he wrote an article in advance of the première to prepare audiences. He also extended his criticism to scenery and costume, compared acting styles in different countries, and was deeply interested in stage spaces and how relationships with audiences might be affected by architecture. Tieck may have been dissatisfied, and his time at Dresden has tended to be viewed as 'a hopeless struggle',[50] but his influence was lasting, and he undoubtedly played an important part in changing dramatic tastes in Germany.

What is intriguing about the cases of Lessing, Schiller and Tieck is the receptivity of German theatre culture to the idea that playwrights and play-makers benefit and develop from a constant interface with a reflective third party. Lessing's experiment collapsed, Schiller's was cut short, Tieck's was far from plain sailing, but managers grasped the wider implications of a progressive project and were not deterred. From the late eighteenth century onwards theatre in Germany, Austria and Scandinavia became far more than a matter of entertainment: it became part of an Enlightenment mission to acculturate audiences, and part of a nationalist agenda to foster a people's identity and their collective values. In Germany, in particular, theatre came to occupy a central rôle in the country's cultural life, and Lessing is just the beginning of a line of exploratory trial and error which can be traced to Brecht and the very many dramaturgs working in Germany today. This fundamental receptivity to the interconnectedness of theory and practice is not a cultural given in the English-speaking West. On the contrary, establishing the seemingly obvious fact that they are not separate territories but are dynamically interrelated was a desperately hard fought, twentieth-century battle for English-speaking thinkers and practitioners. The academy and the theatre industry may mix more than ever before, but their suspicion of each other is still strong.

Leaving aside the theory–praxis debate, the cultural value of establishing and nurturing a high quality of dramatic literature is not difficult to appreciate. The political implications of Lessing's experiment (both positive and negative) have resonated, and it is noteworthy that the first official appointments of dramaturgs or literary managers in any country, East or West, have always come about in the context of a campaign for a national theatre or desire to identify the characteristics of a distinctively home-grown dramatic literature. Those employed in the century after Lessing were invariably playwrights or critics, editors, translators or actor-trainers – some individuals possessed a mixture of these skills and others all of them. One of the first official dramaturgs engaged at a theatre outside Germany was Joseph Schreyvogel (1768–1832), who worked at the Burgtheater in Vienna as Dramaturg und Artistischer Sekretär (Dramaturg and Artistic Secretary) from 1814 to 1832.[51] He displayed a brilliance at selecting classical plays and discovering new talent, as well as fighting off Metternich's censors, securing not just the Burgtheater's reputation as Austria's national theatre, but also giving it an international reputation.[52] In Denmark Peder Rosenstand-Goiske (1752–1803), inspired by Lessing's example, produced Denmark's earliest systematic theatre reviewing, and became Dramaturg at the Danish Royal Theatre from 1780 to 1792. Goiske took his rôle as an educator with the utmost seriousness, his criticism of plays and performers on occasion exacerbating 'audience tumults'.[53] In other countries, official appointments of dramaturgs were delayed because of cultural antipathy to the intellectualisation of theatre, because national theatre movements were not yet underway, as in Britain and America, and/or because the existence of rigid state or imperial controls and theatrical censorship, as in Russia and France, made an oppositional presence in theatre impossible.

Notes

1. Gotthold Ephraim Lessing, *Hamburgische Dramaturgie*, in *Werke*, ed. J. Petersen and W. von Olshausen, 25 vols. (Berlin: Bong and Co., 1925–35), v (henceforth PO, v).
2. See W. H. Bruford, *Germany in the Eighteenth Century: The Social Background of the Literary Revival* (1935; Cambridge: Cambridge University Press, 1980), pp. 1–43; and Mary Fulbrook, *A Concise History of Germany* (Cambridge: Cambridge University Press, 1990).
3. See Michael J. Sosulski, 'Trained Minds, Disciplined Bodies: Konrad Ekhof and the Reform of the German Actor', in *Lessing Yearbook* (1999), 31, pp. 131–56.

4. See J. G. Robertson, *Lessing's Dramatic Theory* (Cambridge: Cambridge University Press, 1939), pp. 20–3.

5. *Ibid.*, pp. 18–20.

6. *Ibid.*, pp. 20–1.

7. Sosulski, 'Trained Minds', p. 132.

8. Lessing had translated extensively from Greek, Latin, French and Italian, and been responsible for translating the dramatic treatises of Riccoboni and Diderot.

9. PO, v, *Stücke* 101–4, p. 407.

10. *Ibid.*, p. 408.

11. *Ibid.*, p. 407.

12. See F. J. Lamport, *Lessing and the Drama* (Oxford: Clarendon Press, 1981), p. 124.

13. *Beyträge zur Historie und Aufnahme des Theaters*, co-edited with Christlob Mylius, a quarterly periodical begun in 1750 and limited to four issues. The intentions behind it were the improvement of taste by examining works of criticism, and the provision of models for the German theatre through the translation of other European plays. See PO, vii.

14. *Theatralische Bibliothek*, a periodical issued from 1754 to 1758 and conceived as a critical history of the theatre.

15. *Briefe, die neueste Literatur betreffend*, a literary weekly which appeared from 1759 to 1765. Lessing was editor until 1760. See PO, ix.

16. Johann Christoph Gottsched, 'Versuch einer Critischen Dichtkunst', originally published in 1730; see *Schriften zur Literatur*, ed. Horst Steinmetz (Stuttgart: Reclam, 1982), pp. 12–196.

17. Lamport insists (quite extraordinarily) on depoliticising Lessing's domestic tragedies, arguing that he just wanted 'to furnish the German theatre with works of timeless, universal human appeal'. See F. J. Lamport, *German Classical Drama* (Cambridge: Cambridge University Press, 1992), p. 25.

18. PO, v, *Stücke* 101–4, p. 409.

19. *Ibid.*

20. PO, v, pp. 23–6.

21. *Ibid.*, p. 25.

22. Letter to Karl Lessing, 2 June 1767, in G. E. Lessing, *Sämtliche Schriften*, ed. K. von Lachmann, 23 vols. (Berlin: Muncker, 1886–1924), XVII, 232.

23. PO, V, p. 25.

24. *Ibid.*

25. Voltaire, Diderot and Corneille are discussed at great length.

26. PO, V, p. 26.

27. PO, V, *Stücke* 101–4, p. 410.

28. Sosulski, 'Trained Minds'.

29. PO, V, *Stücke* 50, p. 215.

30. PO, V, *Stücke* 80, p. 332.

31. PO, V, *Stücke* 101–4, p. 410.

32. See J. G. Robertson's table on p. 47 of *Schiller After a Century* (Edinburgh and London: Blackwood, 1905).

33. Anonymous critic, reprinted in Horst Steinmetz, ed., *Lessing – ein unpoetischer Dichter* (Frankfurt and Bonn: Athenäum, 1969), pp. 73–7 (p. 74).

34. See, for example, Paul Rilla's *Lessing und sein Zeitalter* (Berlin: Aufbau Verlag, 1981), pp. 120–86, in which it is argued that Lessing wrote the *Dramaturgie* to further the bourgeois struggle for power. See also Klaus L. Berghahn's edition and commentary of *Hamburgische Dramaturgie* (Stuttgart: Reclam, 1981). Unhelpfully, Berghahn argues for the work as a 'continuation of *Laokoon*' (p. 532). *Laokoon*, begun in 1763 and published in 1765, was Lessing's treatise on the different means of expression involved in the plastic and the literary arts respectively.

35. Lamport, *Lessing and the Drama*, pp. 151 and 153.

36. PO, V, *Stücke* 95, p. 388.

37. Emil Staiger, ed., *Der Briefwechsel zwischen Schiller und Goethe* (Frankfurt-on-Main: Insel, 1966), p. 756.

38. See Robertson, *Schiller After a Century*, pp. 54–5.

39. From Schiller's inaugural address to the German Society of the Palatinate, 26.6.1784. See H. B. Garland, *Schiller* (London: Harrap and Co., 1949), pp. 84–5.

40. See Schiller's 'Entwurf einer Mannheimer Dramaturgie', in *Sämtliche Werke*, V, 831–3.

41. Letter to Dalberg, 2 July 1884. Friedrich Schiller, *Schillers Werke*, ed. J. Petersen and Hermann Schneider (Weimar: Böhlaus, 1956), XXIII, p. 153.

42. August Wilhelm Iffland (1759–1814), actor and writer of popular sentimental drama, made a mockery of Schiller's position at Mannheim in F. W. Gotter's play *Der Schwarze Mann* in 1784. See Garland, *Schiller*, p. 87.

43. Ludwig Tieck, *Letters*, ed. Edwin H. Zeydel, Percy Matenko and Robert Hendon Fife (Oxford: Oxford University Press, 1937), I, p. 418.

44. Roger Paulin's words: see his account of the institutional politics Tieck faced in *Ludwig Tieck* (Oxford: Oxford University Press, 1985), pp. 275–303.

45. Tieck's play readings were renowned, but beyond the vocal work his acting experience was limited, see Edwin H. Zeydel, *Ludwig Tieck: The German Romanticist* (Princeton: Princeton University Press, 1935), pp. 247–8.

46. *Ibid.*, p. 259; Paulin, *Tieck*, p. 284.

47. Paulin, *Tieck*, pp. 275–6 and 281. Winkler wrote hack-dramas, which went down well in Dresden.

48. *Ibid.*, p. 263.

49. Zeydel, *Tieck*, p. 247.

50. *Ibid.*, p. 261. Paulin is ambivalent about Tieck's tenure, seeing him as a victim of unenlightened intriguers, but at the same time acknowledging his 'not inconsiderable egoism' (*Tieck*, p. 285).

51. He was de facto the theatre's managing director.

52. Shreyvogel discovered Franz Grillparzer, who became Austria's most celebrated playwright.

53. See Laurence Senelick, ed., *National Theatre in Northern and Eastern Europe, 1746–1900* (Cambridge: Cambridge University Press, 1991), p. 28.

3   Dramaturgy in nineteenth-century England

Literary administration and the (actor-)manager 1800–1900

If German entrepreneurs were exploring and developing the function and purpose of dramaturgs, English managers were not. Lessing enjoyed popularity as a playwright, but the *Hamburgische Dramaturgie* remained untranslated in Britain (and America) for much of the century. Without exception a nation's first official dramaturg or literary manager appears in its state-subsidised national theatre, and England not only had none to offer, but lacked the political momentum to acquire one. Commerical success had to be guaranteed for a theatre to stay afloat, so emphasis remained firmly on box-office returns and low-risk strategies. Product, not process, dominated actor-managers' waking thoughts. Dramaturgical functions had nevertheless to be undertaken, and though, as in the eighteenth century, much can be put down to organised chaos, it is clear that unofficial, 'hidden' play readers, advisers, researchers and literary administrators played an important and intriguing rôle at certain theatres.

Theatre historians agree that a major feature of the nineteenth century was the irresistible rise of the manager, and that managers at the main London and regional theatres had normally made names as actors. Another feature of the age was an extraordinary growth in theatre-building: Nicoll lists nine London theatres in regular use in 1800, 89 by 1850 and 144 by 1900; in the English regions, Ireland, Scotland and Wales, he calculates that there were around 58 theatres in 1850 and 351 by 1900.[1] The 1843 Theatre Regulation Act, which abolished the privileges of Drury Lane and Covent Garden, and permitted all theatres to produce (subject to the Lord Chamberlain) any kind of drama, partly explains this rapid growth.

The significant increase of theatres meant that the demand for plays rose, and that managers needed to be doubly industrious in thinking up repertoires, searching out plot lines, commissioning adaptations, seeking new talent and reading unsolicited manuscripts. Managers dominated theatre hierarchy, taking artistic and administrative functions upon themselves, and financed the theatre themselves or via a backer. They bore the risks and took the profits – and before mid-century the risks were considerable. From the 1860s actor-managers increasingly found significant financial gain in presenting long runs of popular plays (mostly melodramas and Shakespearean adaptations), in which they invariably took the main rôle. The long run ushered in an era of effective monopolisation by actor-managers that lasted until 1914, deepening the artistic stagnancy of mainstream stages.

Whilst nineteenth-century English theatres tell the story of the hegemony of the actor-manager, they also encode his or her demise. The plethora of functions most managers took upon themselves led to an impossible workload, and an over-centralised system of management meant that inefficiencies were rife – especially when it came to literary affairs. Managers were officially responsible for every aspect of running a theatre, from hiring actors, backstage and front-of-house personnel, advisers and administrators, to finance, selecting, reading, commissioning, adapting and scheduling plays, supervising rehearsals, organising tours and courting illustrious actors and authors. These were merely the obvious tasks; no list can convey the sheer intensity and complexity of the average manager's working day – especially if they were also performing. Theatre histories have tended to lend a uniformity to styles of management, but individual managers organised their theatres according to their own persuasions and prejudices. Managers were certainly at the apex of the hierarchy, but the professional tiers that existed below them in the state-run theatres in France and Germany were non-existent in England, and while certain officials were charged with specific functions, they were regularly called on to perform others as need dictated. Certain dramaturgical functions, however, became more pronounced, and as the numbers of theatres multiplied and competition grew more intense, managers focused in particular on the search for new plays (overwhelmingly, this meant plot pilfering and adaptations from French dramas), on crowd-pulling angles on the classics and on the need to demonstrate respectable literary credentials. Different managers found different solutions, some employing readers and advisers, and endeavouring to attach the names of successful writers to their establishments.

Some managers (Alfred Bunn, for example) were only too happy to delegate playreading and employ literary advisers; some merely did not want to be *seen* to delegate but did so (Herbert Beerbohm Tree); some (like William Charles Macready) felt that only they were adequately qualified to consult with the writer about preparing and editing a text; and others, if the steady flow of protests from dramatists is to be believed, left new manuscripts to gather dust (Robert Elliston behaved villainously in this respect). Certainly, in the heydays of the 1880s and 1890s, actor-managers proved most reluctant to delegate, and as they took a proliferating, indeed impossible, workload increasingly upon themselves, the conception, preparation, research and writing of a play was often dictated, if not mostly executed, by them – to the detriment of innovative drama.

The sheer stress and fatigue induced by theatre management is a leitmotif of many diaries and memoirs, and the first casualties were usually the unsolicited manuscripts in theatres where there was no designated reader. Macready insisted on reading as many new plays as physically possible, but he heartily resented it:

> Looked over two plays, *Petronius* and *Bertrand*, which it was not possible to read, hardly as I tried. They are utter trash, and it is really trying one's patience to lose so much time over such worthless, hopeless stuff; I cannot longer afford the time.[2]

Macready's diaries are deeply scored with the anxieties of management, which he felt told upon his acting and distracted him from 'ruminating upon my art'[3] – clashes which many actor-managers knew all too well but failed to negotiate adequately. Moments of despair could occur daily: Charles Kean was sometimes at a loss to know why he did what he did: 'What can induce one to encounter the endless turmoil, the dissatisfaction, the risk, the anxiety, the incessant wear and tear, both mental and physical, which are inseparable from the management of a theatre?'[4] In short, actor-managers complained that their schedules were punishing in the extreme, and their work never done. Augustus Harris, manager of Drury Lane from 1879 to 1896, described his pantomime season of 1880 as a life of constant upheaval, of a 'hundred daily interviews' with staff and others connected with theatre business; he was 'besieged from morning till night', and claimed that he went 'without one moment's peace, without time for eating, drinking, or even sleeping'.[5] The toll on managers could be deadly: if Macready sensed the deterioration in his health, Lady Alexander was never in doubt that, like others, her husband, George Alexander, 'really hastened his end by overwork'.[6]

The concentration of dramaturgical functions in the figure of the actor-manager and the subsequent impossibility of ever managing such a workload efficiently or effectively is one reason why the system imploded, but it was also a reason for Harley Granville Barker and William Archer's later theorisation of a *visible, professionalised* tier of intermediary dramaturgical help. The need to find an intermediary to liaise between playwrights and managers, which had suggested itself in the eighteenth century, only grew more urgent as the nineteenth century progressed. Writers still complained of indifferent and exploitative managers. Managers frequently dreaded dealings with established and lesser-known authors alike, and the horror that a rejected dramatist could inspire with their persistent harassment was for certain managers the worst aspect of their profession.[7]

As the century drew to a close actor-managers were increasingly held responsible for what progressive critics saw as the divorce between theatre and literature. Oswald Crawfurd was not alone in perceiving the 'paramount evil' of the actor-manager in what he termed the literary 'degradation' of the London stage:[8]

> It is very evident that the drama suffers by the system, because of the obvious temptation an actor-manager is under to accept plays less with regard to their intrinsic merits or their

adaptability to the various talents of the actors in his company than to the fact of whether or no they contain parts in which he, the autocrat player, can make a conspicuous figure.[9]

Crawfurd saw possible remedy only in an educated, critically active public who demanded theatrical reforms, and the replacement of the actor-manager with 'an impartial board of experienced and instructed men', a theatre with a representative government within itself modelled on the founding principles of the Comédie Française.[10] Crawfurd was representative of those in favour of state subsidy and 'intellectual drama'; actor-managers, not surprisingly, fallaciously claimed that there could not possibly be a better alternative to themselves, and that *if* England had any good dramatists, they would be the first to stage their work. The debate was fierce throughout the 1890s.[11]

Playreaders and literary advisers 1800–1900

Accounts of the functions of Readers and Literary Advisers[12] in this era lie accidentally embedded in dominant narratives about authors' or actor-managers' lives and in the histories of particular institutions. The picture is fragmentary, and most detail is found in connection with the patent and larger theatres in London in the first half of the century, where Readers and Advisers were prominent in competitions to promote their theatre either as a national house of drama or a theatre for 'up-market', illegitimate drama. The large theatres could, of course, afford to make official appointments, which was not necessarily the case elsewhere, and the same informal reading and advising arrangements from the previous century continued in many theatres.

John Russell Stephens's two-page history of officially appointed Readers and Literary Advisers in the nineteenth century, which is all that recent scholarship has to offer, describes a proliferation of posts until the 1850s and a gradual decline into non-existence by 1900.[13] In the early 1880s Dutton Cook gloomily likened the Reader of Plays to 'an extinct animal, whose remains, occasionally discovered, reveal an antidiluvian state of existence'.[14] Cook reflected on the 'very considerable importance' of the post in the 1830s, speculated that it came about as a result of both actor-managers' overwhelming workloads and their insufficiently 'lettered' backgrounds, and attributed its disappearance to the restructuring of theatre managements and the dearth of new plays, play publishers and dramatically inclined readers amongst the public.[15] There is little substantial material to support Cook's claim of the death of the Reader – he himself acknowledges that Readers' positions had previously been rendered invisible – and what Cook observed was, in fact, a trend for the obscuration or deprofessionalisation of Readers and/or Advisers rather than their actual demise.[16]

The work of Readers was no more glamorous in the early nineteenth century than in the eighteenth, but the function was lent a new prestige when Lord Byron joined the Drury Lane sub-committee of management in 1815 and took it upon himself to read and commission new plays. Byron's commitment lasted no more than a year, and his letters testify to drudgery and despair. Apart from the dubious quality of the five hundred plays he rescued from the shelves and divided between himself and others on the committee (not one of those in his share, he claimed, 'could be conscientiously tolerated'[17]), he found the absence of serious, organised discussion and decision-making procedures beyond endurance:

> all *my* new function consists in listening to the despair of
> Cavendish Bradshaw, the hopes of Kinnaird, the wishes of Lord
> Essex, the complaints of Whitbread, and the calculations of Peter
> Moore, – all of which, and whom, seem totally at variance.[18]

He also found dealing with the droves of aspiring writers hair-raisingly stressful:

> The Scenes I had to go through! – the authors – and the
> authoresses – the Milliners – the wild Irishmen – the people from
> Brighton – from Blackwell – from Chatham – from Cheltenham –
> from Dublin – from Dundee – who came upon me! – to all of
> whom it was proper to give a civil answer – and hearing – and a
> reading – ... As I am really a civil and polite person – and *do*
> hate giving pain – when it can be avoided – I sent them up to
> Douglas Kinnaird – who is a man of business – and sufficiently
> ready with a negative – and left them to settle with him –[19]

Unlike the playwrights from whom he recoiled, Byron had never been in the position of having to beg the notice of Readers or theatre managements. He was predominantly a poet and a nobleman of independent financial means, all of which made him an exceptional case; it is no surprise that he soon opted to depart. Official Readers' posts were generally filled by journeymen playwrights, and Frederick Reynolds (1764–1841), Thomas Morton (1764–1838) and Edward Fitzball (1793–1873), all of whom worked as Readers for Covent Garden or Drury Lane at various times in the 1820s–1850s, were at the top of the profession.

All three men were prolific adaptors, editors and playwrights, but were unable, for most of their lives, to earn a living from their plays alone, and all three acquired a special advisory status with successive actor-manager employers. Fitzball wrote of reading 'brainracking M. S. S. [*sic*]' and sitting 'like an owl in a cobwebby corner of the theatre, cogitating over incomprehensibilities';[20] he, in particular, was very conscientious about reading and returning manuscripts and corresponding with unknown authors, his past treatment as a playwright having made him acutely aware of the inefficiencies of theatre managements:[21] 'the fact of remembering that I invariably answered every letter, and, with the best grace in my power, mitigated every disappointment, is to me, at this moment, an unspeakable satisfaction'.[22] As far as Fitzball was concerned a good Reader was a security for all writers, for he guaranteed the efficient organisation of playscripts and could bring an administrative order to what was normatively bureaucratic chaos, engendered by many managers' indifference towards unsolicited manuscripts. Reynolds did his utmost to ensure that new plays were *read*, and not left to gather dust for years, as in the case of one unfortunate writer who waited sixteen years for a response.[23] The 'disappearance' of manuscripts for years on end was not unusual: much of the time it was sheer negligence and lack of organisation, but 'disappearances' also provided convenient exit routes for managers when faced with over-zealous playwrights who wrote lamentable work, and equally could be a face-saving avoidance tactic when dealing with unsuitable or plainly bad plays by well-known writers.[24]

> The great advantage of a reader in a theatre is that no M. S. *can be lost.* It is the duty of the reader, if it will not serve the interest of the establishment, or is unactable, to punctually return a M. S. *kindly,* and with *thanks* to the author; and if that be possible, *without wounding* his *feelings.* I have read as many as two hundred different pieces a season, not one of which could have possibly suited the establishment; but where I saw the *slightest* chance, I always most strenuously urged the manager to *peruse* it.[25]

Fitzball took his advocacy of aspiring playwrights very seriously, but as this indicates, established writers or in-house dramatists were preferred, and Fitzball, Reynolds and Morton would often be engaged in cutting such plays or rendering them dramaturgically sound.[26] Theatre manager Alfred Bunn relied totally on Reynolds's judgement: plays refused by Reynolds were refused by Bunn,[27] who insisted that Reynolds was 'not merely reader of plays but general adviser, to whose experience and wisdom I could at all times safely apply for counsel'.[28] Bunn elsewhere referred him as 'my old and valued friend, my reader of plays and thinker-general, Reynolds the "dramatic wight"'.[29] Reynolds, then, had considerable hidden power: he was, in many respects, the thinker behind the planning and setting of the repertoire, and clearly had remarkable dramaturgical judgement when it came to problematic scripts; to Bunn, those talents were nothing less than magical, and Reynolds was a 'wight', a supernatural conjuror of drama sometimes from the most improbable of scripts and scenarios.

Bunn's previous Reader, Morton, had been no less important to him, though each man had a different *modus operandi.* Morton's relationship with Bunn was on a more formal footing, and Morton wrote reports which either recommended or damned the play concerned:

> *Woman.* – An elegant bit of French comedy – the intrigue clever, the dialogue smart and nimble … Its merits (could it be well played) entitle it to a hearing; but whether that hearing would reward the theatre, you as manager must determine …

The Iron Shroud. – Avoid it …
Imbio, or the *Requital.* – Nonsense.
The Refusal. – No better …
One fool makes Many. – the author, I am sorry to say is,
one of the "many" …
Podesta. – This play could not be advantageously acted. The plot
is complicated – to an audience inexplicable; it has all the
confusion of an Italian feud: but none of the grandeur of a Fiesco,
or a Foscari. There is some poetry, some dramatic power, and
some dramatic situations, but not enough to balance the defects.[30]

Morton's dogged reading of the hundreds of manuscripts that he
received every year simultaneously saved Bunn from an impossible
labour while focusing him on the few scripts that might be of interest.
Bunn was not a man of literary instincts (as his efforts at playwriting
demonstrate), and Dutton Cook's theory of the insufficiently lettered
man needing support is true in this case. Morton was sharply alert to
the politics of plays wanted by Drury Lane and equally attuned to the
needs to fit the play to the company of actors and to the audience. His
reports indicate that he was focused solely on serving the interests of
Bunn (he sees himself as servant rather than equal) and was far less
consumed by desires to show courtesy and encouragement to aspiring
writers. A Reader's work was never done, and the acceptance of such a
post invariably meant that the playwriting career of the individual
concerned was overtaken by their duties. But a good Reader was an
invaluable asset and the financial lure could be tempting; James
Winston was apparently offered the fantastic sum of £1,000 by Robert
Elliston in 1821 to become 'superviser of plays, etc.' at Drury Lane.[31]

From the late 1850s to 1900 officially appointed Readers and
Advisers do not, as Cook asserts, become an extinct species, but they
do become increasingly invisible. There were three major factors: the
ascendant model of the actor-manager as autocrat; the cult of the
actor; and the gradual domination of repertoires by the 'long run'. As
plays began to run for weeks, months or, in some cases, years, the
pressure to find and commission new work decreased. The staple diet
of Shakespeare, comic opera, music theatre, burlesque and melodrama

contented audiences, and actor-managers were not inclined to experiment with new work when they could make lucrative profits from tried and tested (and often cheap) writers. Conscientious actor-managers continued to employ Readers, but generally as a stop-gap measure when they felt that their own workloads and those of their friends and associates offered them no alternative.[32] The status of the Reader therefore fell, and many actor-managers would only appoint them *in extremis*, preferring to read scripts in person. Furthermore, most actor-managers were more interested in the size and potential of their own part than they were in the play itself; and towards the end of the century it became common practice for actor-managers to employ 'secretaries' who weeded out plays that were then passed on to lead actors to read.[33]

There is much to be written on the hidden phenomenon of actor-managers' wives taking on the functions of reading and advising for their husbands in the latter part of the century. A. E. W. Mason's trivialisation of Lady Alexander's rôle with respect to Sir George Alexander's management of the St James's Theatre in the 1890s is a classic example of the way in which such contributions have been marginalised;[34] but Lady Alexander's epilogue paints a rather different picture.

> I read a great many plays, and if one sent me to sleep and another woke me up I felt the latter was the play to produce ... I had a great faculty for being able to tell Alec the plot of a play and to interest him enough to make him read it ... When an author read a play to him I was always present.[35]

Since George Alexander's policy at the St James's was to promote new plays by British authors, he no doubt found his wife's intervention invaluable. Similarly Madge Kendal, joint manager of the St James's from 1879 to 1888 with her husband, W. H. Kendal, and John Hare, worked tirelessly in the capacities of reading and advising, and was particularly interested in nurturing aspiring playwrights.

> Mr Kendal and I get quantities of plays brought to us and we make it a rule to read nearly every one of them ... Sometimes

authors will leave plays with us for three or four weeks, or for as
many months, and then, after a little while, they write and ask us
whether we have read them, and what our opinion is. We often
write a very detailed opinion, which is sometimes shown to
other managers, and used as a lever ... As a rule, my husband and
I, every night of our lives, read something or other, or I go through
a book that perhaps will make into a play.[36]

Shaw was in no doubt about the significant working rôle played by
actor-managers' wives in all aspects of theatre management, and
wrote a humorous sketch celebrating the ironies of husbands receiving
credit for work their wives had accomplished.[37]

By the end of the century there were actor-managers who
thought that admitting to needing literary advice was tantamount to
declaring one's professional inadequacy. Herbert Beerbohm Tree,
whose cavalier attitude to playwrights and their texts was the despair
of many,[38] went so far as to ridicule the necessity of literary advisers
and deny the capacities of Comyns Carr in print. Tree referred to him
as his 'private secretary', but Comyns Carr used the term 'Literary
Adviser' and it was well known on the theatrical circuit that this was
the more accurate term:

> Dear Sir
> I have of late noticed in the Press frequent references to
> 'Mr Tree's literary adviser'. As I have such good reason to be
> grateful to the valued members of my staff, I should be loth to
> burthen any of them with the errors of judgement, of style, of
> grammar and of spelling inseparable from the works of an
> actor-manager. Will you kindly allow me to state that the
> only responsible 'literary adviser' attached to Her Majesty's
> Theatre is your faithful servant,
> Herbert Beerbohm Tree[39]

It was not unknown for Readers and Advisers to get the raw end of both
playwrights' and actor-managers' tongues, and their intermediary status made them convenient scapegoats. Morton had been the subject of
a vitriolic attack by a resentful writer in the 1820s and 1830s,[40] and

by the end of the century there was a more popular, negative view of the Reader or Adviser as an official who existed to do little more than hinder playwrights from direct access to actor-managers – a sign, no doubt, of the growing confidence and empowerment of the professional playwright.[41]

Readers and Advisers did not cease to exist, but their importance was eclipsed by the personalities and working practices of increasingly autocratic actor-managers. Overall patterns of employment at the larger theatres changed from long-term to short-term, and those in full, long-term employment were rendered 'invisible' through a popular tendency to demean their status. This seems to have continued into the early twentieth century: a book written by a full-time Reader who worked at the Stage Society for at least ten years from the turn of the century, and published in 1936 without ascription, was symbolically titled *Anonymous*, and contains a description of the contempt of one playwright when he discovered that his first contact with the theatre had been fixed with the Reader.[42] The author of *Anonymous* was a woman called Agnes Platt and it is significant that she hid her identity; presumably this was a matter of professional discretion and diplomacy, but one also wonders if she felt that in confessing her sex she might be taken less seriously. Officially appointed female Readers are very much harder to locate in historical records than men.

Dramatic criticism

English theatres did not emulate Lessing's radical critical residency, though his plays, like Goethe's, Schiller's and Kotzebue's, were influential in the early part of the century. Lessing's status as a critic of performance was appreciated by a small intellectual minority in England, but the unrelenting earnestness of the *Hamburgische Dramaturgie* was largely lost on a developing tradition of English theatre criticism which favoured vernacular wit over dry scholasticism. Whereas nineteenth-century German critics wrote in a culture which increasingly accepted the centrality of theatre as a 'moral institution',[43] English critics were caught between their desire to write seriously about the theatre and the dangers of associating themselves with an art form that had historically been perceived as intellectually and morally impoverished: satire, self-mockery and coruscating wit were, therefore, often a means of relaying their messages in a way that guaranteed readership and protected their reputations.[44] Lessing's *Dramaturgie* was translated in 1879, albeit in an abridged version,[45] but did not have the impact in England which it had enjoyed in Germany, and Lessing remained predominantly known for his plays and for his aesthetic and philosophical writings.[46]

By the end of the century dramatic criticism had evolved into a distinct and popular subject, and had shifted its ground from the isolated though brilliant essay writing of William Hazlitt, Charles Lamb and Leigh Hunt to occupy dozens of column inches not only in the national and local press but also in the many theatrical journals and newspapers established specifically to cater for mass public demand.[47] Theatre had become a subject of printed debate as never before, and Shaw's dazzling weekly polemics in the *Saturday Review* from 1895 to 1898 represented the zenith of the reviewer's art.[48] From the 1880s onwards dominant general subjects ranged from arguments for and against a national theatre, censorship, and the decline or rebirth of literary drama (depending on your point of view), to debates about the function of criticism and theatre critics themselves. Essays and reviews abounded, but William Archer's *English Dramatists of Today* (1882) provided the first substantial critique of contemporary dramatic writing, with an overview of the material and intellectual conditions for dramatists, of the shortcomings of English theatre criticism and of the supposed philistinism of audiences.[49] Archer had produced a cultural study of theatre and new writing, and his mission to nurture a new national drama had distinct parallels with Lessing's objectives more than a century before.[50]

Despite such progress, French and German intellectual developments still made much English dramatic criticism look amateurish.[51] In the 1890s Shaw and Wilde both complained of the dilettantism of journalistic critical writing, Shaw bemoaning the absence of a professional training and formal career structure, and claiming that accident and opportunism created second-rate theatre critics. Most dramatic criticism published in the newspapers was

'mere street-boy guying',[52] argued Shaw, and was almost entirely
'deficient in technical connoisseurship', though

> never insensible or indifferent to what it calls 'the moral
> tendency' of the drama ... Touch that nerve ever so lightly,
> and we shriek, seeing the downfall of all civil society
> imminent upon the least countenance given to a bad example
> set in serious drama on the stage. Thus we may be bad critics;
> but we are earnest agitators.[53]

Shaw was exaggerating but, in a sense, he was right: theatre criticism
in England did not have the traditions of aesthetic and philosophical
rigour which existed in France and Germany. And he was right again
when he argued that theatre in England had not taken itself seriously
as 'a factory of thought, a prompter of conscience, an elucidator of
social conduct'[54] – politics and censorship had, in fact, made this very
difficult.

Research

The function of research became accentuated as the vogue for so-called
'archaeological' and pictorial stagings of Shakespeare intensified after
J. R. Planché's historical costume research for Charles Kemble at
Covent Garden in the 1820s, and especially after Charles Kean's management at the Princess's Theatre from 1850 to 1859. Planché and Kean
carried out their researches in extraordinary detail, and ultimately both
became members of the Society of Antiquaries (in 1829 and 1857
respectively). It was Kean's practice to produce meticulous documentation of his historical sources, and he employed J. W. Calcraft as an
unofficial research assistant.[55] Calcraft's research function was unusual for the age; managers generally hired established experts such as
artists or architects for a particular project; many did their own dramaturgical research, and some, like the Bancrofts and Beerbohm Tree,
made a point of undertaking research trips abroad in person.[56]
Towards the end of the century actor-managers became more conscious
of the need to explain innovative interpretations of plays to audiences,
and Comyns Carr, for example, was employed by Henry Irving at least
once to research and write explanatory pamphlets for audiences.[57]

In-house criticism

Arrangements for in-house criticism of performances were not formalised and sprang up through a mixture of circumstance and interpersonal relations. Evidence is scattered and points to a multiplication of critical functions during the nineteenth century, though English scholarship has largely been blind to the significance of their existence. Although many established theatre critics had close ties with theatre management and were commonly also aspiring playwrights, actor-managers preferred to rely on friends, professional colleagues and spouses (often friends and colleagues too) for critical feedback. Readers, whose advice or intervention was often sought on the development of the play text, could, when requested, act as unofficial critics of performance to the actor-manager or to the stage-manager, but channels of criticism were not formalised and their views were not necessarily privileged above those of others. At Drury Lane, Fitzball was clear that one of his duties was 'to witness the first night's performance of every novelty and report my opinion to the manager next morning', though he does not indicate whether other members of staff were expected to do the same.[58] What is interesting is that Fitzball's services in this respect are required particularly in relation to new plays: it seems likely that he engaged in the post-production refinement of scripts if they needed it, and was one of the voices that counselled for or against the continuation of production. William Charles Macready dispersed critical, editorial and reading functions among a managerial team of trusted colleagues, and also consulted an array of high-profile intellectual friends when necessary.[59] Critical functions expected of his managerial team included watching plays elsewhere in London, especially at the rival patent house, watching plays in-house during rehearsal and on first nights, and garnering information on promising plays and playwrights for possible future billing.[60] Macready's critical, intellectual circle was sizeable and noted in its day, but his managements of Covent Garden (1837–9) and Drury Lane (1841–3) were nonetheless short-lived and financially ruinous.

Critical feedback to individual actors arose through circumstance. Watching Edmund Kean rehearse *Richard III* at Drury Lane in 1814, playwright and reader Thomas Dibdin discreetly imparted his doubts to Kean about his interpretation of certain passages and was asked to take home the actor's book and mark up his critiques; though Dibdin was unsure of his precise critical rôle in Kean's performance he noted that Kean seemed to adopt every one of his suggestions the following day.[61] Edmund Kean and George Alexander were not unusual in looking to their spouses for appraisals of their own acting performances. Of Kean it has been written that 'It was his practise to rehearse scene by scene to his wife, and to repeat a speech twenty times, until both were satisfied that he had hit the true vein.'[62] Florence Alexander's critical rôle was particular and her description of it revealing:

> I always attended the two last rehearsals before every play because my opinion was worth having just before the play was produced. My remarks were taken down in shorthand and I was always told I was wrong, but in the end my opinions were always taken and proved all right. When an actor has been rehearsing a play for weeks he becomes blind to its faults. I could say things to Alec about his work that nobody else could, and when I went in to the last rehearsals I was called the sledge-hammer.[63]

Florence Alexander did not act, and was not present for the majority of the rehearsals, which meant that she was detached from the production process, but her licence to be critically brutal came directly from the knowledge that her marriage could weather disagreement, and that, however hard the criticism, her judgement could be trusted precisely because she had watched her husband act 'night after night' and had developed a keen analytical sensibility specifically in relation to his productions.[64] The humorous but pointed title of 'sledge-hammer' indicates, however, that her critical power was viewed with ambivalent trepidation, as capable of providing a not wholly welcome jolt to the company.

Of course, actors were also critics for one another. Henry Irving's well-documented reliance on Ellen Terry's critique of his direction came from a professional relationship evolved over two decades together at the Lyceum Theatre, where Irving was actor-manager from 1878. Gordon Craig, Terry's son, wrote: 'The help rendered was incalculable, and to estimate it properly not at all easy ... Neither did she invent a production for or with him. He [Irving] did that, and then, showing it to her bit by bit, would ask her opinion.'[65] Such bonds of professional trust were not uncommon, though no doubt Terry's critical rôle was differently inflected with each production, and as Craig makes clear, it is impossible to apportion creative input into productions – it was a creative partnership and they fired ideas off one another.

Though in-house critical functions were not professionally formalised in any precise way during the nineteenth century, it is clear that there were cases where relationships of professional trust, rehearsal conditions conducive to observation, and managers who cared about acting and production quality could foster productive though limited critical commentary – though prolonged dialogue never seemed to be a goal. Technical vocabularies were only just beginning to develop via journalism and books of dramatic criticism, and the relatively sophisticated, in-house, symbiotic culture of criticism and practice which Lessing's German successors were being asked to reach for as the ideal way to evolve a theatre and its artists did not exist. Criticism was regarded as distinct from practice, and actors and playwrights as other than critics. It was a situation of which Shaw despaired, and he hotly refuted those who claimed 'critic-dramatists' were morally obliged to choose one occupation or the other on the grounds that their judgements would be egregiously partial:

> The advantage of having a play criticized by a critic who is also
> a playwright is as obvious as the advantage of having a ship
> criticized by a critic who is also a master shipwright ...
> Dramatic authorship no more constitutes a man a critic than
> actorship constitutes him a dramatic author; but a dramatic
> critic learns as much from having been a dramatic author as
> Shakespear or Mr Pinero from having been actors.[66]

The cross-fertilisation of practice and criticism, Shaw argued, was entirely necessary to the health of both – but, bar a few like-minded individuals, most obviously Harley Granville Barker and

William Archer, he was very much preaching to the unconverted and the unconvertible.

The promotion of the playwright

As to the profession [...] of a dramatic author's life; many people object to it; parents especially.[67]

The emergence of the official appointment of dramaturgs and literary managers in the second half of the twentieth century is due in part to the legal, artistic and financial battles waged by playwrights the century before. The tail-end of nineteenth-century theatre finally yielded to mounting pressure from various factions, and saw the elevation of the poorly paid, low status and easily exploitable journeyman to respected, well-paid and culturally significant professional, as epitomised by Arthur Wing Pinero, H. A. Jones, W. S. Gilbert and Oscar Wilde in the 1890s. For much of the century London theatres employed resident dramatists or 'hack authors',[68] who could translate, adapt or write a complete new play at the flick of the manager's fingers. W. T. Moncrieff was a high-profile example, and though employed at Drury Lane in the 1820s, where he wrote four to six plays a season, often at twenty-four hours' notice, he considered it 'impossible ... to obtain fair remuneration' for his work, relied on a weekly wage of £10, and was accustomed to being cheated out of anything more.[69] The common experience of most playwrights was to receive nothing at all: James Kenney described the 'bitter and most humiliating' situation of repeatedly having to beg a weekly £10 payment from the management at Drury Lane, despite the fact that his *Massaniello* had played there for 150 nights.[70] Outside London the norm before the 1840s was non-payment of authors, either because managements presumed on writers' gratification that their work had been played at all,[71] or because hack-writers were considered mere 'cookers-up of drama', undeserving of payment, as they were by W. Wilkins, proprietor of the Norfolk theatres.[72] Before the 1890s playwrights were not perceived as high artists, nor was playwriting understood as a craft. It was the actor who featured in criticism by Hunt, Hazlitt and Lewes, and it was only in the 1880s and 1890s through

Archer, Pinero, Jones and Shaw that playwrights and plays came under sustained critical scrutiny. Popular taste for Shakespeare or French and German adaptations did not encourage actor-managers to nurture high-quality original work, but to seek passable adapting skills and writers who could furnish them with formulaically successful parts. Actor-managers such as Macready, Phelps, Kean, Irving and Beerbohm Tree rearranged or restored Shakespeare's texts themselves,[73] and Macready often worked on the editing of new plays himself.

New plays were frequently dashed off at an astonishing rate, and were principally lifted from existing French plays. It was not unusual for the most popular writers to complete over a hundred plays in a lifetime.[74] Words were merely a vehicle for the genius of actors and a necessary prop to spectacle and extravaganza, which most Victorians viewed as vital to theatre. In 1866 Charles Kean opined that the much vaunted 'decline of the drama' could be attributed to the fact that the writing of plays involved far too many risks of failure and offered less financial rewards than writing in a magazine.[75] The play-wright Francis Burnand was convinced that because authors were badly paid it suited them 'better, far better, to adapt foreign plays provided by the managers than to devote time and labour to original work'.[76] For some, the composition of a play had nothing to do with artistic ambition of any kind and everything to do with last resort, as actor-manager J. L. Toole knew all too well:

> Dear Sir, – I am in pecuniary difficulties, and therefore I have written a play. Will you kindly send me the usual fees at once, as I am being pressed.
>> Yours sincerely,
>> Etc., Etc.[77]

Many literati, such as Byron, Browning and Dickens, had little lasting success with their plays. Critics of the time were increasingly confounded by novelists who refused to write for theatre, and though many were indeed hostile to the dramatic form,[78] few critics or prose writers seemed to appreciate the necessity of an active apprenticeship for aspiring drama-tists, or the fact that the vast majority of nineteenth-century dramatists had learned about their craft through participation in theatre business, whether reading, spectating, acting, or stage-managing. English theatre did not have a Lessing to point a way forwards theoretically and practically; nor could it produce one until the right conditions for encouraging and experimenting with original new work began to exist. This did not happen until improvements in copyright law, the institution of matinée performances[79] and, more importantly, the foundation of independent theatre clubs in the 1880s and 1890s, which freed new plays from the formal constraints imposed by censorship.

The situation of dramatists was politically highlighted by three parliamentary Select Committees: the first on Dramatic Literature in 1832; the second on Theatrical Licenses and Regulations in 1866; and the last on Home and Colonial Copyright in 1878. Numerous grievances were aired by playwrights called to speak, but the most predominant were piracy, copyright protection (for performance and publication), non-payment, and other forms of financial exploitation by theatre managers. The 1832 Dramatic Copyright Act and the 1842 Copyright Act were significant steps in the struggle to prevent blatant wrongs to playwrights, stating that copyright was a dramatist's personal property. Case law was equally important in bringing about reform, though it was not until the 1911 Copyright Act that full protection was finally won.[80] Though this was victory indeed the delay had considerable consequences, and Stephens has rightly argued that the international copyright legislation of 1852 'destroyed what it sought to promote' and 'actually inhibited the writing and production of original drama in the British theatre' because 'one clause was understood to give legal sanction to the practice of indiscriminate foreign adaptation'.[81]

Since copyright was such a vexed issue for much of the century, many playwrights did not pursue publication, fearing (justifiably) that their work would be pirated. The Dramatic Authors' Society, set up in 1833, was the first professional body to press for the rights of dramatists, and it organised both fee collection and publication for its members. For those authors who wrote for provincial theatres, organised remuneration made all the difference. By the mid-1880s the organisation was defunct, censorship issues having rather overtaken issues of copyright, but the Society of Authors, with its prestigious set of members, continued the battle for the professional rights of dramatists.[82]

The history of nineteenth-century dramatic publishing is complex, but broadly, while good quality editions of many patent theatre plays were available until mid-century, there was a lull from the 1860s to the 1880s, though cheap acting editions of plays abounded. In the 1890s there was a concerted and successful campaign, led by Pinero, Jones, and Shaw and aimed at a general reading public rather than a special interest group, to foreground plays as (almost novelistic) literary products.[83] Shaw's notorious overuse of stage directions is extreme by today's conventions, but provided a reader's model of a play text which is still largely employed, though far more economically. More to the point, it was Shaw's way of asserting his, the playwright's, authority over the leading actors.

Playwrights and the rehearsal process

In the 1890s the power battles between playwright and manager, which had been brewing since the last century, intensified and moved into a public arena as a new generation of British playwrights began to establish credibility in their own right. Since they were challenging both written and performance traditions, actors needed to be retrained, and Pinero, Jones, Shaw and Gilbert insisted that they had far greater legitimate authority in the rehearsal room than any actor-manager. They were careful to distinguish themselves from hack-writers, and Shaw pressed hard for dramatic authorship to be regarded as a separate and 'highly skilled trade' in its own right: 'a gentleman may be an experienced actor and manager, an enthusiastic student of the stage ... and yet be quite unable to write a play'.[84] Tom Robertson had foreshadowed these developments in his work at the Prince of Wales's in the 1860s, but by the end of the century Shaw, Jones and Pinero had won a reputation for being as autocratic in the rehearsal room as the very actor-managers they condemned. A performance, they argued, should present the author's point of view, and their rehearsals were designed to privilege the text. Pinero took this to an extreme:

All that we call 'business' is in the printed matter that I carry into the theatre. Why should it be altered when it has all been carefully and even laboriously thought out, every detail of it,

during the process of construction? ... Rehearsal is not – or
certainly should not be – a time for experiment. It is to prepare for
the acting together of the players, not for the making of the play.[85]

Given the traditional and commonplace savaging of playwrights'
work, it is not surprising that those who could, vigorously sought to
protect their creations. Shaw has documented a head-on collision with
Beerbohm Tree,[86] as well as the lesson he drew from such encounters:

> But the heart of the matter ... is that the cure for the disease of
> actor-managership (every author must take that pathological
> view of it) is actor-author-managership: the cure of Molière, who
> acted his plays as well as wrote them, and managed his theatre
> into the bargain.[87]

In fact, though he never was a theatre manager, Shaw gradually mano-
euvred himself into a position where he could command the total
direction and production apparatus of his plays. Control of the rehearsal room for Pinero, Jones, Shaw and Gilbert meant that they could
negotiate for more pre-production time and thus help to raise the
standards of crafting plays for stage as well as acting and the nascent
craft of directing – particularly in the case of Shaw.[88] Though Dion
Boucicault had paved the way for the financial independence of
the nineteenth-century playwright through his insistence on profit-
sharing,[89] it was still remarkable, given the situation for dramatists at
the beginning of the century, that a group of playwrights could have
found their way to the upper level of the theatrical hierarchy, and live
very comfortably on the rewards of their profession. In terms of dramaturgy, these playwrights claimed a territory for themselves and
highlighted the importance of textual interpretation and analysis.
The rehearsal process was for them a way of exploring a play text. As
final ratification that playwriting could be a professional as well as a
respectable occupation, Gilbert was knighted in 1907, and Pinero in 1909.

Privileging the literary: the rise of avant-garde theatre

Just as the Hamburg National Theatre had been established to nurture
new plays and playwrights, so the increasing demand for a new drama

of high literary standards came to prevail. During the early and mid-nineteenth century lone critical voices had begun to sound notes of alarm regarding the absence of new, intellectually demanding British drama. Some cries of desperation were more strident than others – *A New Drama or We Faint!* published in 1853 left the reader in no doubt of its message,[90] but it was Matthew Arnold's battle-cry in 1879, '*The Theatre is irresistible; organise the theatre!*', sounded in his article commending the Comédie Française, the French national theatre company, that helped to galvanise critical debate about new drama and state-subsidised theatre (which often went hand in hand) into the early years of the twentieth century.[91] As Arnold saw it in 1879, the English theatre was in a dire condition:

> We in England have no modern drama at all. We have our Elizabethan drama. We have the drama of the last century and of the latter part of the century preceding, a drama which may be called our *drama of the town*, when *the town* was an entity powerful enough, because homogeneous enough, to evoke a drama embodying its notions of life. But we have no modern drama. Our vast society is not homogeneous enough, not sufficiently united, even any large portion of it, in a common view of life, a common ideal, capable as serving as basis for a modern English drama.[92]

Arnold's polemic and his appeal for an end to the 'numberless imitations and adaptations from the French'[93] (as well as his admiration for French national neoclassical theatre) are sharply reminiscent of Lessing's exhortations to the Germans a hundred years earlier. English theatre, Arnold argued, defined itself through mediocre foreign imports or second-rate Shakespearean and Restoration adaptations, none of which reflected the progressiveness of an industrialised nation, to say nothing of England's imperial status. Yet Arnold noted the 'irresistibility' of theatre to the middle classes, finally released from the 'prison of Puritanism', and opined that what brought them was a civilising instinct for conduct, religion, intellect, knowledge, beauty, social life and manners.[94] He saw an opportunity to couple the irresistibility of theatre with a concerted educative mission both to hellenise the middle classes and to 'organise' theatre management and actor training via public subsidy, in order to improve the cultural conditions for those in the theatre professions and thus raise aesthetic standards.

Though Arnold's call was answered by renewed commitment to the foundation of a national theatre rather than the thing itself, his liberal humanist ideology underscored developments in avant-garde theatre and criticism for the next thirty years. William Archer echoed Arnold but identified in *English Dramatists of Today* (1882) a host of factors which militated against an endowed theatre, arguing that the right cultural conditions had to exist before new drama and dramatists could thrive in mainstream theatre. Those conditions included rectifying the culturally deprivileged status of drama (and, by default, drama criticism), elevating plays to the standing of literature as bodies of work to be printed and read, educating audiences to appreciate intellectual modern drama as readers and spectators, and encouraging playwrights to relate their work to modern (middle-class) life, thereby finding points of connection with contemporary audiences.[95] That Arnold's and Archer's opinions were scrutinised, challenged, agonised over and often regurgitated in the next thirty years is evident in the proliferation of articles that appeared in periodicals and newspapers, not to mention the publication of books analysing English theatre, its critics, its champions and its audiences. In 1884 H. A. Jones could assert that what was needed was 'a school of plays of serious intention, plays that implicitly assert the value and dignity of human life, that it has great passions and great aims, and is full of meaning and importance'.[96] Plays, as far as Jones was concerned, very much like his own. The bourgeois ideology of what would become the avant-garde 'New Drama' was gathering speed.[97]

If Arnold's call-to-arms did not result in the actual construction of a national theatre, it did result in organised opposition to mainstream theatre through the foundation of independent theatre clubs from 1891. André Antoine's Théâtre Libre in Paris[98] provided the practical model for J. T. Grein's Independent Theatre Society (1891–7), which was a private club specialising in new foreign and British drama and created with the express intent of providing short runs of literary, intellectual and often controversial naturalist plays not selected by commercially driven, establishment managements. Grein underscored his politics of protest not only by electing to open with Ibsen's *Ghosts* but also by appointing George Moore and Bernard Shaw as his literary advisers, both men of letters, very knowledgeable about theatre, and, significantly, outspoken, pro-Ibsenite critics of prudery and censorship. If the Théâtre Libre was the institutional blueprint for change, Ibsen was the literary one – Shaw, Pinero, H. A. Jones and many of the more minor playwrights were indebted to him, as was the New Drama *per se*. But critical reactions to Ibsen's plays were, in the main, compulsively antagonistic,[99] and theatre managers of mainstream theatres generally practised self-censorship and refused to stage them. The rôle of the independent theatres in the playing of Ibsen was therefore vital. Aside from issues of blasphemy and treason, censorship had in general been easing since the non-renewal of the Licensing Act in 1694; but the reaction against the French Revolution, and the rise (with the high empire) of that extreme Victorian propriety which manifested itself most obviously in the Purity Campaign and the many new statutory restrictions on sexual behaviour that were introduced from the 1880s, generated an increasing repression of any works that did not meet the canons of Good Taste. On the surface, Moore and Shaw had a clear brief to challenge prevailing social and moral codes, though it is interesting to note that Grein mostly tended to play safe with his repertoire.[100]

The Independent Theatre Society challenged the types of plays, acting styles and commercial imperatives that ruled mainstream theatre, and crystallised a desire amongst avant-gardistes for repertory theatre that could provide new, intellectual British and continental drama. Archer experimented with his company, the New Century Theatre, from 1897 to 1899; and the English Stage Society (1899–1939), which sharply developed Archer's critical thinking and Harley Granville Barker's intellectual and artistic practice, was formed to produce unlicensed and/or uncommercial plays, premièred works by Shaw and Barker, and introduced works by Maeterlinck, Hauptmann, Gorky and Tolstoy to the English stage. William Poel's Elizabethan Stage Society (1895–1905), which sought to return

Shakespeare to simple, non-picture-frame staging, also took its organisational remit from the Independent Theatre Society, and exerted a strong influence on a young generation of theatre practitioners, Barker included. Most importantly, these theatre clubs, which foregrounded the playwright as opposed to the actor-manager, were the seedbeds for Archer's and Barker's model of a national theatre, and crucially pointed the way towards the privileging of playreading and play selection processes.

Notes

1. Allardyce Nicoll, *A History of English Drama*, 2nd edn, in 6 vols. (Cambridge: Cambridge University Press, 1955–9), IV, 222–39 and V, 215–28. Nicoll is at pains to point out that his figures cannot be absolute. He gives a separate figure of 44 principal music halls in London between 1850 and 1900.
2. William Charles Macready, *The Diaries*, ed. William Toynbee, 2 vols. (London: Chapman and Hall, 1912), I, 380.
3. *Ibid.*, I, 418 and I, 432.
4. J. W. Cole, *The Life and Theatrical Times of Charles Kean, F. S. A.*, 2 vols. (London: Richard Bentley, 1859), I, 24.
5. Augustus Harris, 'My First Drury Lane Pantomime', *Old Drury Lane Christmas Annual* (London, 1882–3), p. 5, cited in Michael R. Booth, *Theatre in the Victorian Age* (Cambridge: Cambridge University Press, 1995), pp. 29–30.
6. A. E. W. Mason, *Sir George Alexander and the St James Theatre* (London: Macmillan, 1935), p. 233.
7. Dutton Cook, *On the Stage*, 2 vols. (London: Sampson, Low, Marston, Searle and Rivington, 1883), I, 124–5.
8. Oswald Crawfurd, 'The London Stage', *Fortnightly Review* 47 (April 1890): 499–516; see especially pp. 506 and 510.
9. *Ibid.*, p. 505.
10. *Ibid.*, pp. 510–11.
11. See, for example, *Fortnightly Review*: H. Beerbohm Tree, 'The London Stage, I. A Reply' (June 1890): 922–31; Oswald Crawfurd, 'The London Stage, II. A Rejoinder' (June 1890): 931–6; H. A. Jones, 'The Actor-Manager' (July 1890): 1–18; H. Beerbohm Tree,

'II. A Stage Reply' (July 1890): 18–21; Oswald Crawfurd, 'The London Stage' (August 1890): 499–516. *Nineteenth Century*: Bram Stoker, 'Actor-Managers I' (June 1890): 1040–51; Henry Irving, 'Actor-Managers II' (June 1890): 1052–3; Charles Wyndham, 'Actor-Managers III' (June 1890): 1054–8.

12. I use upper case because these were official job titles.

13. John Russell Stephens, *The Profession of the Playwright: British Theatre 1800–1900* (Cambridge: Cambridge University Press, 1992), pp. 148–9.

14. Cook, *On the Stage*, I, 116–17 and 137.

15. *Ibid.*, pp. 118 and 137. A typical evolution of the position, to Cook's mind, was actor-manager's Reader to actor-manager's Adviser.

16. Cook says of the Reader: 'Who first filled this post would be hard to say; the necessity of such an appointment was not perhaps immediately perceptible, or was a matter of gradual growth.' *Ibid.*, p. 118. Stephens cites Edward Fitzball and Tom Taylor as evidence of the decline of the Reader, but again these sources are highly subjective: see Stephens, *Profession of the Playwright*, p. 219, note 17.

17. Byron, *Letters and Journals*, ed. Leslie A. Marchand, 12 vols. (London: John Murray, 1973–82), IX, 35.

18. *Ibid.*, IX, 296, letter to Thomas Moore (12 June 1815). All persons named are connected with the management of Drury Lane.

19. *Ibid.*, IX, 35–6.

20. Edward Fitzball, *Thirty-Five Years of a Dramatic Author's Life*, 2 vols. (London: T. C. Newby, 1859), II, 268.

21. *Ibid.*, I, 262.

22. *Ibid.*

23. The writer was John Tobin and the play *Honey Moon*. See *1832 Report from the Select Committee on Dramatic Literature* (Shannon: Irish University Press, 1968) [British and Parliamentary Papers: Stage and Theatre I], p. 113, q. 1984. Miss Mitford's play *Rienzi* lay at Covent Garden for four years, *ibid.*, p. 118, q. 2074.

24. Leigh Hunt's play *Look to your Morals* was returned after his death, many years after he had written it; see Leigh Hunt,

Autobiography of Leigh Hunt, ed. Roger Ingpen, 2 vols. (London: Archibald Constable and Co., 1903), II, 228–9. Charles Wyndham mused on the many plays that were 'lost' in nineteenth-century theatres: T. Edgar Pemberton, *Sir Charles Wyndham* (London: Hutchison and Co., 1904), p. 100.

25. Hunt, *Autobiography*, II, 200.

26. Reynolds, for example, adapted and cut Byron's *Sardanapalus*.

27. Alfred Bunn, *The Stage: Both Before and Behind the Curtain*, 3 vols. (London: Richard Bentley, 1840), I, 156.

28. *Ibid.*, I, 155.

29. *Ibid.*, III, 77.

30. *Ibid.*, III, 158–62.

31. James Winston, *Drury Lane Journal. Selections from James Winston's Diaries 1819–1827*, ed. Alfred L. Nelson and Gilbert B. Cross (London: Society of Theatre Research, 1974), p. 34.

32. As manager of Covent Garden (1837–9) and of Drury Lane (1841–3), Macready had a team of literary friends whom he consulted, but in July 1837 the volume of new plays obliged him to employ a reader, whom he paid £3 a week. See William Charles Macready, *Reminiscences and Selections from his Diaries and Letters*, ed. Frederick Pollock, 2 vols. (London: Macmillan, 1875), II, 78.

33. Henry Irving, for example, had his 'private secretary' Louis Austin, who was prized by other actor-managers for his literary advice (though, interestingly, his nickname was 'the Dodo'). See John Martin-Harvey, *The Autobiography of Sir John Martin-Harvey* (London: Sampson, Low, Marston and Co., 1933), p. 114. In a coruscating letter to an unpromising playwright, Shaw wrote: 'You are mistaken in supposing that plays are not read. Not only managers but actors who are waiting to become managers until they have a few good plays in hand, spend their days in drudging through manuscripts, 99% of which are hopelessly bad ... Refusals mean nothing: a play may be a masterpiece and yet not suit this or that particular manager. Besides the actual managers, you may take it that almost every "leading man" in London – Fred Terry, Yorke Stephens, Forbes Robertson, Arthur Bourchier, &c. &c. &c. would read anything on the chance of picking up something good enough

to start with.' See Bernard Shaw, *Collected Letters 1874–1897*, ed. Dan H. Laurence (London: Max Reinhardt, 1965), letter to Arthur Clark (18 May 1895), p. 533.

34. Mason claims that Lady Alexander's concerns were mainly with the 'private lives' of the actors. See Mason, *Sir George Alexander*, p. 100.

35. *Ibid.*, pp. 231 and 234.

36. From an article by Mrs Kendal in *Dramatic Opinions*, 1890, and reprinted in Russell Jackson, *Victorian Theatre* (London: A. and C. Black, 1989), pp. 342–3.

37. See, Cyril Maude, *Behind the Scenes with Cyril Maude* (London: John Murray, 1927), pp. 163–73.

38. Shaw placed Tree in the same genre of actor-manager as Irving: men who saw play texts as no more than a 'literary scaffold' on which to exhibit their own actorly creations. See Max Beerbohm, ed., *Herbert Beerbohm Tree* (London: Hutchinson and Co., 1920) p. 241.

39. *Ibid.*, p. 129. Printed as a Letter to the Editor in the *Referee* (22.9.1901).

40. Dutton Cook describes the contents of a pamphlet written by an outraged author and entitled *Epistolary Remonstrance to Thomas Morton, Esq., Dramatic Writer and Professed Critic and Reader to Captain Polhill and His Majesty's Servants of Drury Lane Theatre*. Cook, *On the Stage*, pp. 118–21. I have been unable to trace the original.

41. See Mason, *Sir George Alexander*, p. 23.

42. See [Agnes Platt,] *Anonymous* (London: John Murray, 1936). Platt read freelance for other actor-managers and was an experienced and prized newspaper critic and reader of plays.

43. Friedrich Schiller, *Sämtliche Werke*, ed. Gerhard Fricke and Herbert G. Göpfert, 5 vols. (Munich: Hanser, 1980), v, 818–31.

44. See Leigh Hunt's self-parodic essay 'Rules for the Theatrical Critic of a Newspaper', in *Dramatic Essays*, ed. William Archer and Robert W. Lowe (London: Walter Scott, 1894), pp. 124–7.

45. G. E. Lessing, *Selected Prose Works*, ed. E. Bell, trans. E. C. Beasley and Helen Zimmern (London: George Bell and Sons, 1879). Zimmern

had published *G. E. Lessing: His Life and Works* (London: Longmans, Green and Co., 1878).

46. Thomas Carlyle, for example, was influenced by much of Lessing's work but scarcely referred to the *Dramaturgie*. See Charles Frederick Harrold, *Carlyle and German Thought 1819–1834* (London: Archon, 1963).

47. To name but a few: *Era* (1838), *Theatrical Times* (1847), *Dramatic Magazine* (1829–31), *Dramatic Gazette* (1830–1), *Dramatic and Musical Review* (1842–4), *Theatrical Inquisitor* (1812–21), *Theatrical Observer* (1821–76), *Theatrical Examiner* (1823–8) and *Theatrical Journal* (1839–73).

48. Collected in George Bernard Shaw, *Our Theatre in the Nineties*, 3 vols. (1932; London: Constable and Co., 1948).

49. William Archer, *English Dramatists of Today* (London: Sampson, Low, Marston, Searle and Rivington, 1882).

50. The French critic Filon saw the significance of Archer's work at an early stage and noted his similarity to Lessing. See Augustin Filon, *The English Stage*, trans. Frederic Whyte (London: John Milne; New York: Dodd, Mead and Co., 1897), p. 202.

51. Henry James, in particular, thought English theatre vulgar, low-brow and culturally marginalised in comparison to French theatre. See Allan Wade, ed., *Henry James: The Scenic Art* (New Brunswick: Rutgers University Press, 1948), pp. 3–12 and 93–111.

52. Shaw, *Our Theatre in the Nineties*, I, 76.

53. *Ibid.*, III, 152–3.

54. *Ibid.*, I, vi–vii.

55. Hazelton has described Calcraft (whose pseudonym was J. W. Cole) as Kean's 'official historian', but, as she points out, this was not his title and he was employed as a managerial assistant to Kean. See Nancy J. Doran Hazelton, *Historical Consciousness in Nineteenth-Century Shakespearean Staging* (Ann Arbor: UMI Research Press, 1987), p. 101. Undoubtedly, Calcraft had a unique rôle as a historical researcher for Kean (amongst other roles), but the extent of his work remains uncertain and Calcraft's official biography of Kean (supervised by Kean) does not expound on his research functions. See Cole, *Life and Times of Kean*.

56. See Marie and Squire Bancroft, *The Bancrofts* (London: John Murray, 1909), pp. 203–6, in which they describe their trip to Italy for *The Merchant of Venice*, and Beerbohm Tree, ed., *Beerbohm Tree*, p. 211, in which Tree mentions his research in Egypt for *Anthony and Cleopatra*.

57. See Percy Fitzgerald, *Henry Irving. Twenty Years at the Lyceum* (London: Chapman and Hall, 1893), p. 265.

58. Fitzball, *Thirty-five Years*, II, 243.

59. Macready mixed with literary celebrities such as Dickens, Thackeray, Browning, Carlyle and Bulwer-Lytton.

60. Macready, *Reminiscences and Selections*, I, 439 and 457. Macready's managerial team was constituted of play and prose writers, journalists, lawyers and financiers.

61. Thomas Dibdin, *Reminiscences of Thomas Dibdin*, 2 vols. (London: Henry Colburn, 1827), II, 29. Of course, Dibdin may be exaggerating the full extent of his contribution.

62. Cole, *Life and Times of Kean*, I, 50.

63. Mason, *Sir George Alexander*, p. 231.

64. *Ibid.*, p. 233.

65. Gordon Craig, *Henry Irving* (London: J. M. Dent and Sons, 1930), p. 125. See also Christopher St John, ed., *Ellen Terry and Bernard Shaw. A Correspondence* (London: Constable and Co., 1931), p. 80.

66. Shaw, *Our Theatre in the Nineties*, I, 248.

67. Fitzball, *Thirty-five Years*, II, 399.

68. Moncrieff's description of himself. See *Select Committee 1832*, p. 175, q. 3124.

69. *Ibid.*, p. 227, q. 3124; p. 175, q. 3129–32; p. 176, q. 3148.

70. *Ibid.*, p. 227, q. 4082.

71. *Ibid.*, p. 209, q. 3747. Mr Raymond of the Liverpool Theatre never paid authors. It was common practice to try out new plays outside London to see if they might merit production in London.

72. *Ibid.*, p. 210, q. 3767.

73. Richard Foulkes, *Shakespeare and the Victorian Stage* (Cambridge: Cambridge University Press, 1988), pp. 3–5.

74. Nicoll's figures are approximate but, for example, Tom Taylor wrote at least 76 plays, Francis Burnand 149, James Robinson

Planché 153 and Thomas Dibdin 266. See Allardyce Nicoll, *A History of English Drama 1660–1900*, 6 vols. (1930; Cambridge: Cambridge University Press, 1955–9), III–V.

75. *Report from the Select Committee on Theatrical Licences and Regulations 1866* (Shannon: Irish University Press, 1970) [British Parliamentary Papers: Stage and Theatre II], p. 232, q. 6636.

76. F. C. Burnand, 'Authors and Managers', *Theatre* (February–July 1879): 17.

77. See Pemberton, *Sir Charles Wyndham*, p. 264. The letter is undated and anonymity has been preserved – though one also wonders whether this might be a spoof. Toole managed the Charing Cross Theatre (renamed Toole's Theatre in 1882) from 1879 to 1895.

78. Adaptations of novels met with great success on the Victorian stage, and it was assumed that novelists would be interested and skilled enough to dramatise their own works.

79. Matinée performances offered playwrights an invaluable chance to learn about practical dramaturgy and did not involve commercial risk to the actor-manager. Beerbohm Tree and Alexander, in particular, encouraged new writers in this way. See Stephens, *Profession of the Playwright*, pp. 153–5.

80. See *ibid.*, ch. 4, pp. 84–115 for a detailed history.

81. *Ibid.*, p. 102.

82. *Ibid.*, pp. 174–83.

83. *Ibid.*, ch. 5, pp. 116–42.

84. Shaw, *Our Theatre in the Nineties*, III, 203.

85. Hamilton Fyfe, *Sir Arthur Pinero's Plays and Players* (London: Ernest Benn, 1930), p. 259.

86. Mason, *Sir George Alexander*, p. 245.

87. *Ibid.*, p. 251.

88. See Bernard F. Dukore, *Bernard Shaw, Director* (London: George Allen and Unwin, 1971).

89. Stephens, *Profession of the Playwright*, pp. 53–7.

90. See Mario Borsa, *The English Stage of Today*, trans. and ed. Selwyn Brinton (London and New York: John Lane, 1908), p. 50. Borsa describes the discovery of this 'little book' but does not specify its author.

91. Matthew Arnold, 'The French Play in London', *Nineteenth Century* 6 (August 1879): 228–43.

92. *Ibid.*, p. 238.

93. *Ibid.*

94. *Ibid.*, p. 240.

95. Archer, *English Dramatists*, pp. 1–19.

96. From a lecture entitled 'The Dramatic Outlook' delivered at the Playgoers Club on 7 October 1884 and reprinted in H. A. Jones, *Renascence of the English Drama* (London and New York: Macmillan, 1895), pp. 153–91.

97. See William Archer, *The Old Drama and the New* (London: William Heinemann, 1923). Archer includes Haddon Chambers, Wilde, Barrie and Galsworthy in the New Drama, and argues that Tom Robertson's work in the 1860s was the first signal of 'an intellectual movement', p. 338. For background see Jean Chothia, *English Drama of the Early Modern Period 1890–1940* (London and New York: Longman, 1996), pp. 54–87.

98. For a detailed analysis, see Jean Chothia, *André Antoine* (Cambridge: Cambridge University Press, 1991). Another significant influence, also inspired by Antoine's initiative, was Otto Brahm's work at the Freie Bühne in Berlin from 1889 to 1894.

99. Archer comments on the four years following the Novelty Theatre's staging of *A Doll's House* in 1889, since when, he claims 'the compact majority of English theatrical critics has been assiduously, energetically, one may almost say unintermittently, occupied in building the mausoleum of Ibsen'. See 'The Mausoleum of Ibsen', *Fortnightly Review* 54 (July 1893): 77–91, reprinted in Michael Egan, ed., *Ibsen: The Critical Heritage* (London and Boston: Routledge and Kegan Paul, 1972), pp. 304–12. Without doubt the most apoplectic in his moral outrage was Clement Scott, critic for the *Sunday Times*, 1863–5, for *London Figaro*, 1870, and for the *Daily Telegraph*, 1871–98.

100. Kenneth Richards points out Grein's conservatism. See T. W. Craik, general ed., *The Revels History of the Drama: 1880 to the Present Day*, ed. Hugh Hunt, Kenneth Richards and John Russell Taylor (London: Methuen/New York: Barnes and Noble, 1978), VII, 107.

4 William Archer and Harley Granville Barker: constructions of the literary manager

Archer and Barker's construction of the office of Literary Manager was framed within their campaign for a national theatre and emerged from what leading late-nineteenth-century literary and cultural figures agreed was a crisis in English theatre. The term first appeared in the 'Blue Book', *Scheme and Estimates for a National Theatre*, privately printed and distributed in 1904 and published in 1907, when it became a focus of the national theatre debate.[1] In *Scheme and Estimates* Archer and Barker constructed an alternative model to the prevailing autocracy of actor-managers by creating a new functionary, the Literary Manager, and inserting him into the artistic hierarchy. The inscription of this new official into theatre management theoretically achieved three key things: it highlighted the centrality of dramatic literature to the national project, posited the Literary Manager as guardian of literary standards, and secured a playwrights' advocate at the heart of theatre. In these respects Archer and Barker's invention of the Literary Manager can be understood as a manifestation of the wider ideological mission of the late nineteenth-century theatrical avant-garde and literary canon shapers in England, ardently campaigning for the elevation of dramatic literature and of the playwright's status. Archer and Barker's proposal preceded practice by over half a century, and if they overestimated the public will for a national theatre, they underestimated the determined conservatism of actor-managers.

The background to the Blue Book

The call for a National Theatre was not new. Geoffrey Whitworth has suggested that Garrick's Jubilee Celebration of Shakespeare at

Stratford-upon-Avon in 1769 presaged nineteenth-century calls for a national playhouse, and cites Effingham Wilson's 1848 'Proposition for a National Theatre' as the first officially recorded proposal of its kind in England.[2] Wilson's proposition, made just after the Shakespeare Committee had purchased Shakespeare's birthplace, emphasised:

> the importance and expediency ... of purchasing by national subscription, on the part of and for the people, some theatre wherein the works of Shakespeare, the "world's greatest moral teacher", may be constantly performed.
>
> That the said theatre should be opened at such reasonable charges as shall be within the reach of all ...
>
> That the Government for the time being, or any other body of men agreed upon, should hold the said theatre in trust for the nation, appointing a committee for the management of the same.
>
> That the said National Theatre should be made to act as a great and true dramatic school, at which alike the poet and performer, the creator and the embodier (in the highest walks of the dramatic and histrionic arts), should receive their diplomas, living genius and talent being so fostered and sustained.[3]

If bardolatry with its concerns to preserve and monumentalise was vital to the thinking behind a national theatre project,[4] so too was a mission to 'enlighten' national and imperial audiences and aver England's moral legitimacy as a world power. Irving notably gave a paper on the subject at a Social Science Congress in 1878. Victoria's imperial zenith was symbolised by the Jubilees of 1887 and 1897, and many of the country's theatrical and literary élite lent their voices to the idea of a national theatre: institutions such as the British Museum and the National Gallery had opened as long ago as 1759 and 1838, and the lack of a theatrical equivalent was glaring.

William Archer (1856–1924) strongly advocated a national theatre from the early 1880s, seeing it as a means of promoting avant-garde reforms, setting new dramatic standards for national and international drama, and catalysing a sea change in cultural attitudes to theatre and drama. As a would-be playwright,[5] a perspicacious critic whose writings challenged the parochialism of the London theatre world, and the prime translator-champion of Ibsen, Archer moved at the heart of the New Drama. Archer's whole-hearted crusade for Ibsen began in earnest in 1880 with the first Ibsen production in England – *The Pillars of Society*,[6] which Archer translated and promoted – and lasted much of his life, his eleven-volume collected Ibsen appearing in 1906–8. Archer first encountered Barker (1877–1946) via correspondence in 1898, in his capacity as literary adviser (*inter alia*) at the New Century Theatre, when he rejected Barker's *The Weather-Hen* (Barker had to chase Archer for a response and the manuscript).[7] The following year Archer was invited to a production of the same play,[8] was intrigued by the elliptical qualities of the dialogue, and arranged to meet Barker; and his relationship with Barker gave him a new lease of life.

Barker's theatre apprenticeship had involved acting and collaborative playwriting, but he was uninspired by the narrow remit that commercial theatre allowed both activities.[9] His Richard II in a production by Poel brought Barker under the critical spotlight, and stimulated his directorial ambitions, but it was his acting and directing for the Stage Society that established his talent for interpreting plays of different genres and styles, and which confirmed him as a consummate Shavian actor (he and Shaw developed a close if turbulent friendship).[10] Successful as the Stage Society was, it was marginal in terms of mainstream commercial theatre, and Barker and Archer were in complete agreement that a new kind of theatre, a national theatre, was needed to forge a model path of innovation. In 1900 they established a committee with theatre scholars Spenser Wilkinson, Gilbert Murray, A. C. Bradley and writer Hamilton Fyfe to foster the idea of a national theatre, but after a series of meetings Archer and Barker came to understand that to harness serious intellectual and monetary support they needed to provide a detailed theoretical document outlining not just the objectives, functions and ideals of such an institution but also its financial, administrative and artistic structures.[11] Thus they began work on the 'Blue Book', completing it in 1904, the same year that Barker began his practical experiments at the Court Theatre in a direct attempt to put theory into practice.

The Blue Book and the literary manager

Since the construction of the Literary Manager is at the centre of the artistic politics of the Archer–Barker national theatre project, and driven by their socialist ideals,[12] it is helpful to sketch their mission statement. In their 1904 preface they specified that the imagined theatre was to be a 'Central Theatre, to be situated in London ... worthy of the Empire', and an institution which 'may give a healthy impulse to theatrical progress throughout the English-speaking world'.[13] Their plans would 'place England abreast of France and Germany in theatrical organisation',[14] and it is clear throughout that French and German (as well as German-speaking) national and regional repertory theatres, particularly the Théâtre Français, provided a yardstick. They explicitly presented their repertory model as an alternative to the 'harmful predominance' of the actor-manager system, the long run, and the profit-seeking stage, and emphasised their hopes that it would lead to reform of the British theatre system.[15] Repertory theatre for Archer and Barker was understood to mean that 'a number of plays shall always be ready for performance, and shall be performed in alternation, and no play shall be acted more than two or three times in unbroken succession'.[16] Anxious to avoid controversy and play down their avant-garde reputations, they stressed that they did not envision a pioneer theatre or a place for literary élitism – a paradoxical self-betrayal which Shaw bitterly rebuked[17] and Barker later lamented.[18]

The costings, the organisational, production, legal, contractual and salary details, the numerous play lists, casts and front-of-house and behind-the-scenes outlay, not to mention the comparative analyses of theatre conditions elsewhere, are extensive and impressive, and Archer and Barker's invention of a theatre persuaded leading theatrical celebrities, including actor-managers – Henry Irving, Squire Bancroft, J. M. Barrie, Helen D'Oyly Carte, John Hare, H. A. Jones and A. W. Pinero – to patronise it.[19] Archer and Barker envisaged a purpose-built theatre with a capacity of 1,500; a mixture of subscription and 'ordinary' seats at lower prices than the West End; an ensemble of sixty-six actors (42 males, 24 females) on three-year contracts; a board of fifteen trustees[20] responsible for ownership and government as well as appointing the Director and General Staff;

a training school for actors; special royalty arrangements for living writers; and a repertoire including 'the best English (and some foreign) dramatic literature'.[21] For all this they saw any hope of government subsidy as 'a waste of time'[22] and insisted private sponsorship was the only remedy. Their sense of urgency and instinct that the time was right for change made them confident that sponsors would rapidly be found, Barker imagining that the project would be realised in little more than a year.[23] In fact, neither lived to see the founding of the National Theatre.

There is no record of how Archer and Barker lighted on the title Literary Manager, and there was no sustained usage of the term between 1859, the *OED*'s earliest date, and the publication of the Blue Book – though 'literary editor' and 'literary advisor' had currency in journalism and publishing. Certainly, the term gained new life through Archer and Barker, but its current usage was popularised through Tynan. In his last work on the project, *A National Theatre* (1930), Barker defensively labelled the term 'awkward' but showed no inclination to change it.[24]

The authors state in the first line of the job description that the new functionary corresponds to the German notion of the dramaturg, and Archer, in particular, knew of such posts from his extensive travels and research into German and Scandinavian theatre systems. Given existing biographical data on Archer and Barker, Lessing's influence seems certain. The growing interest in theatre criticism and explosion of continental influences on English theatre in the late nineteenth century fuelled translations of avant-garde foreign drama, and Lessing's *Hamburgische Dramaturgie*, first translated in an abridged version in 1879, was reprinted in 1905.[25] It seems clear that Archer and Barker would have been interested; Archer no doubt knew of Lessing through investigations in Germany, and had apparently been compared to Lessing in his critical thinking;[26] and Shaw in 1895 made a characteristically witty, trivialising but lingering, high-profile reference to Lessing, a barbed back-handed compliment:

It was Lessing, the most eminent of dramatic critics (so I am told by persons who have read him), who was reproached by Heine for

not only cutting off his victims' heads but holding them
afterwards to shew that there were no brains in them. The
critical profession, in fact, is cruel in nature, and demands for
its efficient discharge an inhuman person like myself.[27]

Asserting Lessing's mastery as critic, Shaw declares he has read none
of his critical work, hinting that his prolixity is too dull to be worth
study. Shaw's phrasing postures: Archer could certainly have told him
about Lessing, but Heine had only superlative praise, calling Lessing the
'literary Arminius, who liberated our theatre from foreign domination';[28]
and in his almost monstrous construction of Lessing Shaw seeks comparison with his supposed critical barbarity.[29] Such suspicion and
caricature only served to foster prejudice and sheer indifference in the
already problematic English reception of Lessing's work as resident critic.

The hierarchy of General Staff for Archer and Barker's national
theatre comprises five officials: the Director,[30] Literary Manager,
Business Manager, Solicitor and Reading Committee Man:

1. *The Director*, who should have absolute control of everything
   in and about the Theatre, engagement of actors, casting of
   parts, &c., &c., excepting only the selection of plays. For this
   purpose, he would have one vote in a Reading Committee of
   three, to be hereafter provided for. In all other matters, there
   would be no appeal from the authority of the Director, except
   to the Trustees.

2. *The Literary Manager*, an official answering to the German
   Dramaturg. His duties should be to weed out new plays
   before they are submitted to the Reading Committee;
   to suggest plays for revival and arrange them for the stage;
   to follow the dramatic movement in foreign countries,
   and to suggest foreign plays suitable for production; to
   consult with the scene painter, producers, &c., on questions
   of archæology, costume and local colour. The Literary
   Manager would be a member of the Reading Committee, but
   in all other matters would be subordinate and responsible to
   the Director.

3. *The Business Manager*, who would (subject to the Director) control the whole financial working of the Theatre, keep its accounts, sanction all expenditure, and check the estimates of subordinate officials.

4. *The Solicitor*, who should act as Secretary to the Board of Trustees, and advise the Trustees in the investment of the Guarantee Fund, Sinking Fund, &c., and the Director on contracts and other legal matters connected with the management of the Theatre. He would not be expected to give more than a portion of his time to these duties.

5. *The Reading Committee Man*, a third member of the Reading Committee, who ought to have no other function in connection with the Theatre, and to be, so far as possible, outside its atmosphere. He would not be expected to give more than a portion of his time to the work of the Committee.[31]

These sketches are on closer examination somewhat confusing, none more so than the Literary Manager. Greater clarity is perhaps not to be expected, given the absence of an indigenous tradition of the dramaturg, but in their anxiety to address what they saw as the principal flaws in mainstream theatre Archer and Barker subsumed very disparate functions into one official. What is significant is that their job description places a literary specialist at the centre of artistic decision-making and privileges processes of playreading and play selection within an international, and not just a local frame. They do not specify an ideal apprenticeship for such a specialist: analytical textual skills are clearly essential, but so too, given the requirement to 'arrange' texts for revival, are editing and playwriting credentials. At least two foreign languages are also required if the Literary Manager is to judge the merits of non-English language productions visited at home or abroad, and to 'supervise the translation' of such plays in any rigorous way.[32] The problem of the skilled and efficient reading and filtering of plays, which heretofore occurred only haphazardly, is recognised and a systematised answer found through the intervention of the Literary Manager, who saves the Director time and an onerous playreading workload. In addition, the Literary Manager is recognised as providing the access and contact route for playwrights,[33] is therefore by default made responsible for developing writers, and thus also mediates between author and Director, or author and producer.

The idea of the Reading Committee integrates an idea of democratic debate into decisions concerning play selection, and the need for majority vote checks and balances the domination of either Director or Literary Manager. It is designed to promote and work by compromise and consensus, not divide and rule:

> It is evident that the Director might conceivably wreck the fortunes of a play which he disliked; but even if his loyalty to his colleagues did not check this tendency, care for his own reputation would not permit its frequent indulgence. At the same time it would only be natural and not undesirable, that his colleagues should be chary of forcing a production upon him, very much against his will. He would, in fact, have a sort of suspensive veto upon any given production, to be overruled only in cases which, to his colleagues, seemed matters of principle.[34]

The reassuring language of this passage conceals a political minefield, which was painfully exposed when Laurence Olivier and Kenneth Tynan eventually became Artistic Director and Literary Manager of the National Theatre in 1963. Questions of 'loyalty' and 'matters of principle' mean different things to different people, and Archer and Barker understandably suppose in their ideal construction of the Reading Committee that all three will share the same literary, political and personal outlooks. Quite how they expected the Reading Committee Man to function with any authority, given that his only connection to the theatre was to be at committee meetings themselves, is not clear; no qualifications are specified; and it is difficult to see how he could avoid becoming a mere yes-man to the Literary Manager.

The authors specifically rejected the suggestion that the Director should be allowed any independent power of selection and production of plays, because they felt it would undermine the Reading Committtee altogether and could too readily be abused.[35] Although

Archer and Barker did not point out that the position and ethos of the Literary Manager would be severely curtailed by such a power, they must have seen that it would lead them back to an official uncomfortably close to the autocratic theatre manager, and that the 'critic of high authority'[36] who had suggested it was suspicious of collaborative decision-making procedures. In fact, such was Archer and Barker's determination to do away with the self-promoting actor-manager that they stipulated in the 'Statutes':

> The Director shall in no case be an actor, practising his art for fee or reward. Should he be a retired actor, the Trustees shall decide, by fixed regulation or otherwise, on what exceptional occasions (and in no case for personal profit) he shall be allowed to reappear at other theatres. He shall in no event play any part on the stage of the … Theatre.[37]

By curbing the self-interestedness of the Director, the authors were focusing as far as possible on the merits of the dramatic literature under discussion, and giving ballast to the Literary Manager's function as a standard-bearer of literary excellence.

In the Literary Manager's job description the authors also specify a consultative rôle 'with the scene painter, producers, &c., on questions of archæology, costume and local colour',[38] which implies a responsibility for aesthetic control, probably anti-commercial in principle and aimed at the prevention of over-lavish spectacle for its own sake – though the danger was, as Barker later recognised,[39] that the Literary Manager could impose uniformity of design, inhibiting visual experiment and innovation precisely because he was a textual and not a scenic specialist.

Compared with the playreaders and literary advisors of the past, Archer's and Barker's Literary Manager has an unprecedented executive status, power and visibility. Far from a shadowy figure in a backroom, the Literary Manager is second in the hierarchy with a salary of £1,000 – half that of the Director and equal to that of the Business Manager.[40] His real artistic power resides in preselecting what the Director and Reading Committee Man read in the first place; he need only 'indicate' to the committee plays which seem 'manifestly

impossible'.[41] His judgement is, in this respect, absolute: there are of
course other avenues by which the Director may learn of a new play or
be influenced in his thinking, but the Literary Manager's scope for
strategic manipulation of the Reading Committee is very great, and for
Archer and Barker this was precisely the point.

If the multiplicity of functions for the Literary Manager seems
daunting, the competing ideological remits implied by the authors'
specimen repertory are a further complication. The categories are:
New Plays (5 sample but fabricated British plays are named);
Shakespeare (9 plays); Elizabethan Comedy (1); Restoration Comedy
(1); Eighteenth-Century Comedy (1); Nineteenth-Century Comedy –
pre-1870 (2); Modern English Plays – since 1870 (9); Foreign Classics (1,
French); and Modern Foreign Plays (4 French and 1 German).[42] In one
season Archer and Barker calculate that:

> 326 performances are devoted to English plays – 37 to foreign
> plays; 106 performances are devoted to new plays, 257 to revivals;
> 124 performances are devoted to Shakespeare, 34 to old English
> plays, other than Shakespeare, and 62 to revivals of recent
> English plays.[43]

By implication the Literary Manager is primarily responsible for shaping and regulating this canon. His criteria, in order of priority, are:
(i) the preservation of Shakespeare, revival of classic British plays, and
related questions of textual transmission and fidelity; (ii) the codifica-
tion of a modern British canon (plays since 1870); (iii) the recognition
of new plays of significance; and (iv) the representation of the best
plays from foreign dramatic canons. But almost immediately Archer
and Barker express their dissatisfaction at the domination of
Shakespeare and suggest the proportion of new and Shakespearean
plays be reversed,[44] which weakens their case for a house of ancient
and modern standard-bearing drama, and highlights a profound conflict between the desires to present an acceptably conservative
national repertoire and to promote an avant-garde theatre of social
and aesthetic reform.[45]

How this reversal would affect the Literary Manager is not
explored, but expertise in new playreading and development would

clearly have to become the priority. Archer and Barker's construction of the Literary Manager is caught between two conflicting ideologies, the canon-shaper in the main text and the pioneer reformist/experimenter implicated in Barker's 1907 preface. These constructions were in turn prey to the complex politics of the endeavour to produce a publicity and fund-raising document to assert the commercial viability of the project while paradoxically appealing for private funding, and they obviously felt constrained by the need for pertinence and functionality. The main problem with *Scheme and Estimates* is the desire for the national theatre to be all things to all people, and the rôle of the Literary Manager as canon-shaper is over-compacted and over-determined (Barker's 1907 preface moots the need to redefine the rôle). Despite these confusions, Archer and Barker's document provided the first serious recognition and description of an in-house, high-status, distinct, professional literary specialist in England, and by placing such a functionary at the centre of theatre management offered a radically different model for English theatre.

The exemplary theatre

Barker's *The Exemplary Theatre*, published in 1922, made little impact at the time and the few critics who note it at all have marginalised it as obscure and pedantic, Kennedy finding it significant for its influence on the national theatre debate but otherwise 'dry' and 'high-minded',[46] and noting that it marked Barker's turn to scholarly writing and abandonment of acting, directing and playwriting. Barker wrote it to assuage his keen disappointment that there had been no realisation of a national theatre, and to turn his mind 'to a reconsideration of theatre's whole position'.[47] He appraised the book as 'a plea for the recognition of theatre as an educational force',[48] and outlined a paradigm of theatre as both playhouse and training school engaged in applied theory and practice, offering a repository of great dramatic literature and occupying, in Schillerean tradition, a central position in the social and intellectual advancement of society.

The structural basis of Barker's exemplary theatre rested on his premise that intellectual and artistic advancement could only be made through commitment to a reflexive process of critical learning and practice, an idea derived from Lessing but anticipating Brecht in the thoroughness of Barker's organisational and artistic planning. Barker was still preoccupied by the lack of training for actors in England, but insistent that actors and playwrights had to be taught a critical language in order for their practice to develop intellectually and creatively: 'For in England the art [of theatre and acting] is neither studied, practised nor appreciated even by its professional devotees with any sustained intelligence.'[49] 'The true theatre', argued Barker, was 'the place for the study and development of the dramatic art';[50] an apprentice actor's opportunity for study and experiment was more important than performance *per se*, while for the fully qualified actor, director and designer no boundary between playhouse and training centre should exist.[51] Production in England lacked concurrent criticism, he complained, while the notion of what he called 'co-operative' (collaborative) criticism was not provided for at all.[52] Creating fertile training environments for actors, writers and dramaturgs, not to mention breaking down boundaries between criticism and practice, was to be Brecht's speciality, and the young German playwright, then unknown in England, was in the early stages of his collaborative experiments when Barker was writing. And, as for Brecht, it was Max Reinhardt's influence as well as Stanislavski's rigorous critical training of his actors that inspired Barker and reinforced his conviction of the poverty of intellectual analysis among English theatre practitioners.[53] It was not only English anti-intellectualism, argued Barker, but the antipathetic, commercially driven conditions of play production in England which made research and experimentation during rehearsals an impossibility and meant that economics not ideas, a stock cast not an ensemble, and shortage of time not artistic integrity all too often governed a director's vision.[54]

In *The Exemplary Theatre* Barker focuses on playreading and selection processes much more keenly and fleshes out the functionaries (the plural matters) required to fulfil these tasks in some detail. There are reasons for the precision of redefinitions: his travels and researches in German theatre before and after the war; and his practical experience as manager of the Court Theatre with J. E. Vedrenne (1904–7), his seasons of work at the Savoy (1907–8) and the Duke of

York's (1910–11), and his management with Lillah McCarthy of various seasons at various theatres (1911–14).[55] He had confronted problems and pitfalls at first hand and learned directly what worked and what did not. In theory, Barker knew about the work of continental dramaturgs at the time of *Scheme and Estimates* but probably had only second-hand information from Archer, who had travelled extensively and was responsible for the lion's share of the research for the national theatre project.[56] Barker's own subsequent travels abroad enlightened him considerably. In 'Two German Theatres', published in 1911, Barker expressed admiration for the management of the repertoire and the division of labour at both the Düsseldorfer Schauspielhaus and the Deutsches Theater under Max Reinhardt (the theatre at which Brecht was appointed dramaturg a decade later).[57] Reinhardt, Barker noted, encouraged a healthy ethos of self-criticism among the actors and employed 'two or three *dramaturgen* to read and advise upon plays, correspond about them, and do the literary work of the theatre generally'; furthermore, he employed the specific services of Felix Holländer, a novelist and literary specialist, to advise him on repertoire.[58] Barker was particularly impressed with the scholarly dramaturgs at the Düsseldorfer Schauspielhaus, Dr Ernst Leopold Stahl, who gave weekly public lectures 'on almost every conceivable literary and artistic subject', and Dr Reinhardt Bruck, who wrote for a weekly journal on theatre and related disciplines.[59] For Barker these theatres were models for the centrality of literary management as well as the critical and intellectual education of artist and audience, and the plurality of dramaturgs made him rethink the construction of a Literary Manager.

The practical knowledge Barker gained through running the Court, a repertory theatre specialising in new plays, cannot be overestimated. The innovatory nature of the repertory idea and working ethos of the Court company have been expounded by others,[60] but, broadly, it was Barker and Archer's chance to find an alternative working model for a politically radicalised theatre, and to locate the playwright and their work at the centre of the production process. Barker officially chose the repertoire but had Archer and Shaw as unofficial literary advisers, thereby furnishing himself with two of

the most formidable critics and agitators for British, Irish and continental avant-garde drama. Shaw rapidly established himself as the
Court's most popular playwright, took to directing his own work,
advised on the direction of other plays, and helped Barker with finance
and organisation. Of 988 performances during the Vedrenne–Barker
management, 701 were plays by Shaw (11 plays in all), 82 by Barker
(including collaborations with Housman), 48 by Euripides (3 versions
translated by Gilbert Murray), 29 by Galsworthy, 27 by Hankin (2 plays),
23 by Elizabeth Robins, 13 by Ibsen (2 plays), 2 by Hewlett (2 plays), 9 by
Hauptmann, 9 by Schnitzler, 9 by Yeats, 8 by C. Harcourt, 8 by Masefield,
6 by Maeterlinck, 2 by R. V. Harcourt and 2 by Fenn.[61] The Court was
unquestionably a theatre for playwrights run by playwrights, and a
model theatre for new writing. The two playwright-directors, Barker
and Shaw, established the ethos that actors were vehicles for the text
and not vice versa. The rigour which Barker brought to the discipline of
interrogating text in performance demanded much of his actors and
raised rehearsal and production standards. Archer's critical contributions also came from outside the theatre: in the *World* he kept up a
commentary on plays and performances at the Court and challenged
Barker and Shaw to think of stretching themselves in new ways – and
though not a resident critic in a formal capacity as Lessing had been,
Archer's knowledge was highly specialised, allowing him to straddle
the internal aesthetic politics of the Court and the external demand for a
contextualisation of the experiments staged there.

The legacy of the Court was felt in Scotland and the English
regions, not in the London commercial sector, which given the levels
of demand and ready profit had little reason to change. It provided the
model for a literary and committedly intellectual theatre with high
production standards, and appealed to the reformist zeal of progres-
sives who wanted a theatre that could inspire and affirm a sense of
national and local identity. By the end of 1913 there were four major
repertory theatres outside London, in Manchester (1908), Glasgow
(1909), Liverpool (1911) and Birmingham (1913). Initially they fash-
ioned repertoires mostly from authors favoured by the Court, and
often had direct influences through actors who had worked at the
Court, so that Barker and Shaw's methods of working scrupulously

on text were emulated. Theatres for literary plays in turn attracted new playwrights, and, most notably, Ben Payne and Lewis Casson as successive manager-directors at the Gaiety Theatre in Manchester nurtured what came to be known as the 'Manchester school'.[62] In Glasgow the Scottish Repertory Company (i) promoted the new literary drama and high acting standards, (ii) stimulated 'a popular interest in the more cultured, important and permanent forms of dramatic art' and (iii) encouraged 'the initiation and development of a purely Scottish Drama'.[63] Barker promoted repertory theatre as a means of completing the 'civilisation of the drama' and providing a home for new work,[64] and a way of rethinking and restructuring playreading and play selection processes.

The exposure to German models and much greater practical knowledge of management profoundly affected Barker's thinking. Though written in a fallow period for theatre after the First World War, when many theatres had not survived financial hardship, Barker's *Exemplary Theatre* does not make a case for literary, intellectual theatre but takes its necessity as given. More philosophical and theoretical than *Scheme and Estimates*, the book simultaneously bears the imprint of Barker's intervening managerial experience in the sections of its practical, problem-solving detail. To begin with, much more emphasis is placed on the reading system of an exemplary theatre, and the Director's duties in this respect are far more pragmatically delineated:

> Another limiting of power and lightening of responsibility wants careful compassing. We must deal at length with the problem of the choosing of plays. For purely practical reasons a director must, over this, if not delegate his powers, at least contrive to extend his faculties very considerably. He cannot hope to read a tithe, or even to consider upon a fair report a half, of the manuscript plays such a theatre is likely to receive. Yet this reading, and the encouragement or considerate discouragement of the author, is a most important part of the theatre's work, too important to be entrusted to private secretaries (who in any case would not be found capable of doing it), or to be left at the point of

vague and polite letter-writing. Apart for the moment, from the theatre's relations to the authors of established reputation, and from its concern with the playwriting work of its students, its touch with potential authorship, its fostering of a future supply of play material, must be a matter of great importance. It is not that one would try to 'attach' playwrights to the theatre; no return to even a remote likeness of the tamed hack, turning his stuff out to order, would either be possible (one hopes) or desirable ... for nobody is it more important than the dramatist to escape from this vicious tendency, common to all institutions and their inmates, to revolve perpetually in the circle of his own ideas.[65]

Barker acknowledges here a problem throughout the late eighteenth and nineteenth centuries – the sheer volume of scripts – and takes into account the proliferation of other functions that a Director has to accomplish. There is a stern recommendation for delegation of reading to specialists, and condemnation of delegation to unskilled readers such as private secretaries, whose response to plays was often confined to cursory rejection letters – a practice common in many commercial theatres. Reading manuscripts and interlocution with authors, Barker now asserts unequivocally, 'is a most important part of the theatre's work'; in fact, they have become critical functions on which the vitality of a country's theatrical world depends. The fostering of playwrights is particularly delicate for Barker, requiring a shrewd, full-time and dedicated diplomat who can liaise with writers, stimulate and encourage them, and draw the good ones into their theatre's orbit.[66] He does not advocate resident writers, fearing the return of the nineteenth-century hack, the stagnation of the theatre's artistic policy and the playwright's gifts; instead he proposes a mutually supportive relationship between theatre and writer mediated via the reader-cum-diplomat (and Barker insists on this even though he recognises that the abolition of residencies is very hard on writers in their pupillage).[67]

The play selection processes in Barker's exemplary theatre retain the idea of control by a triumvirate, but the thinking behind the personnel and their functions is more advanced. The triumvirate involves Director, Playreader, and a 'third chooser of plays'[68] – Barker refers readers to the same triarchy in *Scheme and Estimates*, though the third authority, while retaining intellectual independence, now appears to be a full-time employee and fulfils specific functions for which the Playreader has limited time. The Playreader, Barker says,

> must be in any important theatre someone of authority and understanding whose chief business it will be to deal with plays and – more importantly – with playwrights. He must have authority, because a good man will not work without it; and only a good man, a man of individual ability, will be listened to by people whose independence of the theatre is their very virtue. And he must probably be given a playreading secretary, so that his mind is not hopelessly lowered by the contemplation, day in and day out, of the miles of manuscript upon which there is no possible comment but 'Thank you'.[69]

There are two crucial points in this passage: Barker argues that a Playreader's time is more fruitfully spent dealing face to face with (by implication) promising writers than lurking amidst 'miles of manuscripts'; and he is relieved of the daily slog of reading cheerless plays through the services of a playreading secretary. The suggestion that there should be a designated official in the theatre who could enter into intellectual, artistic dialogue with a writer with a view to stimulating their creativity and helping them to formulate ideas and works of art, someone who could, in modern parlance, 'develop' writers, was new in England. The notion that a Playreader should have a secretary was also new and it was recognised that the Playreader needed to be available and his skills deployed the moment a play's promise had been determined, and that burdensome administration should not detain him from the pursuit of finding good plays and playwrights. Though the need for a secretary seems minor, Tynan later understood all too well how his whole rôle could have been radicalised with adequate administrative help.

Barker reflects on the inadequacies of current literary management strategies and analyses the Playreader as development specialist in detail:

Today the best intentioned theatre can do little but accept a play or reject it ... But while rejection is easy enough, acceptance of a play is, for any theatre, the beginning of responsibilities which few people and very few authors seem to realize. Anything like a reckless policy of experiment is really not possible. For not only the author and the finance of the theatre is involved in failure. A play is, indeed, very much a house of art.[70]

Acceptance for Barker does not simply mean full-scale production, but also encompasses an acknowledgement of talent and commitment to developing that talent. The Playreader should not fall back on the 'cheap commodity of advice' in all cases, but should concern himself particularly with apprentice playwrights of promise and seek to give them practical understanding of theatre processes, practical knowledge of how the written word differs from spoken performance by allowing them direct access to the theatre for a number of weeks.[71]

A man's work might be brought, perhaps, to the preliminary stages of production, there being admittedly no chance of taking it further. But it might be handed for a few days to a seminar of students, or discussed with the author and playreader by a committee of such of the actors and actresses as would be likely players of it; talks even with producers and designers would not be ... barren of result. Not only the contact with individuals would count, but the dramatist's entry, even for that little time, into the theatre's general scheme of collaboration. Attendance at rehearsals, at play readings, at the discussion of productions: these are things that cannot be offered by the ordinary theatres of today.[72]

Barker's concern to bring the playwright into the thick of creative interrogation with performers, directors and designers, the thick of play-making itself, foreshadows Brecht's collaborative experiments at the Berliner Ensemble. With the resources of the theatre at his disposal, the Playreader's task is to find the best means of aiding the apprentice playwright to understand the complex, multifaceted craft of play-making, the interpretative contribution and collaboration of actor and director. Barker stops short of describing what are now known as writers' workshops, and does not suggest the professional crossover of writing, acting and directing in the manner of Brecht, but he does put forward a new blueprint for an *active, practical* rôle for the Playreader. Doubtless the idea came from Barker's knowledge of Reinhardt's dramaturgs, but the concept of 'development' is understood in England as post-1960s, and Barker has never been credited with sowing its seeds forty years before.

Barker is chary of specifying precise qualifications for the Playreader, but recognises that the success or failure of a theatre depends upon their proficiency.

> For the gist of such a task one can lay down few laws; its very feasibility will depend upon the playreader's personality. But such men (and women, though as yet, with their own worlds to conquer, more rarely) do exist: men whose personal ambitions have been absorbed in an unselfish regard for their art. Theirs are not very dynamic natures, perhaps, but they are receptive and sympathetic. They have dropped the burden of their egoism, have broken the many mirrors of their youthful minds. If ill-luck has left them disappointed that trait may yet be sweetened with humour. They look now to find their account in the passing of the torch to swifter runners.[73]

This is heroic rhetoric as well as an uncharacteristically vague passage in the book, but Barker seems to envisage an older person with extensive theatrical knowledge, who once harboured ambitions as a playwright. The key aspect of the personality appears to be a lack of self-interest coupled with a fervent desire to further the careers of others in the pursuit of art; the opposite of the stereotypically egotistical actor-manager. Barker's ideal Playreader is approachable, supportive and uncontentious, and oddly to be found teaching at university (though he warns against ossified species of academic).[74] By contrast, the third member of the triumvirate is the dissenting voice:

> there is the perennial danger of hardening taste and narrowing mind, in no direction likely to be greater than in the choice of

plays. The third authority, then, must be someone who can keep themselves as free as possible from this particular risk. And, while the playreader would try to bring the playwright into tentative collaboration with the theatre's work, the part of this third chooser of plays would be to keep out of touch with it altogether. He should never be tempted to consider plays from the point of view of the ease with which the theatre could produce them, never for their sheer effectiveness or their chances of immediate success. Ideally he should possess one of those sceptical, critical, troublous minds, unattachable to any movement, frankly at odds with acquiescence. He should be a discoverer of talent that would not be drawn into the theatre's orbit. One sees him, perhaps, travelling on its behalf. He would be constantly out-voted in the committee of three. That would not matter. The flavour of his opinion would abide.[75]

The third chooser of plays, then, is a maverick and an agitator, not expected to confine himself to thinking in line with artistic policy but to challenge the Playreader's and Director's strategies, bringing danger and provocation to discussions. He is open to different dramatic traditions, seeks out plays and playwrights in less obvious venues, and broadens debate through visits to theatres in other lands. Licensed like the King's fool to say the unsayable and think the unthinkable,[76] to turn custom and convention on their head, he operates as an in-built interrogatory mechanism to check the dominant power of the other triumvirs and ensure they do not shirk controversy at the expense of art. In short, he is a thorn and a trouble-maker, and Barker is not blind to the fact that the whole system depends upon an unknowable mix of character and chemistry.

I have dwelt on *The Exemplary Theatre* because I believe it is a crucial document for theatre historians. It anticipates two central concerns of English twentieth-century theatre practitioners: the need for theatre companies to develop an artistic policy[77] and thus be able to communicate and market a specific creative identity to their chosen constituency, and the need for specialist literary advisers and readers to be involved in the decision-making procedures of theatres to invigorate and interrogate company policy. These preoccupations make

Barker a man far ahead of his time in England, and had there been swifter development of a national theatre, or greater understanding of his insights, or a willingness to furnish him with subsidy for long-term experiment, he would have made an even more concrete impact on the English theatre system. It seems clear that Barker withdrew from theatre practice not, as much received criticism suggests, under the supposedly insidious influence of his second wife, Helen Huntington, nor because he had always harboured a secret longing for retreat to academe, but because (like Peter Brook forty years later) he was alienated by a theatre system which, as he saw it, precluded intellectual and artistic integrity and crushed any chance of developing innovative and challenging ways of working on new and classic texts. As Kennedy phrases it, 'He left the theatre because its conditions were antagonistic to his genius, and he became less and less willing to compromise his ideals.'[78] Had he left for Germany (as he apparently once wondered whether to do[79]), he would have been taken seriously and found the cultural conditions for play-making for which he cried out in England. It is disturbing to think of the consequences of the misapprehension of his aims.

The national theatre revisited

Barker updated *Scheme and Estimates* as *A National Theatre*, published in 1930. His commitment to the idea of a national theatre had not wavered, and his conviction that it was inevitable had only grown stronger.[80] The broad changes in his thinking related to finance – he acknowledged that costs had increased dramatically – funding – which he no longer thought could be entirely by private donation – training – he no longer perceived the need for a school since the foundation of such academies as the Royal Academy of Dramatic Art – company size, which he increased, and the need for two stages, one large and one small.

In *A National Theatre* the Literary Manager still forms an integral part of the project, but there is a significant change in the hierarchy of the General Staff (see table 1). The Literary Manager now receives less than half of the Director's salary and has been demoted in favour of the Business Manager. He is still accorded considerable power and licensed to 'take artistic control in the Director's

Table 1   Salaries of the General Staff

Director	£4,500 p.a.
Business Manager	£2,500 p.a.
Literary Manager	£2,000 p.a.
Reading Committee Man	£750 p.a.[81]

absence',[82] but financial expertise supersedes play selection and play-reading. Barker, in other words, recognises that since subsidy is required for such a venture, the need for financial accountability and direction is essential. 'Efficiency in this post would be the only economy ... A good man would save the amount of his salary over and over again.'[83] The lesson that Barker learned from his management of repertory theatres, especially the Court, was that they could not survive without subvention, and even then he underscores the importance of a policy of calculated risks, balancing 'safe', profit-orientated classical plays against risk-taking new plays. As a consequence the job description of the Literary Manager is modified:

> his chief business would be with the texts of the classics, the quality of translations (he would need to be something of a linguist), and, most importantly, with the reading of new plays. With much more than their mere reading, however.[84]

This is the first time Barker explicitly registers the necessary linguistic qualifications for the Literary Manager; he also places far more emphasis on the need for a specialist reader and fosterer of *new* plays: 'Upon a catholic and enlightened choice of new plays the best fortunes of the theatre would depend.'[85] Barker is sharply aware that the expertise involved in detecting promise is not ordinary: 'the new thing in drama lies close hid in a mere manuscript and may well escape all but the keenest eye'.[86] Indeed, he is inclined to develop this side of the Literary Manager's portfolio at the expense of the other:

> The fact is that good plays, like other good things, need cultivating. Dramatists need to be encouraged to write them.

This Literary Manager, then would not have to be a man who sat in his office and read what came to him; he would need to be out and about, seeing new plays at home and abroad, and above all, in sympathetic personal relationship with dramatists – of the younger school as well of the old. Upon his personality and critical flair would depend the freedom of the theatre from the reproach which is apt – and quite unnecessarily – to fall upon all academies of being behind the times.[87]

In fact, the tension between the Literary Manager's supposedly 'chief business' with classic texts and his restless engagement with the search for new plays is not sustainable. Barker seems to conflate two specialist posts into one, and since the Literary Manager is also expected to read the bulk of the manuscripts without assistance (even of a secretarial kind), his portfolio is once again decidedly over-determined. The rôle of the Reading Committee Man has been scaled down, partly subsumed into the remodified Literary Manager, though his insurrectionary purpose remains:

he would not have to wade through the bulk of the manuscripts, though he might well bring some for consideration on his own account. One sees a man of letters in the post, sympathetic to the drama, of course; a critic, perhaps, but not necessarily or even advisably a dramatic critic. Nor, I now think, should the appointment be a permanent one. Its object would obviously be better served if the divergent current of ideas were drawn from a fresh source every three years or so.[88]

Barker's mention of a drama critic for the post is interesting given his past partnership with Archer, and prescient of Tynan, although his concern that they may be too set in their views is perhaps over-cautious. In the main he insists on independence of mind, and while the Reading Committee Man's three-year tenure guards against artistic induration, the regular disturbance potentially makes it hard for the triumvirate to negotiate relations of trust, or, as Barker phrases it, to resolve 'their properly discordant opinions into harmony'.[89]

Barker's Literary Manager was born from a particular proto-socialist ideology and implicated in the promotion of the New

Drama. By the time Barker wrote *A National Theatre* that particular political battle had been won, and the Literary Manager became associated with the search for innovative and experimental drama *per se*. Barker's two sketches of the Literary Manager are rich with internal contradictions and tensions, and the play selection and playreading processes described within the context of a national theatre are underdeveloped by comparison with the pragmatic administrative thinking in *The Exemplary Theatre*. This is not surprising given the breadth of repertoire that a national theatre is obligated to represent, and to some extent the paradoxes of the position illustrate the imponderability of the enterprise itself. It is significant that Barker's description of literary management processes has greater clarity in *The Exemplary Theatre*, for Barker concentrates on systems and structures designed for finding and developing new plays and is less torn by the need to represent classical repertoire and demonstrate financial accountability. His persuasion of the necessity for a specific functionary to encourage and develop new playwrights becomes increasingly emphatic in the three works, and anticipates a post-1960s boom in such posts. Remarkably, Barker's theorisations of structures and systems for literary management are in their thinking the most advanced printed documents written by an English hand on the English theatre. Though his writings have been superseded by different models of practice, it is a remarkable testament to Barker that he was emphatic about literary management at a time when no one else in England gave it serious attention; even today theories of literary management are evolved only by working Literary Managers and dramaturgs themselves, who develop their practice but who are as yet heeded by very few in academia. Perhaps a portion of Barker's attentiveness to playreading and play selection processes came from his multiple points of view as playwright, director, actor, critic, scholar and manager, an astonishingly versatile range which made him, like Brecht, a highly unusual combination of the practical and the theoretical. Barker's theory of literary management inspired the early planning phases of regional repertory theatres in England, and his influence on the development of repertory theatre, new writing theatres, and the National Theatre has been acknowledged by many:

> Few men have entered the profession with as many talents as Granville Barker, and none in England or America has ever combined his resources to the same extent. His influence has been profound, more profound than is generally recognized, and continues to affect the life of the theatre in our time.[90]

But all have failed to recognise him as the first serious progenitor of literary management in England.

Notes

1. For the official publication the title was altered, see William Archer and H. Granville Barker, *A National Theatre: Scheme and Estimates* (London: Duckworth and Co., 1907).
2. Effingham Wilson, 'Proposition for a National Theatre', reprinted in Geoffrey Whitworth, *The Making of a National Theatre* (London: Faber and Faber, 1951), pp. 26–9. In the first instance Wilson sent his proposition to newspapers and journals, then discussed it in pamphlets entitled *A House for Shakespeare; a Proposition for the Consideration of the Nation* (London: Mr Hurst, King William Street, Strand, 1848; London: Mr Mitchell, Red Lion Court, Fleet Street, 1848). Whitworth provides a comprehensive history to 1949 of the movement to found a national theatre.
3. Whitworth, *Making of a National Theatre*, pp. 28–9.
4. The trend for Shakespeare to become a national institution had increased since *c.* 1700. See Michael Dobson, *The Making of A National Poet* (Oxford: Clarendon Press, 1992), and Jonathan Bate, *Shakespearean Constitutions: Politics, Theatre, Criticism 1730–1830* (Oxford: Clarendon Press, 1989).
5. In his twenties Archer had worked hard at writing plays but never had lasting success; see Peter Whitebrook, *William Archer* (London: Methuen, 1993), p. 32. His play-reading skills and dramaturgical knowledge, however, were much sought after: see his book on structuring drama, William Archer, *Play-Making* (London: Chapman and Hall, 1912).

6. Produced as a matinée at the Gaiety Theatre, 15 December 1880.
7. Whitebrook, *Archer*, p. 222.
8. Produced as a matinée at Terry's Theatre, 29 June 1899.
9. Barker had worked on plays with Berte Thomas since the age of 17. For futher details of Barker's pre-Stage Society apprenticeship, see Dennis Kennedy, *Granville Barker and the Dream of Theatre* (1985; reprinted with corrections, Cambridge: Cambridge University Press, 1989), pp. 5–7.
10. *Ibid.*, pp. 8–11. Barker's stint with the Stage Society lasted from 1900 to 1904.
11. Barker recalls the origin of the idea for the Blue Book in Harley Granville-Barker, *The Exemplary Theatre* (London: Chatto and Windus, 1922), pp. v–vi. (Barker began to hyphenate his name in published works after 1921.)
12. The inflection is decidedly Arnoldian, and the epigraph a passage containing Arnold's summons to *organise the theatre!*
13. Archer and Barker, *National Theatre*, pp. xvii, xxi.
14. *Ibid.*, p. xv.
15. *Ibid.*, pp. xvi–xix.
16. *Ibid.*, statutes, p. 129, no. 13.
17. See Granville-Barker, *Exemplary Theatre*, p. vii. Shaw condemned the repertory as 'a musty list of plays' and said 'that if [Archer and Barker] hadn't the courage of our opinions [they] deserved to be ignored.'
18. Barker opines that they may have overdone their concern to appear disinterested and free of rigid artistic convictions. 'Helping you with this book today, I should unhesitatingly, both from motives of good policy and personal taste, advocate the inclusion in our repertory list of every author whom we so carefully excluded a year ago – Ibsen, Hauptmann, d'Annunzio, Shaw and the rest. I hope I could even find other names to add.' *Ibid.*, p. xi.
19. Archer and Barker, *National Theatre*, see p. v.
20. The trustees were to be made up of nine members nominated by the sponsor/s, two from London County Council and one each from the Royal Academy and the Universities of Oxford, Cambridge and London. Charges of literary élitism are hard to counter. Archer and Barker, *National Theatre*, p. 10.

21. *Ibid.*, p. xxiii.

22. *Ibid.*, p. xix. They do not say why, though puritanical prejudices against theatre as an art worthy of intellectual attention let alone public subvention were still widespread and ingrained.

23. Granville-Barker, *Exemplary Theatre*, p. v.

24. See Harley Granville-Barker, *A National Theatre* (London: Sidgwick and Jackson, 1930), p. 40.

25. See G. E. Lessing, *Selected Prose Works*, ed. E. Bell, trans. E. C. Beasley and Helen Zimmern (London: George Bell and Sons, 1879).

26. Maris Borsa, *The English Stage of Today*, trans. and ed. Selwyn Brinton (London and New York: John Lane, 1908), p. 263.

27. Bernard Shaw, *Our Theatre in the Nineties*, 3 vols. (1932; London: Constable and Co., 1948), I, 263.

28. Heinrich Heine, *Werke und Briefe*, 10 vols. (Berlin and Weimar: Aufbau Verlag, 1980), V, 25 [*Lessing war der literarische Arminius, der unser Theater von jener Fremdherrschaft befreite*].

29. Shaw's remark could also have been infected with the widespread anti-German sentiments which took root in Britain after the Franco-Prussian war in 1870 and the consequent shift in the European scale which made Germany Britain's likeliest military foe; see Peter Keating, *The Haunted Study: A Social History of the English Novel 1875–1914* (London: Fontana Press, 1991), p. 359.

30. This term corresponds to the modern notion of AD. Archer and Barker specify that two full-time Producers (directors) are among the full-time 'behind-the-scenes' staff. See Archer and Barker, *National Theatre*, p. 68.

31. *Ibid.*, pp. 12–13.

32. This function is added in the 'Regulations', *ibid.*, p. 133, no. 5. The specimen repertory cites examples of French and German plays only; see p. 48.

33. A function which appears in the 'Regulations', *ibid.*, p. 132, no. 5. 'It shall further be the duty of the Literary Manager to conduct special negotiations with authors.'

34. *Ibid.*, pp. 14–15.

35. *Ibid.*, p. 15.

36. *Ibid.*

37. *Ibid.*, p. 129, no. 12.
38. *Ibid.*, p. 13.
39. See 1907 preface, *ibid.*, p. ix. Having seen modernist experiments in Berlin, Barker argues that a new professional, the 'artist designer', should have a place within theatre production.
40. *Ibid.*, p. 16. The salaries of the Solicitor and Reading Committee Man are £300 each. The two Producers rank below the Literary Manager, receiving £750 p.a.; see p. 66.
41. *Ibid.*, 'Regulations', p. 132, no. 5. The authors do not seem to take into account that this would hardly be workable given the volume of plays the Literary Manager would be likely to receive.
42. *Ibid.*, pp. 47–8. Note that Archer and Barker, like many of their time, often used the term 'English' inaccurately – under the rubric 'Modern English Plays (since 1870)' they include Wilde and Yeats.
43. *Ibid.*, p. 48.
44. *Ibid.*, pp. 48–9.
45. Tension that Barker admits in his 1907 preface, *ibid.*, pp. x–xi.
46. Kennedy, *Granville Barker*, p. 201. There has been a tendency to bisect Barker's life and to characterise him as a man who betrayed his artistic gifts in order to become a critic and scholar, but of course he never ceased to have an acutely perceptive understanding of all these disciplines, which he saw as complimentary and overlapping. For Kennedy's review of received biographical accounts, see pp. 2–4.
47. Granville-Barker, *Exemplary Theatre*, p. viii.
48. *Ibid.*, p. 1.
49. *Ibid.*, p. 39.
50. *Ibid.*, p. 77.
51. *Ibid.*, p. 154.
52. *Ibid.*, p. 124.
53. *Ibid.*, pp. 229–30. Barker clearly absorbed Stanislavski's method in significant detail at the Moscow Art Theatre, and evidently talked to him at length. See his article 'At the Moscow Art Theatre', in *Seven Arts* 2 (1917): 659–61.
54. Granville-Barker, *Exemplary Theatre*, pp. 221–2.

55. Mainly the Little Theatre, the Kingsway, the Savoy and the St James's. See Kennedy, *Granville Barker*, pp. 212–13 for listings.

56. Barker acknowledges the imbalance of their contributions in *Scheme and Estimates*, p. xiv, and again in *Exemplary Theatre*, p. vi.

57. H. Granville Barker, 'Two German Theatres', *Fortnightly Review* 89 (January–June 1911): 60–70. For further information on Barker's impression of German theatre, see Kennedy, *Granville Barker*, p. 196.

58. Barker, 'Two German Theatres', p. 64.

59. *Ibid.*, p. 64.

60. See for example, Desmond MacCarthy, *The Court Theatre 1904–1907* (London: A.H. Bullen, 1907); P.P. Howe, *The Repertory Theatre: A Record and a Criticism* (London: Martin Secker, 1910); Jan McDonald, 'Shaw and the Court Theatre', in Christopher Innes, ed., *The Cambridge Companion to George Bernard Shaw* (Cambridge: Cambridge University Press, 1998), pp. 261–83; Eric Salmon, ed., *Granville Barker and his Correspondents* (Detroit: Wayne State University Press, 1986).

61. Information from MacCarthy, *Court Theatre*, p. 123.

62. Including playwrights such as Allen Monkhouse, Stanley Houghton and Harold Brighouse.

63. See Howe, *Repertory Theatre*, pp. 65–6. Howe's book gives clear and valuable information on the early formation of the repertory movement, and explains why the idea of repertory at the Court could not be as fully developed as Barker wished; see pp. 34–5.

64. H. Granville Barker, 'Repertory Theatres', *New Quarterly* 2 (1909): 491.

65. Granville-Barker, *Exemplary Theatre*, pp. 183–4.

66. *Ibid.*, p. 188: 'it must rest with the playreader of the theatre to see that no playwriter [*sic*], bringing anything of dramatic value, is either let go quite empty away or, indeed, quite let go.'

67. *Ibid.*, p. 184.

68. *Ibid.*, p. 192.

69. *Ibid.*, p. 185.

70. *Ibid.*, p. 186.

71. *Ibid.*, p. 189.

72. *Ibid.*, pp. 189–90.

73. *Ibid.*, p. 188.

74. *Ibid.*, p. 188n. I wonder if Barker was thinking in part about Archer, who started as a playwright, had practical theatre credentials, and turned to criticism, translation and scholarly work. Barker certainly thought of him as a dramaturg and academic, and they explored setting up as Artistic Director and Dramaturg at the New Theatre in New York in 1908 (see Whitebrook, *Archer*, p. 271). In some ways the description applies to himself, though Barker pursued his scholarly career as an independent writer. Perhaps the preference for a university scholar is simply an insistence on the intellectual and pedagogical aspects of the Playreader's role.

75. Granville-Barker, *Exemplary Theatre*, p. 192.

76. I am thinking of King Lear's fool and of Goneril's description of him as 'your all-licensed fool'. See William Shakespeare, *King Lear*, ed. R. A. Foakes (Walton-on-Thames: Thomas Nelson and Sons, 1997) [Arden Shakespeare, 3rd series], 1.4.191, p. 203. Looking ahead to Tynan, Barker's description of a 'sceptical, critical, troublous' mind is apt.

77. Granville-Barker, *Exemplary Theatre*, p. 191. 'The choice of plays will be a dominant part of the theatre's policy, and it must, above all things, show consistency of purpose.'

78. Kennedy, *Granville Barker*, p. 205.

79. See C. B. Purdom, *Harley Granville Barker: Man of the Theatre, Dramatist and Scholar* (Westport, CT: Greenwood Press, 1956), p. 121. Barker's credentials in Germany were impeccable because of his association with Reinhardt. He was involved with Reinhardt's 1911 production of *Oedipus Rex* in London, in which his then wife, Lillah McCarthy, played Jocasta. See J. L. Styan, *Max Reinhardt* (Cambridge: Cambridge University Press, 1982), pp. 80–4.

80. Barker, *National Theatre*, p. viii: 'There is apparently no other way by which the best of our drama can be kept in being … no one … can doubt, surely, that a generation will rise, if it has not already risen, to whom such a theatre will seem a necessity.'

81. *Ibid.*, p. 38.

82. *Ibid.*, p. 40.

83. *Ibid.*
84. *Ibid.*
85. *Ibid.*, p. 42.
86. *Ibid.*, p. 41.
87. *Ibid.*
88. *Ibid.*, p. 42.
89. *Ibid.*
90. Kennedy, *Granville Barker*, p. 4.

5 Bertolt Brecht: the theory and practice of the dramaturg

Brecht's theory and practice of the dramaturg have brought systematic institutional and artistic reforms to German-speaking, central and Eastern European theatre. There dramaturgs in Brecht's mould are at the heart of theatre practice and operate quite uncontroversially. In Canada and the United States the professionalisation of the dramaturg has occurred since the 1970s and is now well established, though always accompanied by a good deal of hotly contentious debate. In non-German-speaking Western Europe the appointment of dramaturgs is a familiar practice in Scandinavia, Holland and France, whereas in Britain and Spain dramaturgs tend to be deployed on short-term projects, are not regarded as integral to theatre-making, and there is a greater confusion about what they do. In Britain, whilst there is no question of Brecht's international status as a playwright, nor of his place as one of the most significant theatrical thinkers of the twentieth century, the official recognition of dramaturgs is much more recent and the numbers employed have sharply increased over the last five years. What is most odd is that although the practice of Brechtian dramaturgs has demonstrably had an enormous influence in the West since the 1960s, Brecht's actual theorisations on the dramaturg have scarcely been addressed at all. This has led to considerable misunderstanding and misrepresentation.

Brecht's theory and practice of the dramaturg spread to the English-speaking West in the 1960s and 1970s, mainly through the discipleship of directors and dramaturgs either working at or formerly employed at Brecht's theatre, and through John Willett's 1965 translation of *Der Messingkauf*. In the United States and Canada the importance of the dramaturg is reflected not just in the number of positions existing in mainstream theatres and companies – over three hundred, but in the plethora of university courses on dramaturgy, many of them high-profile, perhaps none more so than the Yale School of Dramaturgy founded in 1977.[1] The professional association LMDA, the Literary Managers and Dramaturgs of America, was established in 1985, has a membership of hundreds (including many from outside the USA), and its annual meeting is a hothouse of discussion. In a pattern which is the opposite of the one in Europe, American and Canadian curiosity in the Brechtian dramaturg grew out of the universities and spread to theatres:[2] one clearly influential figure is Carl Weber, Professor of Directing and Dramaturgy at Stanford University since 1984, who trained under Brecht from 1952 to 1956 and continued directing with the Berliner Ensemble to 1961.[3] In Britain Brecht's influence is most obviously traceable through Tynan's appointment as Literary Manager at the National Theatre in 1963. In the last decade many British theatre companies and directors have shown increasing willingness to employ an extra functionary to undertake dramaturgical tasks which are Brechtian in conception, yet there is little consciousness of Brecht's theory or practice. Many western practitioners, on the other hand, have tended to assume a false transparency and consistency of dramaturgical practice, often unwittingly basing models on practices developed at the Berliner Ensemble *after* Brecht's death. Western academics fare worse: there has been no substantial analysis specifically centred on Brecht's theory of the dramaturg, nor any systematic investigation of Brecht's strategic training and deployment of dramaturgs at the Berliner Ensemble from 1949 to 1956. This chapter is a first step and seeks to illuminate the complex reception of Brecht's theory and practice of the dramaturg.

I: Theory
Der Messingkauf

Written sporadically between 1939 and 1955, the definitive edition of *Der Messingkauf* runs to 174 pages and includes fragments of dialogue, poems, notes, essays, plans and actors' exercises.[4] It is this edition, the

Berlin and Frankfurt edition, to which I shall refer, not Werner Hecht's version *Dialoge aus dem Messingkauf* (1963) translated by Willett.[5] Brecht's plans in the text itself, and commentaries in his journals, make it clear that his intention was to produce both a theoretical document and a performance text.[6] It is the dialogues, and Brecht's division of them into four nights, which provide an organisational pattern for the editors and clear structural direction for the reader; and though the *dramatis personae* names five characters – the Philosopher, Actor, Actress, Dramaturg and Technician – it is the Philosopher and Dramaturg who embody the dialectical design of the text and bring theoretical coherence to the dialogues.

Der Messingkauf has received scant attention from western academics: there are Willett's translation and notes, Kenneth Tynan's interest in a private London performance of it in 1965, and a few passing references in studies of Brecht. Interest in Brecht's theory was obstructed by the political prejudices of early commentators, who presented his œuvre as fixed and unchanging, viewing it 'as either dogmatic, communist-inspired abstraction or revered holy writ',[7] or choosing to sever Brecht's plays from his politics.[8] Although this has changed, Brecht's influence has primarily been through productions of his plays, as Michael Billington, the *Guardian's* theatre critic, confirmed in an article on the centenary of Brecht's birth: 'What do we remember Brecht for? Great roles, as well as great plays.'[9] To date, Willett's *Brecht on Theatre* and *The Messingkauf Dialogues*, the *Brecht Sourcebook*[10] and *Brecht on Art and Politics*[11] – a tiny proportion of Brecht's theoretical writings – are all that is widely available on the English-speaking market.

Willett's *The Messingkauf Dialogues* created additional problems of reception: the majority of English-speaking readers do not know what a dramaturg is, but Willett's introductory note serves only to obfuscate:

> A *Dramaturg* is a playreader and literary odd-job man, and is part of the staff of most German-language theatres. He may occasionally direct a play. Often he is a playwright himself, as Brecht was when he was one.[12]

This is a misleading definition, signally failing to contextualise the historical significance of the dramaturg in German theatre or to distinguish the dramaturg's principal rôles of resident critic and literary consultant from those of the playwright and director. By reducing the dramaturg to a 'literary odd-job man', Willett makes nonsense of Brecht's insistence on his centrality to theory and practice. Furthermore, persuaded that *Der Messingkauf*'s incomplete and hybrid form renders it theoretically mutant and obscure, Willett has habitually presented it as a 'problem'[13] text or a 'great torso'.[14]

This situation does not improve. Margaret Eddershaw aims to focus 'on the challenges and problems set by Brecht's dramaturgy, theatrical theory and politics for British practitioners',[15] yet erroneously believes that Brecht 'abandoned' *Der Messingkauf* after four years,[16] and alludes to the work only six times without elaborating on its content or indulging in analysis. As early as 1980 Jan Knopf argued that it should finally be recognised by the West for its unique form and as 'Brecht's most significant theoretical achievement',[17] a plea that has elicited only token responses.[18] The dominant understanding of Brecht's theories is that *A Short Organum for the Theatre* is his most significant work, although he called it 'a potted version' of *Der Messingkauf*.[19] Brecht was haunted by the idea of *Der Messingkauf* for at least sixteen years, a clue to its importance for him. In any history of twentieth-century dramaturgy it is the core text.

In *Der Messingkauf* Brecht recognises that redefinition of the traditional model of the dramaturg is central to the successful institutional implementation of epic theatre. The tradition of Lessing, Tieck and their successors offered Brecht a model of the dramaturg as intellectual, often combining the rôles of playwright, translator, reader, literary consultant and distinguished critic, but expressly set dramaturgy apart from involvement in performance practice. In *Der Messingkauf* Brecht imagines the traditional dramaturg's process of transformation from a defender of naturalist, 'Aristotelian' drama into the ideal dramaturg of Brechtian epic theatre, and so provides a model for the conversion he expects the dramaturg to undergo.

The Dramaturg[20] in *Der Messingkauf* represents the conventional qualifications of his post in three principal ways: first, he is a writer and analyst of play texts with a thorough understanding of dramaturgical structures; second, a formidable theatre historian, with encyclopædic knowledge of theatre history from scholarly research in libraries and dedicated spectatorship of plays; and third, an incisive, receptive and articulate comunicator-critic. But, radically reversing tradition, the decision of Brecht's Dramaturg to conduct the four nights of discussion on stage, not in his cold, inhospitable office with its innumerable unread play scripts,[21] symbolically relocates the dramaturg from the exile of the writer's and reader's garret to the site of performance. Just as the backdrop to the discussion is the dismantling of a stage set,[22] the metaphorical tearing down of traditional organisational structures, so the constituents of the new theatre represent a new collaborative configuration of personnel; playreading, research, writing and analysis are no longer functions isolated from acting and directing, but are undertaken in a collaborative space that brings together all those involved in the writing, speaking and staging of the text. The Dramaturg is no longer a back-room figure whose function extends no further than the selection and delivery of a text to the rehearsal room, but is positioned within the rehearsal process and made its dynamic facilitator.

The *dramatis personae* of *Der Messingkauf* shows a significant shift in status for the new Brechtian dramaturg:

The Philosopher wishes to apply theatre ruthlessly to his own ends. It must furnish accurate images of incidents between people, and allow the spectator to adopt a standpoint.

The Actor wishes to express himself. He wants to be admired. Story and characters serve his purpose.

The Actress wishes the theatre to inculcate social lessons. She is interested in politics.

The Dramaturg puts himself at the Philsopher's disposal, and promises to apply his knowledge and abilities to the reconstruction of the theatre into the thaetre [*sic*] of the Philosopher. He hopes the theatre will get a new lease of life.

The Lighting Technician represents the new audience. He is a worker and dissatisfied with the world.[23]

While the Dramaturg in *Der Messingkauf* is represented as binding himself to realise the Philosopher's ideas, it is clear in their discussions that the Philosopher is powerless to radicalise theatre practice without the Dramaturg's specific intellectual and practical skills, which ironises the classically privileged status of the Philosopher. The Dramaturg's pre-eminent critical presence within the institution of theatre provides the Philosopher with a point of contact, negotiation and entry, but also with a figure capable of masterminding the transplantation of his ideas into an experimental, practical arena. The traditional presences of the rehearsal process, the Actress, Actor and Lighting Technician, though less developed, are constructed as passive voices expressing present dissatisfaction and desire for change, while the Dramaturg and the Philosopher, the new occupants of this space, are depicted as agents of change. Whereas the traditional dramaturg's decision-making powers remained implicit, held in check by organisational structures which marginalised him, Brecht's Dramaturg is endowed with real and extended powers that shift him to the forefront of shaping and implementing artistic policy in practice.

The Dramaturg's conversion to the 'scientific', Marxist laws of epic theatre is more than the imagining of an individual's journey; a conscious depiction of the Dramaturg in the act of facilitating the conversion of the Actor, it foreshadows his rôle as teacher and ideologue, his most significant task over the four nights of discussion being to mediate between Philosopher and Actor, facilitating their struggle to find common ground for their opposing views. Just as the Dramaturg is redefined, so, reciprocally, is the Philosopher, whom Brecht liberates from Marx's formula, widely quoted in the GDR as aphorism and motto:

> Philosophers have only *interpreted* the world in different ways; what matters is to *change* it.[24]

Brecht enables the Philosopher to act, and has him posit theatre as a laboratory for the study of human behaviour, while the Actor defends Aristotelian principles and naturalist theatre: the formulation is Science versus Art, and by the fourth night both Philosopher and

Actor have come to understand, through a dialectic, that Science and Art can be merged into a dynamic reformulation of theatre. But the renegotiation of their respective positions has come about only through the intervention of the Dramaturg: just as the Actor requires the Dramaturg to act as a formulator and spokesman for the articulation of his own craft, so the Dramaturg is the only member of the theatrical team who can talk to the Philosopher on equal intellectual terms. It is the Dramaturg's questions and his contextualising statements about theatre history and practice that provide a logical structure for the exposition of both sides of the argument, his concern with the clear articulation of complex ideas, and provision of definitions and background information, that allows Actor and Philosopher to comprehend each other's territories. The Dramaturg can identify, analyse and articulate all aspects of the processes of theatre-making and construct a frame for the debate through his presence; his successful mediation demonstrates that his professional ability to span theory and practice is the means by which practical implementation of epic theatre can occur. For Brecht the Dramaturg is the vital tool for forging an historic encounter between Marxist theory and theatre practice, and the catalyst of dynamic possibilities in their new dialectical relationship.

This dialectical relationship is investigated in the way that the Dramaturg constructs the discussion itself as a site of interrogation for epic theatre:

> While we are talking about theatre here, we can also feel that we're holding a discussion in front of the audience, that we ourselves are performing a little play. And now and again that will allow us to stage a small experiment or two to help clarify matters.[25]

From the outset the Dramaturg frames the debate as experimental performance and mines it for its value as a practical learning strategy for the participants. One of the principal tasks of Brecht's Dramaturg is therefore represented as the conceptualisation and development of a 'didactics' of epic theatre. This didactics is aimed at actors and writers in that it seeks to develop a pedagogy to help them understand the dramaturgical components of the epic play; but also aims at audience, for the Dramaturg serves to emblematise the implied spectator through his presence as observer and critic. The need for this duality is explained in an entry in Brecht's *Journals* which elaborates the principles of *Der Messingkauf*:

> Skimmed through the *Messingkauf*. The theory is relatively simple. It deals with the traffic between stage and auditorium, and how the spectator must master the incidents on the stage. As Aristotle states in the *Poetics*, the theatrical experience comes about through an act of empathy. So defined the adoption of a critical position cannot be among the elements which constitute empathy, and the greater the empathy the less room for criticism there must be. Criticism is stimulated with reference to the way empathy is generated, not with reference to the incidents the spectator sees reproduced on the stage.[26]

For 'traffic' Brecht uses the word *Verkehr*, which might also be translated as 'communication', or loosely (but perhaps more meaningfully) as 'dialogue'. This dialogue is monitored by the Dramaturg, strategically located in the space between stage and auditorium: during rehearsals he critiques the Actor and ensures that he is thinking about the historical and social context of the material he is presenting, not seeking to submerge his critical faculty in identifying with character. Simultaneously the Dramaturg also critiques the overall performance from the point of view of the spectator and assesses whether the Philosopher's Marxist objectives have been achieved. This involves two levels of enquiry: are the laws posited for the actions of human beings living under specific historical and social conditions clearly discernible? And are the alternative courses of action open to the actors on stage clearly identifiable? If not, the Dramaturg intervenes and may suggest alterations to the text, experiments for the actors, or areas of research and investigation which need to be pursued before a solution can be found. The Dramaturg's very presence is thus constructed as a self-reflexive reminder that the premise of epic theatre rests on a dialectical relationship between practice and criticism, and between stage and auditorium.

Brecht's ideal spectator is a social historian, a *Gesellschafts-historiker*,[27] and the Dramaturg stands in relation to this as a specialist in theatre history and Marxist theory, who can help the Philosopher realise a new theatre practice that awakens the critical faculties of the spectator and offers Marxist doctrine as a tool for social change. In the words of the Philosopher, the new 'thaetre' will mean that 'The spectator will no longer flee from the present times to history; the present times will become history.'[28] But the new 'thaetre' requires scripts specifically written for this purpose, if not new plays, then adaptations of classical plays. Not surprisingly Brecht's ideal Dramaturg not only has a complete understanding of the structural components of dramatic forms, of everything, in Brecht's words, relating to 'the laws of drama',[29] but is also a skilled adaptor. As the Dramaturg explains, the adaptor must possess a wide knowledge of classical plays, in particular by authors such as Goethe, Schiller and Shakespeare, and is required to bring about the full-scale transformation of the dramatic narrative into a workable starting point for rehearsal; in the case of foreign authors this means that the adaptor may also be a translator. It is the Dramaturg's rôle to teach the process of adaptation to both writers and actors; this process, he argues, means the radical alteration of structure and plot where necessary, the invention of new scenes, modifications in characterisation, and extensive cutting. One of the most likely reasons for the failure of an adaptation, he explains, is conservatism of the adaptor's ambitions: 'What's important when you alter the text is that you have enough courage and skill to alter it sufficiently.'[30] For the purposes of the Philosopher's 'thaetre' the Dramaturg recommends that textual modification takes place through a collective process, with adaptor and actor working through a text together, testing its logic and efficacy on page and stage; thus Brecht uses the Dramaturg to activate and facilitate collaboration in a bid to break down the traditional social separation of writing and acting.

The pedagogical rôle of Brecht's Dramaturg extends to the broader development of actors' skills and the evolution of the ensemble as a whole. He makes a series of suggestions for creating texts to be used as actors' exercises, practical experiments on techniques of

Verfremdung: these include the use of legal documents reporting actual court cases, adaptations of well-known novels and rewriting historical events in a vernacular style.[31] In a single fragment entitled 'The Dramaturg's Speech' the Dramaturg stresses the importance of continually stretching an actor's abilities by avoiding typecasting and star turns, and implicitly makes clear that his own rôle in casting is significant.

Brecht strengthens the Dramaturg's power base from the top down, implicitly anticipating his control over the selection of plays for performance and his identification of 'incidents of sufficient public interest'.[32] Demolishing the fixed location of the traditional dramaturg, Brecht frees his ideal Dramaturg to act as a roving agent, intervening at any point in the preparation and rehearsal of text to acquire the 'right answer to the people's questions'.[33] By bringing the Dramaturg's critical acuity to bear at the site of practice, Brecht creates a new form of interactive performance criticism, which feeds directly into methods of writing, acting and directing; but at the same time he also ensures a new means of intervention and a different conduit for ideological commentary.

Beyond *Der Messingkauf*

Brecht's ideal Dramaturg is a paradoxical construct of considerable ambiguity, required to negotiate constantly between his synthesising rôle (as the critical articulator of process) and analytical rôle (as a representative member of the audience): the former positing involvement and the latter critical detachment. An adaptor, historian, scholar, teacher, experienced practitioner, Marxist ideologue and critic, the Dramaturg possesses a formidable armoury of intellectual and practical skills, and, no longer excluded from performance processes, his influence extends across the whole concept of a production from the director, writer, designer and actors to figures such as the technical crew, stage hands, make-up artists and set builders. He is ubiquitous and intentionally controlling, and it is telling that Brecht denies him the full breadth of his power in the *dramatis personae* by describing his rôle as a willing act of sacrifice to a higher ideological truth. In doing this Brecht consciously situates the Dramaturg at a point of symbolic overlap, where scholar and critic coincide with director, writer and actor, and actor with audience; thus he signifies a point of crossover between theory and practice, and between object and subject. The traditional model of containment and exclusion has been replaced with one of authority and infiltration: having no clearly demarcated territory of his own, the Dramaturg now has the possibility of moving between sets of variable relationships and crossing all boundaries within theatre, including that between stage and auditorium. By forcing a construction of the Dramaturg as willing resource for the Philosopher, Brecht obscures the extent of the Dramaturg's power base; no doubt Brecht intends readers to accept that the Dramaturg is indeed acting on the instructions of the Philosopher, has yielded up his knowledge, and is content to be used as an instrument in the Philosopher's grand plan; but if that premise is not accepted, and the Dramaturg is exploiting the Philosopher's idea to strengthen his own power base – and after all, the whole enterprise of promoting the acceptance, practice and propagation of epic theatre is unrealisable without the Dramaturg – then he becomes a rather sinister figure. Even accepting Brecht's deliberately naive model of the Dramaturg as the practical facilitator and intellectual resource for the growth of epic theatre, he clearly wields a power which subtlety could manipulate.

If driven to its logical extreme, Brecht's model Dramaturg can turn into an ominous political censor, an ultimate instrument of surveillance who dictates rather than democratises and becomes the Marxist shadow and political inverse of the Nazi *Reichsdramaturg*.[34] While Brecht certainly mooted the ambiguity of his power and made him an ideological construct, he did not construct him as an extremist; rather, he intended the Dramaturg to be an ideal composite of the combined intellectual and practical skills required to implement epic theatre. Yet, given the lack of information on Brecht's actual practice and its frequent confusion with his theory, and in the absence of a long-term tradition of institutional dramaturgy, many western practitioners tend to the ideologically extreme construct of the dramaturg. Thus, the work of many dramaturgs is construed as representing 'the ideological stranglehold of the past' or perceived as 'the theatrical thought police'[35] – Graham Whybrow, Literary Manager at the Royal

Court, can shrink from the horrors of 'using the D-word',[36] and American director Terry McCabe can expatiate against the evils of dramaturgs, gratuitously invoking the names of Stalin and Trotsky.[37]

In sober theory, the figure of the Dramaturg provides Brecht with a continuum between old and new theatre practices. In institutional, historical and artistic terms he can be seen as the 'pivotal man', the transformative dynamic on whom the success of the project depends; I use the term 'pivotal man' in both a local sense to denote the Dramaturg's centrality to epic practice, and in its specific historical sense to underline his privileged position in the national reconstruction of post-war German theatre.[38]

II: Practice
Collaboration and experimentation before 1949

Brecht's organisation of dramaturgical practices at the Berliner Ensemble was the culmination of many experiences and practical experiments made before 1933, when he left Germany, and during his exile, from 1933 to 1949. This section examines Brecht's own training as a dramaturg and his persistent creation of literary and theatrical collaborations, in order to contextualise his later systematisation of working practices with the Berliner Ensemble.

The most striking pattern in Brecht's development as playwright, critic, theorist, director and dramaturg is his persistent need for and generation of teams of creative individuals to fuel his own artistic energy. Throughout his life he positioned himself at the centre of literary and theatrical circles, both private and professional, from which he sought ideas, discussion, collaboration and a willing audience. As early as his schooldays Brecht gathered friends around him, read them poems, sang songs, wrote and performed poems and plays with them, and encouraged both their individual work and cross-fertilisations of literary, musical and artistic talents.[39] Even then he was insistent that everyone should write copiously and keep a journal to record any idea, conversation, event, book or story which seemed significant to them:[40] this, as it turned out, was the seedbed for note-taking and documentation – two major functions of Brecht's later practice and a substantial part of his training for dramaturgs.

Brecht's first joint playwriting project, a version of Marlowe's *Edward II*,[41] was written with an established novelist, Lion Feuchtwanger (1884–1958); the collaboration enabled Brecht to learn from an experienced literary craftsman and gained him an admirer and mentor. During the 1920s Brecht transformed his informal collaborative experimentation into the formal but fluid constellations of 'Brecht collectives', composed of actors, directors, dramaturgs, writers, musicians, designers and other intellectuals who operated in various combinations on Brecht's projects and productions from the winter of 1924 until Hitler came to power in January 1933. By the time *Mann ist Mann*[42] was performed in 1926, Brecht was at the centre of a collaboration which included significant names such as Emil Hesse Burri, Slatan Dudow, Elisabeth Hauptmann, Caspar Neher and Bernhard Reich: Burri and Hauptmann were writers in their own right, Dudow a student of cinema, Neher a designer, and Reich a dramaturg in Moscow. This multiply creative team became a typical feature of Brecht's way of working since it challenged and informed his evolution as a thinker and creator in all aspects of theatre practice. In Hauptmann's words:

> The collective was the fundamental principle of his working method. Wherever he was, there was always a circle of friends, of collaborators who helped him during the work process and with whom he talked about his plans and his projects.[43]

Brecht's closest working relationships were with women, particularly Elisabeth Hauptmann (1897–1973), Ruth Berlau (1906–74) and Margarete Steffin (1908–41). Though Brecht at this stage called them *Mitarbeiter*, collaborators, not dramaturgs, they were a recognisable step towards what he eventually theorised in *Der Messingkauf*. Hauptmann was his key working partner from 1925 to 1932, before emigration made contact more sporadic; and at the Berliner Ensemble she later functioned as an executive dramaturg. Berlau and Steffin met and worked intensively with Brecht in Denmark from 1932; later at the Berliner Ensemble Berlau was named as a dramaturg with specific archival functions.

Their functions varied and sometimes overlapped. Hauptmann was indispensable to Brecht as an editor, literary consultant in foreign – especially English – literature, translator, researcher, writer, note taker and documentor of discussions, literary agent, secretary and intellectual debating partner. In a reference written for her in 1934, Brecht described her as *meine beste Mitarbeiterin*, 'my best collabora-tor', noted her 'extraordinary linguistic gifts' and credited her with 'an active and critical input in all my dramatic works'.[44] From 1925 to 1932 Hauptmann dedicated herself to Brecht's intensive work regime, moving into a flat adjacent to his and often working round the clock to fulfil tasks she had been set.[45] Hauptmann's wide reading and transla-tions exposed Brecht to new ideas and forms; among her most notable works were translations of Arthur Whaley's Nô plays, Gay's *The Beggar's Opera*, and Kipling's poetry, all of which Brecht incorporated into plays to some degree. Hauptmann's contribution to the dramatic structuring of Brecht's plays was very considerable; it was often her task to present Brecht with variable dramaturgical structures once an idea had been formulated: 'Ideas for a play came to Brecht quickly, usually in ten to twenty pages, but trying to find a dramatic structure for them was the hard part.'[46] But Hauptmann's talents also went beyond this; as a writer she was substantially responsible for *Mann ist Mann* and the *Lehrstücke*, wrote *Happy End* (under the pseudonym Dorothy Lane) and had a significant rôle as researcher and writer on most of Brecht's other plays from the mid-1920s to 1933.[47]

Margarete Steffin, a translator and playwright, served both these and administrative functions. She was Brecht's principal colla-borator on *Die Horatier und Kuratier*, *Furcht und Elend des Dritten Reiches*, *Die Gewehre der Frau Carrar*, *Das Leben des Galilei*, *Das Verhör des Lukullus* and *Der Aufhaltsame Aufstieg des Arturo Ui*. Brecht valued her in particular as an authentic voice of the proletariat and representative member of his intended audience; and her critique of his work constantly pressurised him to consider clarity for the spectator.[48] Ruth Berlau initially operated as Brecht's translator,[49] secretary and literary agent in Denmark, but Brecht undertook the task of teaching her his methods of reading and critiquing plays and trained her to reduce any narrative to its barest dramatic elements – five or six sentences, a preparation for conveying his theory of the *Fabel*. She was given exercises, and Brecht made her a book in which he wrote down his corrections of her work. For the purposes of research she was taught to write down everything – her thoughts and experiences, other peoples' stories – and then to work it into a condensed dramatic structure.[50] In doing this Brecht gained potential material for his writing, but also clarified the techniques he would later use to train dramaturgs at the Berliner Ensemble. Berlau characterised her rôle as that of *Aufschreiberin*, note taker or writer-down, and joked that this should be her professional title in her passport.[51]

All three women embodied aspects of Brecht's ideal Dramaturg in *Der Messingkauf*, but what cut across this, and has no place in the theory, is the sexual politics, though issues of personal power are complex and relevant. The details of these collaborations have been much discussed following the controversy surrounding John Fuegi's *Brecht and Company*.[52] Fuegi's book is pathologically hostile towards Brecht, displaying almost McCarthyite paranoia, and has been the subject of lengthy denunciation by other academics.[53] His thesis appears to suggest that the name and figure of 'Brecht' is merely a cynical marketing concept for works written by his dramaturgs. Brecht is painted as a ruthless dictator and literary thief, a sexual predator and a profound misogynist. His female dramaturgs are represented as sorry victims. Dubious scholarship aside, Fuegi's case is weak: neither Hauptmann's nor Berlau's own testimonies support his argument, and though they undoubtedly suffered emotionally and professionally, they made a choice to devote their lives to Brecht.[54] There are certainly disturbing personal aspects to Brecht's relationships with his female dramaturgs, but the historical contexts for collective creativity and communism must also be taken into account. The sorrier aspects of Brecht's professional and sexual relationships with these women need no rehearsal here; what is clear is that Brecht was developing an expanding nucleus of dramaturgs and positioning them at the core of his theatrical enterprise.

One underexplored facet of Brecht's life in 1919–33 is the time he spent observing or participating as writer, director or dramaturg in rehearsal processes. He had begun his critical observation of performance as a theatre critic on various publications in 1914–22.[55] By 1933 there had been sixteen premières of Brecht's plays and adaptations, seven of which he directed. Whatever his rôle, Brecht spent as much time as possible in rehearsals, setting the pattern of immersing himself in practice and subjecting his texts to repeated rewriting and experimentation.

Brecht's first employment as a professional dramaturg was at the Munich Kammerspiele in 1922–3, which provided him with access to actors and directors and also with the debate and discussion he needed to stimulate his thoughts and develop theories. His second appointment as dramaturg, from September 1924 to autumn 1925, was at the Deutsches Theater in Berlin under the artistic directorship of Max Reinhardt. Reports of Brecht's apprenticeship are conflicting. Carl Zuckmayer, employed by the Deutsches Theater as a dramaturg at the same time, satirically claimed that the experience was insignificant:

> At such theatres the dramaturg was either a lowly official who managed the archive and so on, or more or less an intellectual ornament ... Brecht ... wanted sole power, the exclusive right to select the repertoire according to his ideas and to rename the theatre the 'Epic Smoking Theatre' because he posited the thesis that people were more inclined to think if they were permitted to smoke. Since he was refused these things he limited himself to collecting his wage every now and then.[56]

Elisabeth Hauptmann, however, claimed that Brecht saw Reinhardt's rehearsals as deepening his practical understanding of theatre.[57] It seems unlikely that Brecht would have shrugged off the opportunity to see an acknowledged master like Reinhardt at work: observing actors had never been a passive act for Brecht, and he noted in 1920 that critically engaged visual and aural observation required the discipline to train oneself to discard one's dramatic expectations and learn to appreciate the new.[58] If Brecht spent his time as a dramaturg watching rehearsals and little else, it was because he wanted to learn about making theatre at its most practical level and to train his critical eye for performance. Nevertheless, Zuckmayer's comments are interesting, revealing the moribund state, even superfluity, of the dramaturg's rôle in German theatre of the 1920s, and demonstrating that

Brecht, even at this early stage, identified the need to develop his theory and practice in a theatre company over which he had full control.

As Brecht acknowledged in *Der Messingkauf*, it was Erwin Piscator's model of the 'dramaturgical collective' that most shaped his thinking regarding the practical training and deployment of dramaturgs.[59] Brecht was hired by Piscator for the first season of the Piscator-Bühne in 1927–8. Piscator's model of revolutionary Marxist theatre, and his radically technological vision of the theatrical spectacle, were the spur Brecht needed to commit himself to a sustained intellectual and practical project in order to develop his own theories and methods for writing and staging epic texts. Piscator's political mission was one that Brecht shared: the creation of a German theatre that could respond in subject matter and form to traumatic recent history, mass industrialisation and the brooding threat of political extremism. Like Piscator, Brecht sought a propagandistic reinvention of a Schillerian theatre of the moral tribunal, but with the representation of working-class lives and concerns at centre stage.[60] Yet if Piscator was a great director, he was not a writer. He needed skilled playwrights to find ways of presenting new subject matters within a broad historical sweep, and needed to adapt their writing to the radical design concepts of his work. Brecht was one of a team of politically committed literary specialists and researchers, and found the system creatively inspiring. In *Das Politische Theater*, Piscator explained how he had redefined traditional dramaturgical practice:

> Because of the significance of the dramaturgical process in our theatre, the selection of dramaturgs was crucial ... For us the dramaturg's tasks were not restricted to the same tasks that existed in other theatres such as the drawing up of the repertoire, making casting suggestions, seeking out new scripts and cutting superfluous passages in the text. What I required from a dramaturg in the specific circumstances of our theatre was a genuinely creative collaboration with myself or the respective playwright. Our dramaturg had to be capable of reworking texts in the light of

our political standpoint and to develop text and shape scenes with the closest possible adhesion to my directing concept.[61]

Though Piscator's experiments were short-lived, Brecht had seen the value of deploying a team of researchers and dramaturgs and would replicate it at the Berliner Ensemble.

Brecht continued his experiments in America in 1941–7, albeit less grandly, and continued writing *Der Messingkauf*. He moved mainly amongst a German-speaking circle of refugee intellectuals; Hauptmann and Berlau continued as administrators, researchers and translators, but collaboration was much less intense. Brecht's plays were not well received: *Furcht und Elend des Dritten Reiches*, translated by Eric Bentley, played in New York in 1945 but received a lukewarm critical response. Brecht's most valuable collaboration was with the actor Charles Laughton on *Das Leben des Galilei*, performed in Beverly Hills in 1947, where Berlau began to experiment with photographing the rehearsal process, stimulating Brecht's creative energies as writer and director in new ways. But generally Brecht was treated with suspicion, indeed ultimately targeted as an enemy, notoriously so during his examination by the House Committee on Un-American Activities on 30 October 1947. He left for Europe the next day.[62]

The foundation of the Berliner Ensemble

Brecht returned to the Russian-occupied zone of Berlin on 22 October 1948, having already spent months negotiating for a state-funded theatre where he could apply his own methods of work and select his own ensemble. His return was noted with excitement by a depleted artistic intelligentsia and his instatement as a founding member of the Academy of Arts the following year officially confirmed his status as one of the most powerful cultural figures in the country. Berlin lay in ruins, however, and no suitable building was available, so that although Brecht initiated the Berliner Ensemble in January 1949, it was March 1954 before he could move the company into their permanent base at the Theater am Schiffbauerdamm; until then the Deutsches Theater was used for performances.

State sanction for the Berliner Ensemble was granted rapidly. On 1 April 1949 the Socialist Unity Party (SED) approved the formation of an ensemble under the artistic directorship of Brecht's wife, Helene Weigel, and allocated DM 1,465,500 towards running costs and expenses for the 1949/50 season.[63] These decisions were taken by those at the centre of the state political machinery, members of the Politburo, and on 18 May 1949 the Central Department for the Arts at the SED confirmed the official status of the Berliner Ensemble as an 'institution of the German Department of Education'.[64] Within six months of his return to Berlin, which he described as 'the heap of rubble outside Potsdam',[65] Brecht had negotiated himself to the forefront of artistic and educational policy, and for the first time in his life had the economic and material means to organise his working methods as he saw fit. His situation was happy; the birth of a new country with a communist mission meant he was both well placed to contribute to new cultural life, and expected to set an exemplary theatrical agenda.

Brecht's vision of an ensemble was from the first a company committed to a radical dialectical relationship with its subject matter and audience. His primary objective remained what it had always been: the awakening and development of the spectator's sociopolitical critical faculty as the key to class-consciousness, empowerment and the gradual transformation of society. Brecht saw his task as both national and international. In his view the cultural destruction of German theatre had worked so deep because of the absence of any mainstream theatre-making that adequately sought to engage with and sociologically interrogate man's conditions. Furthermore, the skills and training needed for practitioners committed to a theatre aimed at social change had all but died out or been destroyed:

> The poetic had degenerated into the declamatory, the artistic into the artificial; the trump card was outward show and false emotion. The representative stood in the place of the exemplary, temperament in the place of passion. A whole generation of actors had been selected from the wrong point of view and trained in false doctrines.

How could we go about staging new performances for new spectators with such a depraved, with such a spiritually and technically ruined theatre?[66]

From such rhetoric it is not hard to deduce that Brecht was positioning the Berliner Ensemble as the central instrument in any theatrical regeneration for East Germany. From the beginning he intended the Berliner Ensemble to act as the national model for collaborative play-making, exemplary in its selection, writing and directing of texts, acting method and mechanisms for research, self-critique and documentation. If communist East Germany was to establish a cultural identity, then theatre, with its nationally and historically privileged status, would play a major rôle in forging that identity. The foundation of the Berliner Ensemble suited the Politburo as much as Brecht, though interests did not by any means converge perfectly. The positioning of Brecht's ensemble under an educational remit meant that Brecht's central official function as play-maker was one of systematic instruction, and Brecht, who had rejected the official doctrine of Socialist Realism,[67] sometimes had to invent imaginative strategies to pit against the authorities in the struggle to uphold a dynamic relationship between play-making and ideology at the expense of party dogma. But as James K. Lyon has argued, Brecht overwhelmingly 'sought the acceptance and approbation of authority figures in the East German state', becoming a 'dissident conformist, with the emphasis on the "conformist"'.[68]

Organisation and training at the Berliner Ensemble

The organisational structure of the Berliner Ensemble evolved gradually as Brecht identified his requirements. Weigel, as *Intendant*,[69] initiated and managed all matters related to production, finance and administration – a gargantuan task, ranging from negotiating contracts and wages, and organising the construction of an office and rehearsal space, to finding accommodation and food rations for employees.[70] She was constantly having to respond to the complications of post-war strife, and the fragmentary archive records of the first two years reflect the necessity to concentrate energies on the practical rather than bureaucratic aspects of running the Ensemble. Brecht made the artistic decisions and decided on the appointment of actors, directors and dramaturgs.[71] The structure that evolved was conceived and dictated by Brecht, and he was always at its centre – Weigel ensured that everything ran to his satisfaction. It was a formidable husband and wife team. In Wekwerth's view Brecht could not have built up the Berliner Ensemble without her.[72]

Actors, directors, dramaturgs and writers trained in conventional techniques were of no use to Brecht: he needed actors who understood acting methods centred on narration, *Gestus*, and *Verfremdung*; directors who were keen observers of the dialectics between the verbal and the visual; and dramaturgs who understood the principles of playwriting and play analysis as well as the theoretical and practical dynamics of text-in-performance. Brecht himself provided plays and supervised and arranged adaptations; he had no need of, nor interest in, established professional playwrights. His mission therefore had to incorporate the methodical instruction of his techniques to a generation of apprentices. From 1949 to 1956 Brecht systematised a large and complex training operation, carefully selecting mostly young individuals of distinction and promise, and providing them with a thorough knowledge of his working methods while using them to fuel both his theory and practice. In those years the Berliner Ensemble staged *Mutter Courage, Herr Puntila und sein Knecht*, J.M.R. Lenz's *Der Hofmeister*, Gorky's *Die Mutter*, *Das Verhör des Lukullus*, *Die Gewehre der Señora Carrar*, Erwin Strittmatter's *Katzgraben*, *Die Dreigroschenoper*, *Der Kaukasische Kreidekreis* and J.R. Becher's *Winterschlacht*.

In relation to Brecht's practice at the Berliner Ensemble, the Dramaturg in *Der Messingkauf* can best be understood as a composite configuration of various literary, critical, pedagogical and administrative functions, which were undertaken not by a single person but by a team. Brecht insisted that the skills required by the dramaturg, critic and director were the same, and that the literary and analytical functions mastered by traditional dramaturgs could not be isolated from the functions of staging a text and critiquing its efficacy. Determined to end the rigid compartmentalisation of their respective skills, he established a training programme which was founded on principles of interdisciplinarity, and specifically set out to make transparent what had always been distinct and 'secret' preserves. Brecht's dramaturgs and directors therefore underwent the same training. This broke radically with the past; its singularity is graphically highlighted by a letter from one of Brecht's dramaturgs to a disappointed old-school dramaturg who had not understood the reasons for his rejection:

> The difficulty of offering you employment with us is a curious one. Brecht works only with young people, whom he has trained himself. Dramaturgs, in the traditional sense, do not exist in our theatre at all. Our dramaturgs work as assistant directors and *vice versa*; our directors work in the Dramaturgy Department. This way of working has probably come about as a result of Brecht's own activity as a writer, dramaturg and director.[73]

The significance of this dismantling of the boundaries between specialised professions[74] has not been fully recognised by western critics and is under-researched, no doubt because the concept is unfamiliar and the area of overlap in their training makes describing the input of individual dramaturgs and directors difficult. It was a difficulty acknowledged in house, and in a meeting called specifically so that different practitioners and departments of the Berliner Ensemble could give an account of their tasks, Weigel drew attention to it, at the same time explaining that it was inevitable since the work of directors and dramaturgs was 'inextricably bound together'.[75]

As a rule, Brecht selected potential actors, writers, dramaturgs and directors from arts academies, universities and schools,[76] but this did not prevent the employment of anyone else who came to Brecht's or Weigel's attention and was considered suitable. The élite members of the team were the *Meisterschüler* from the Academy of Arts, who had already demonstrated exceptional capabilities and were expected to work most closely with Brecht; one rank down were the *Studenten* from universities and colleges; and below this were the *Élèven* from schools. The privileged *Meisterschüler* started joint training as directors and dramaturgs straight away; *Studenten* and *Élèven* generally undertook the bulk of dramaturgical tasks involving documentation and administration, and had to wait for a chance to direct, with no guarantee of an opportunity.[77]

Brecht's training path for his *Meisterschüler* is documented in a letter to the Ministry of Education, outlining the contents of the course and the credentials required. There are two criteria for entry: a school-leaving examination from a Workers' and Peasants' Faculty or secondary school, or failing these, evidence of attendance at a social science course; and the submission of a short study of a play or performance seen in the GDR.[78] It is clear that Brecht wanted to assess the strength of applicants on critical ability, powers of analytical thought, and not just experience of, or talent for, writing, acting or directing. In his letter Brecht demanded the right of successful applicants to attend lectures at university and rehearsals at leading Berlin theatres.[79] He also documented the functions in which new recruits would be initiated at the Berliner Ensemble:

5. The pupils will participate in the regular activities of the assistant directors and dramaturgs of the Berliner Ensemble. They will attend conferences with stage designers, mask makers, costumiers and stage technicians, in addition to rehearsals. They will take notes on production problems. At certain points in their training they will direct amateur groups in factories on their own.

6. They will take part in the work of adapting plays. (So far *Der Hofmeister* by Lenz, and *Der Biberpelz* and *Der Roter Hahn* by Gerhart Hauptmann have been adapted by the Berliner Ensemble. Shakespeare's *Coriolanus* is in the process of adaptation.)

7. The training is to take two to three years and should enable the pupil to become a dramaturg, a director, or a theatre critic.

8. Maximum number of students: 6.[80]

Brecht's system of training was strictly hierarchised and hierophantic, and the dramaturgs who displayed both a literary and visual stage literacy were valorised more than others. While Brecht accepted six *Meisterschüler* a year, there were anywhere from twelve to twenty trainee dramaturgs, paid and unpaid, in the company at a time, and this does not include the senior staff team of dramaturgs, with variously allotted specialist rôles: the core included Peter Palitzsch as *Chefdramaturg* (or Head Dramaturg, a title reflecting not overall management of others, but expertise in public relations and publicity), Hauptmann, Berlau, Hans Bunge and Claus Hubalek. Brecht's system was a phenomenally efficient and productive machine, which administratively had little to do with democracy and everything to do with hierarchy, facts repeatedly misunderstood and misrepresented in the western reception of Brecht's practice.[81] Besides learning to analyse text and adapt plays in the context of collaborative performance, processes described in detail in Käthe Rülicke's *Die Dramaturgie Brechts*,[82] the trainee dramaturgs' functions fell into three broad categories: criticism, research and education.

Brecht's method of teaching critical skills involved compulsory attendance throughout prerehearsal and rehearsal stages of those plays to which a dramaturg had been assigned. Again, there was a strict protocol, and trainee dramaturgs were required to make critical notes, *Notate*,[83] later assessed by a senior dramaturg and usually read through by Brecht himself. They were expected to observe and to intervene verbally only when Brecht called for their opinion. The 'assessment' of the *Notate* (the German verb is *verwerten* or *auswerten*, 'to extract the value from something') was a means by which useful critical observations could be identified and fed back into the writing and acting processes the following day; it was simultaneously an opportunity for the trainee to ask questions and to be monitored.[84] Furthermore, once the *Notate* were approved, the dramaturg typed and filed them. Thus the dramaturgs provided exhaustively detailed documentation of the entire process of the research, writing and development of a text, and the *Notate* were in themselves valuable reference materials. Once the play was in performance the same dramaturgs, in rotation with others, were expected to write a *Vorstellungskritik*, a critique of the performance, acting and audience response, and if Brecht found points valid they were communicated to the cast. Brecht's systematisation of the *Notate* was ingenious; it gave young trainees, new to professional theatre practice, a formal means of giving feedback, and prevented theoretical discussion from dominating what for Brecht, as writer and director, had to be the practical arena of problem-solving. The direct intervention of the Dramaturg theorised in *Der Messingkauf* was therefore not granted to trainee dramaturgs at the Berliner Ensemble; this powerful province Brecht reserved for himself.

From the outset Brecht established the Berliner Ensemble as a centre of research and development, and his fascination with documenting process led him to appoint Berlau director of an in-house photographic archive. Berlau was deployed to organise photographic documentation of every production, and to index the growing archive for publicity and teaching purposes. This vast undertaking grew more complex when Brecht instituted experiments with film. Berlau needed two assistant dramaturgs with specialist technical knowledge, and even then described the work of creating the archive as *eine Sisyphusarbeit*, a Sisyphean task, with all its implications of a grinding slog, the impossibility of completion and divine punishment.[85]

Hans Bunge was the senior dramaturg charged with building an archive of materials collected by company dramaturgs and research exercises undertaken by them. Brecht encouraged the serious academic research of every aspect of his productions, ranging from broad historical and sociological investigations to a specific prop or costume. Audience research was conducted by questionnaire, and dramaturgs filed reports on talks or lectures they had given. This archive was effectively an in-house library for use by all the company, and the dramaturgs were expected to keep it stockpiled with reference material. Brecht often set his dramaturgs the task of researching subjects he wanted to investigate in his practice, such as Stanislavskian theory or form in Shakespeare, and research for programme material was extensive. Trainee dramaturgs were also expected to attend lectures at the university and write reports on current political and aesthetic debates. Bunge extended his archival responsibilities when he began recording rehearsals on tape and subsequently started a sound archive.

In their systematically myriad functions, dramaturgs were the linchpins of Brecht's wider educational mission. They were involved in writing publicity material and programmes, and the title *Werbedramaturg*, 'publicity dramaturg', was accorded those who worked besides Palitzsch in the publicity department. Palitzsch developed a model for programmes combining text, illustrations and photographs, and used the latest print technologies. It was pocket-size for convenience and produced as a small book, so that audience members would be encouraged to keep and read it properly at home, and it was a point of principle that programmes could be bought as soon as tickets went on sale. Programme contents concentrated on the political message of the play and on its contemporary relevance to society, and Brecht wanted dramaturgs to learn to write in ways that would make the reader 're-evaluate' (*umwerten*) their attitude to theatre by adopting critical distance.[86]

The *Modellbücher*, which documented productions by juxtaposing play text and photograph and which also included contextual information and essays, provided constant work for trainee dramaturgs, so much so that at times any spare hand was drafted in to help.[87] John Rouse suggests that they are 'perhaps the most successful attempts at production documentation in the history of the theatre'.[88] Usually dramaturgs worked on the *Modellbuch* for the play they had observed. Brecht profited doubly: he disseminated books that gave a detailed insight into his production aesthetics, and trained dramaturgs to develop an understanding of his creation of stage pictures and an eye for the dialectics of word and image. The *Modellbücher* also ensured that under Brecht's supervision the senior dramaturgs Berlau, Hubalek, Palitzsch and Rülicke compiled and edited *Theaterarbeit*, described as 'the most thorough investigation of a company's working practice ever published' and 'a manual of theatre crafts that has not yet been surpassed'.[89] It was an important part of Brecht's campaign for transparency, presenting his core theory and practice in a format that was accessible both to initiates and to those unfamiliar with his work.

Trainee dramaturgs did not just communicate to the audience via publicity and publications; they also arranged talks and discussions about Brecht's work in schools and universities, and arranged and supervised amateur performances of Brecht's work in factories and community centres across the GDR. In some cases they provided the performers with research material which they then helped them shape into a didactic piece, but mainly they relied on the *Lehrstücke* to drive home the message. If their intervention was tightly regimented in professional productions, it was a vital part of their work as educators on amateur productions, and this was the arena in which they usually got their first taste of the Brechtian power of being both director and dramaturg.

The one dramaturg set apart from the others was Hauptmann, who closely resembled the traditional model, and sat in her office reading and translating foreign plays, compiling a register and record of foreign dramatic literature, and making suggestions to Brecht about repertoire. Brecht still deployed her as a personal researcher, and a letter he sent to her in spring 1949 reveals the extent to which he relied on her for exhaustive background material:

> Dear Bess,
>
> Re: *Eulenspiegel*:
>
> Material about the Peasant War; look especially for a phase when it seems to be, or really is, going well for the peasants.
>
> I want to show how the peasants are in too much of a hurry to think they've won, they go home to their harvests, fight among themselves, and relapse into their old feudal relationships with landowners, etc.
>
> What did those knights who sided with the peasants do about their own peasants (as regards their working obligations)?
>
> Why did they side with the peasants?
>
> At what point did they leave the peasants in the lurch?
>
> What was the attitude of the burghers?
>
> Was there a big meeting of the appropriators of the peasants' land to decide how the campaign was to be carried on?
>
> Was there much starvation?
>
> What were the peasants' main mistakes?
>
> Was there guerrilla warfare?
>
> Was there clandestine resistance?
>
> Sabotage on the farms? Punishment for it?
>
> Were the sons of peasants fighting for the enemies of peasants?
>
> Did the universities take part? Who were the students? What did they study? Who were the judges? On what basis did they judge?

Are there any contemporary satires (about the priests,
the *Ius primae noctis*, the overlords of the towns, the robber
barons, etc.)?
Luther's writings against the peasants.
What was the reaction to them?
Re: *The Commune*:
Documentation of mistakes.
The different tendencies among the Communards.
Were any big businesses threatened?
What about war profits?
What connection were there between Paris businessmen and the
victorious Germans?
Food prices. Black market.
Bureaucracy in the Commune?
What about the students?
Jokes and anecdotes.
The journalists.
Attitude of the Goncourts. Zola.
Is there anything by Maupassant? Baudelaire?
Attitude and rôle of England.
Did the Church agitate (against the Commune)? What was the
attitude of the lower clergy?
Were some of them favourable?
Were there shifts of mood?
Cabaret songs?
Love
b[90]

Whether Hauptmann undertook all this research herself or delegated to other dramaturgs is unrecorded, but Brecht patently thought
nothing of setting her a gargantuan task, indicating that she was used
to research briefs of this kind. The range of disciplines she was
expected to cover is striking: journalistic, religious, political, legal
and economic questions mingle with the literary and anecdotal,
and in several cases any answer would demand substantial archival
investigation.

Hauptmann continued to act as Brecht's official editor and translator, and resumed the publication of Brecht's plays, poetry and miscellaneous writings under the title of *Versuche*. She negotiated the Berliner Ensemble's tours abroad, kept an eye on noteworthy international work, and was regularly consulted by trainee dramaturgs and directors on a whole range of day-to-day matters.[91] Manfred Wekwerth thinks her input and influence were so extensive that there is no adequate title to describe all she did, further asserting that Palitzsch, Bruno Besson and himself were as much students of Hauptmann as they were of Brecht.[92] She was perceived by all to be quite differently employed to anyone else, to be, as Werner Hecht puts it, 'the classical dramaturg in the truest sense of the word'.[93] Brecht's systematic training and organisation of dramaturgs at the Berliner Ensemble was the result of over thirty years of experimental private and professional collaborations. Once he had a theatre company of his own, Brecht had to balance practice with theory, and knowing the areas where he needed support, trained his dramaturgs in different specialisms and deployed them accordingly. Brecht's status as the premier theatre practitioner in the country afforded him the luxury of a generous state-funded base, but his selection of young trainees also meant that he could keep wages low while promoting his own ideas. He and Weigel were always flexible, and the number of unpaid, unofficial placements there were is hard to gauge, but there was certainly no shortage of keen applicants. Brecht's management structure for dramaturgs was multitiered, with trainees at the bottom and himself at the top; to save his time and energy for writing and directing he deployed the middle-management tier of senior dramaturgs not just to work in their specialist areas but also specifically to instruct the new entrants. Brecht's strict hierarchy was reinforced by the terms *Assistent* or *Mitarbeiter* (collaborator) that he generically used to describe his dramaturgs, directors and designers. By implication they were all assistants to him or collaborators with him, Brecht remaining the controlling force, and though this terminology was coloured with communist utopianism it was also convenient for him to exploit, not least because it constantly enhanced his own identity as playwright, dramaturg and director.

Comparing Brecht's practice at the Berliner Ensemble with his theory in *Der Messingkauf*, Brecht himself appears to embody the unification of the ideal Dramaturg and Philosopher and be controller of the means of production to boot. But the symbolic conversion of the ideal Dramaturg in *Der Messingkauf* remains centrally relevant. Brecht's most devoted dramaturgs were committed communists prepared to sacrifice themselves to a sometimes inexplicable extent. It is interesting that while Brecht redefined the model of the dramaturg established by Lessing and created a new theory and practice, he did not shelve the idea of the traditional dramaturg, but in the figure of Hauptmann allowed it a complex, dialectical coexistence with the new model.

Post-Brechtian practice and the Berliner Ensemble

A significant element of the western reception of Brecht's practice has unconsciously rested on the formulations of dramaturgs and directors who have described and propagated a post-Brechtian system of working practice at the Berliner Ensemble. One of the immediate effects of Brecht's death in 1956 was the collapse of the joint training of dramaturgs and directors which underpinned his philosophy of practice – a fact which Heiner Müller always mourned.[94] Though subsequent attempts were made to reinstitute the system, they were never sustained. Instead, a working party of seventeen senior dramaturgs and directors (including Weigel) was created to discuss repertoire and make decisions about analysis of texts, casting and staging.[95] Palitzsch remained *Chefdramaturg* until 1961. Hauptmann also maintained her unique position, editing an eight-volume *Collected Works* which appeared in 1967,[96] and became the 'most important'[97] dramaturg of the company through the sheer breadth of experience she had acquired working with Brecht for over thirty years. Productions followed a pattern of director – dramaturg partnerships. With Brecht the benevolent dictator gone a predictable battle for territory broke out and the division of labour became increasingly stratified and determined, with the result that dramaturgs were channelled into specialism. Thus, in the 1970s Hecht identified the general areas of dramaturgs' work as repertoire, work with writers and directors, education and documentation. At the same time Hecht stressed the need for individual dramaturgy departments to have more autonomy and created for himself the post of *Leiter der Dramaturgie*, Director of Dramaturgy, which oversaw all dramaturgical functions.[98] Dramaturgs appointed to support directors were specifically developed as *Produktionsdramaturgen*, 'production dramaturgs', with special responsibility for research, developing the directing concept with director and designer, and an accentuated critical rôle in rehearsals, writing *Notate* and programme material. It is this concept of the *Produktionsdramaturg* that has reached the West, sometimes in garbled ways, and often without any understanding that the *Produktionsdramaturg* was only one component of a sophisticated apparatus.

Joachim Tenschert's interview 'What is a dramaturg?' in 1960 is an example of the way in which some post-Brechtian commentary fed misunderstandings of Brechtian practice proper. Employed as a dramaturg at the Berliner Ensemble in 1958 after Brecht's death, Tenschert gave a homogeneous view of the dramaturg as dogmatic ideologue:

> The director does the practical work, and the dramaturg does the theoretical work ... He [the dramaturg] has to analyse the text systematically, explain it, define its ideology ("what I want to show") and translate this concept into a theatrical language which is accessible to everyone right up to the night of the dress rehearsal. In parallel he works on documentation which will give the necessary pointers to the stage work ... The director is controlled by the dramaturg during rehearsals. Less absorbed by details, the dramaturg is more attentive to the general through-line of the work.[99]

Tenschert failed to specify that he was talking of a production dramaturg, and gave no indication of the numbers of dramaturgs employed at the Ensemble, nor of their various functions. He overstressed his case, and by falsely asserting that the dramaturg controlled the rehearsal process gave an impression that the dramaturg was a conceptual dictator rather than a facilitator. Given the Cold War climate, many western theatre-makers and critics were ideologically suspicious of Brechtian dramaturgs anyway, and descriptions such as Tenschert's of a controlling entity, concerned only with Marxist doctrine, reinforced prejudice and wariness. This is far removed from Brecht's emphasis on the dramaturg as a practical and theoretical worker with a profound understanding of directing. Tenschert's dogmatism reflected the growing entrenchment of an increasingly gerontocratic East German government during the later 1950s and 1960s.[100] The Berlin Wall (built in 1961) restricted access in and out, and the Berliner Ensemble, despite notable successes abroad, including London, began to turn in on itself.

In the 1970s there was a slight political thaw, and, following accusations that the Berliner Ensemble had become little more than a museum, promising writers were given posts as dramaturgs in order to develop a new body of dramatic literature; thus Volker Braun, Heiner Müller, Thomas Brasch and Karl Mickel all spent their apprenticeships working in a system which still insisted on the presence of dramaturgs throughout preproduction and performance.[101] Brecht had not needed trainee playwrights, but times had changed, and the new writers were employed to write plays, their training as dramaturgs in the Brechtian sense overlooked.[102]

Even in East Germany, while Brecht's terminology continued to be employed, the coherence and understanding of the system which he evolved and to which he had been central gradually broke down, and disparate voices claimed a 'Brechtian' authenticity of practice. It is not surprising that confusion and puzzlement arose amongst western academics and critics, most of whom lacked experience of theatre in the East, frequently had poor German, and did not allow for certain traditions of dramaturgy nor the absence of those traditions in their own countries.

Reception in the West

In the German-speaking world there is a network of two hundred well-funded state, regional and municipal theatres all with ensembles, without which the dramaturgy department, *Dramaturgie*, would be unthinkable.[103] *Dramaturgien* also exist in major theatres throughout

Central and Eastern Europe[104] and in Scandinavia. Many of these departments pre-existed Brecht, initially emulating Lessing's model of the resident playwright/critic. A large-scale theatre employs a *Chefdramaturg* to head the department and liaise with the Artistic Director on repertoire, and usually two or three other dramaturgs to work on adapting or cutting scripts, revising translations and producing programme and publicity material about the play. Post-Brecht these dramaturgs, more often than not, are assigned to particular productions and operate as *Produktionsdramaturgen* for a director, doing research, acting as a sounding-board and observing rehearsals – participating in them as a consultant when required (the matter might be scenic, textual, to do with sound or image, or anything the director requires information on). Unlike Brecht's model, the division of labour between director and dramaturg is organised in a way that separates their functions and thus their professions: a dramaturg with aspirations to direct is generally viewed negatively and, strangely, deficient as a dramaturg. Overwhelmingly, dramaturgs are now expected to be theatre historians, researchers and textual specialists; they are not expected to stray on to other terrain unless they are asked.[105]

The western reception of Brecht's training and deployment of dramaturgs has been mixed. In Britain the transfer of theory and practice has been fraught with difficulty, dogged until very recently by general ignorance of the term. But progress in the English-speaking West has also been obstructed by failures to recognise or understand *Der Messingkauf* as Brecht's central theoretical document. The fact that only a small percentage of Brecht's theorisations have been translated into English is also a major problem. There are no full translations of *Der Messingkauf*, *Theaterarbeit* nor the *Modellbücher*, indeed it seems as though all three are still considered marginal to Brecht's œuvre precisely because they theorise practice. Furthermore, the more informed lessons of German scholarship have not been collated to put together a coherent picture of dramaturgical practices before or after Brecht's death – a distinction which is barely recognised. Apart from Ruth Berlau's *Lai-Tu* (itself rendered problematic by posthumous editing), none of the principal works by Brecht's dramaturgs – Rülicke's *Die Dramaturgie Brechts* or Wekwerth's *Schriften: Arbeit mit Brecht* and *Notate*, offering detailed accounts and analyses of practice at the Berliner Ensemble – have been translated.

Reception in the English-speaking West has also been affected by an anti-intellectualism among many theatre professionals, and by academic prejudices about the analysis of theatre practice – this is particularly true of Britain, though Robert Brustein has commented on the hostility of the struggle to establish dramaturgs in the United States.[106] Brecht's theory was regarded as awkward territory by early western converts, who knew that Brecht's communism would make him decidedly unpalatable to the establishment. But it was also diffi-cult for westerners to compehend precisely because it depended on an understanding of practice. Hauptmann was struck by Willett's 'fear of too much theory' in his publications on Brecht, and Weigel told him quite specifically that he lacked sufficient knowledge and intellectual rigour when it came to dramaturgy and directing.[107] In France the conflicts of opinion expressed in a journal devoted to dramaturgy in 1986 broadly reflect debate in Spain, Portugal and Britain: directors Michel Bataillon, Jean Jordheuil and Roger Planchon acknowledge the seminal influence of Brecht on the appointment of dramaturgs, while Antoine Vitez voices a deep political hostility to their appearance and likens them to ideologues, 'a Stalinesque redeployment of an old system'.[108] Despite such prejudices, dramaturgs are established in France, and as the same journal makes clear, dialogue with German dramaturgs and directors is lively. France is unusual in having a bril-liant teacher of Brecht's practice: Bernard Dort, both dramaturg and academic writer, is a champion of Brecht's dramaturgy and has exer-cised a very significant influence on his positive reception in France.[109]

Some degree of obfuscation of the work of dramaturgs can be led back to Brecht himself: given the thoroughness of *Theaterarbeit* in its description of agency and process, and the fact that four of Brecht's dramaturgs worked with him to compose it, it is curious that the various functions of the dramaturgs are not set down and explained. The omission may have been accidental, a classic and collective blindness to self in the dramaturgical core of Brecht's enterprises, or a deliberate cloaking by Brecht of the work done by his principal collaborators to serve his own sexual, political and creative agendas, and it continues to impede the research of even those who read German; but in either case the omission has compounded all the other difficulties of cross-cultural transmission.

The fact remains, though, that in Britain there is still very little understanding of the myriad functions performed by Brecht's dramaturgs at the Berliner Ensemble. Reception is still dominated by reported caricatures of the ideal Dramaturg in *Der Messingkauf* (always tending to the monolithic and coloured by disparagements of theory), and by the political prejudices and judgments about communism that have always dogged reception in the West. The theoretical and practical complexities behind Brecht's utilisation of the dramaturg continue to be ignored or attacked rather than investigated and applied, and without a substantial and fundamental reassessment of what has become the received account of Brecht's work the misunderstandings can only continue.

Notes

1. For a description of how it developed see, Robert Brustein, 'From "The Future of an Un-American Activity"', in *Dramaturgy in American Theater*, ed. Susan Jonas, Geoff Proehl and Michael Lupu (New York: Harcourt Brace, 1997), pp. 33–8.
2. Jonas, Proehl and Lupu, eds., *Dramaturgy*, p. 57.
3. Eric Bentley was the earliest and most important proselytiser of Brecht in America and Canada. See *The Playwright as Thinker* (New York: Reynal and Hitchcock, 1946), pp. 249–72, and *Bentley on Brecht* (New York and London: Applause, 1981).
4. See *Der Messingkauf* in *Bertolt Brecht: Werke*, ed. Werner Hecht, Jan Knopf, Werner Mittenzwei and Klaus-Detlef Müller, 30 vols. (Berlin: Aufbau Verlag/Frankfurt-on-Main: Suhrkamp Verlag, 1988–98), XXII.II (1993), 695–869. The editors organise the fragments into four chronological sections according to the times when Brecht is known or thought to have been working on *Der Messingkauf*: 1939–41; 1942–3; 1945; 1948–55. No exact chronology for the

writing of the text is known, nor what was added, removed or lost from the four bundles of documents labelled as *Der Messingkauf*.

5. See *Brecht: Schriften zum Theater*, ed. Werner Hecht (1957; 6 vols., revised edn, Frankfurt-on-Main: Suhrkamp, 1963), v. Apart from changing the title, Hecht chose to conflate fragments with a common theme or subject. He also omitted many fragments, some essays, most actors' exercises and poems.

6. See *Messingkauf*, pp. 695–6 (para. A2), pp. 696–7 (A4); and Bertolt Brecht, *Journals 1934–1955*, ed. John Willett (London: Methuen, 1993), pp. 20–1 (12.2.1939).

7. Peter Brooker in *The Cambridge Companion to Brecht*, ed. Peter Thomson and Glendyr Sacks (Cambridge: Cambridge University Press, 1994), p. 185.

8. The obvious perpetrator of the view that Brecht is really a poet whose language transcends theory and ideology is Martin Esslin in *Brecht: A Choice of Evils* (London: Eyre and Spottiswoode, 1959). For a balanced account of the British reception of Brecht's plays and practice to 1980, see Jan Needle and Peter Thomson, *Brecht* (Oxford: Basil Blackwell, 1981), pp. 1–22.

9. Michael Billington, *Guardian*, 10.2.1998, G2, p. 9. His title, 'The other Marx brother', casts Brecht as Marx's right-hand man, but the allusion to the Marx brothers undermines any serious intent. While Billington is convinced Brecht's influence has affected British dramaturgy and acting, he cannot say how or why: 'Brecht is somehow invisibly present … Brecht still has much to teach us, and this seems as good a time as any to start learning'. But he does not suggest how we might learn, or refer to any individual theoretical work by Brecht.

10. Carol Martin and Henry Bial, eds., *Brecht Sourcebook* (London: Routledge, 2000).

11. Tom Kuhn and Steve Giles, eds., *Brecht on Art and Politics* (London: Methuen, 2003).

12. Bertolt Brecht, *The Messingkauf Dialogues*, trans. John Willett (London: Methuen, 1994), p. 10.

13. See *Brecht on Theatre*, trans. and ed. John Willett (London: Methuen, 1987), p. 169.

14. Brecht, *Messingkauf Dialogues*, p. 108.
15. See Margaret Eddershaw, *Performing Brecht: Forty Years of British Performances* (London: Routledge, 1996), p. 1.
16. *Ibid.*, p. 18.
17. See Jan Knopf, *Brecht-Handbuch: Theater* (Stuttgart: J. B. Metzler, 1980), pp. 452–3.
18. Mews's companion to Brecht annotates *Der Messingkauf* as 'Probably Brecht's most important theoretical treatise – albeit less well known than "Short Organum"', but there are only passing references in the main text and there is no attempt to redress the wrong. See Siegfried Mews, ed., *A Bertolt Brecht Reference Companion* (Westport, CT: Greenwood Press, 1997), p. 402.
19. *Journals*, p. 392 (18.9.1948). See *Brecht on Theatre*, p. 205; Willett has written: 'Failing completion of "Der Messingkauf", the "Short Organum" became (and remained) Brecht's most important theoretical work.'
20. I capitalise the word when referring to the character in the text.
21. *Messingkauf*, p. 773.
22. *Ibid.*
23. *Ibid.*, p. 696. Translations are my own unless otherwise stated.
24. Karl Marx, *Feuerbach-Thesen*, in *Marx-Engels-Werke*, Institut für Marxismus-Leninismus beim ZK der SED, 43 vols. (Berlin: Dietz Verlag, 1958), III, 7, no. 11.
25. *Messingkauf*, p. 773.
26. *Ibid.*, p. 697. See also *Journals*, p. 81 (2.9.1940).
27. Bertolt Brecht, *Über die epische Schauspielkunst*, in *Werke*, ed. Werner Hecht et al., XXII.II, p. 672.
28. *Messingkauf*, p. 736.
29. Ruth Berlau, Bertolt Brecht, Claus Hubalek, Peter Palitzsch and Käthe Rülicke, eds., *Theaterarbeit: 6 Aufführungen des Berliner Ensemble* (Dresden: Desdener Verlag, 1952), p. 431. This is Brecht's glossary definition of the word *dramaturgisch*: 'dramaturgical'. The word 'dramaturg' is not included.
30. *Messingkauf*, p. 773.
31. *Ibid.*, p. 708.
32. *Ibid.*

33. *Ibid.*
34. Rainer Schlösser was appointed by Hitler on 12.1.1933 with a remit to ban all 'degenerate' plays and performances and to develop Nazi propaganda through the vast spectacles of the 'Thingspiel'. See Glen Gadberry, 'The Thingspiel and Das Frankenberger Wurfenspiel', *Drama Review* 24.1 (March 1980): 103–14, and Jeffrey T. Schnapp, *Staging Fascism* (Stanford: Stanford University Press, 1996).
35. Ben Payne, 'Six Managers in Search of the Author', *New Playwrights Trust Newsletter* 98 (1996): 3–7, p. 1.
36. Interview with the author, 28.1.1998.
37. Terry McCabe, *Mis-directing the Play* (Chicago: Ivan R. Dee, 2001), p. 70.
38. See *OED* 2: 'Pivotal ... 1.a. Of, pertaining to, of the nature of, or constituting a pivot; being that on which anything turns or depends: central, cardinal, vital. 1.b. *pivotal man,* a man considered to have an important part to play in the re-establishment of industry and commerce after the war of 1914–1918, and hence eligible for early demobilization.' Obviously, I am drawing a parallel with World War Two.
39. See Hans Otto Münsterer, 'Recollections of Brecht in 1919 in Augsburg', in Hubert Witt, ed., *Brecht As They Knew Him*, trans. John Peet, 3rd edn (London: Lawrence and Wishart, 1980), pp. 23–31. His close friends were Caspar Neher, who later collaborated with Brecht as a designer, Georg Pfanzelt and Otto Müller, but other followers were included if Brecht felt they would complement the group.
40. See Klaus Völker, *Brecht,* trans. J. Nowell (London: Marion Boyars, 1979), p. 12.
41. Premièred 19 March 1924 at the Munich Kammerspiele, directed by Brecht. Brecht collaborated again with Feuchtwanger from November 1942 to spring 1943 on *Die Geschichte der Simone Machard.*
42. Premièred 26 October 1926 at the Landestheater, Darmstadt, directed by Jacob Geis.
43. Elisabeth Hauptmann, *Julia ohne Romeo,* ed. Rosemarie Eggert and Rosemarie Hill (Berlin: Aufbau Verlag, 1977), p. 185.

44. See Paula Hanssen, *Elisabeth Hauptmann: Brecht's Silent Collaborator* (New York: Peter Lang, 1994) [New York Ottendorfer Series, no. 46], p. 7.

45. See Hans Bunge, ed., *Brechts Lai-Tu: Erinnerungen und Notate von Ruth Berlau*, 2nd edn (Darmstadt: Hermann Luchterhand, 1985), pp. 106–7.

46. From the documentary film *Die Mit-Arbeiterin – Gespräche mit Elisabeth Hauptmann*, director Karlheinz Mund, broadcast by Deutscher Fernsehfunk, Channel 1, 3.12.1972.

47. See Sabine Kebir, *Ich Fragte Nicht Nach Meinem Anteil: Elisabeth Hauptmanns Arbeit mit Bertolt Brecht* (Berlin: Aufbau Verlag, 1997).

48. *Brechts Lai-Tu*, p. 107.

49. See Ruth Berlau's account of her first collaboration with Brecht in Witt, ed., *Brecht As They Knew Him*, pp. 89–92.

50. *Ibid.*, p. 59.

51. *Ibid.*, p. 256.

52. John Fuegi, *Brecht and Company: Sex, Politics, and the Making of the Modern Drama* (New York: Grove Press, 1994). Also published as *The Life and Lies of Bertolt Brecht* (London: HarperCollins, 1994).

53. See *Brecht Then and Now*, Brecht Yearbook 20 (Madison: International Brecht Society, 1995), pp. 239–367.

54. See Sabine Kebir, *Ich fragte nicht nach meinem Anteil: Elisabeth Hauptmann's Arbeit mit Bertolt Brecht* (Berlin: Aufbau Verlag, 1997) and *Ein akzeptabler Mann? Brecht und die Frauen* (Berlin: Aufbau Verlag, 1998); John Willett, 'Bacon ohne Shakespeare? The problem of Mitarbeit?', in John Fuegi, G. Bahr and John Willett, eds., *Brecht, Women, Politics* (Detroit: Wayne State University Press, 1983); James K. Lyon, 'Collective productivity – Brecht and his Collaborators', in *Intersections*, Brecht Yearbook 21, pp. 1–18.

55. Brecht wrote contributions for the *Augsburger Neueste Nachrichten*, *Augsburger Volkswille*, *Der neue Merkur* and *Berliner Börsen-Courier*.

56. Carl Zuckmayer; see Werner Mittenzwei, *Das Leben Bertolt Brecht*, 2 vols. (Berlin: Aufbau Verlag, 1986), II, 222.

57. *Die Mit-Arbeiterin – Gespräche mit Elisabeth Hauptmann.*

58. Bertolt Brecht, *Werke,* ed. Hecht et al., II.I, 50.

59. *Messingkauf,* pp. 720, 763, 794–5, 814–16.

60. See Piscator's *Über Grundlagen und Aufgaben des Proletarischen Theaters* in *Schriften,* ed. L. Hoffmann 2 vols. (Berlin: Henschelverlag, 1968), II, 9–12.

61. Erwin Piscator, *Das Politische Theater* revised Felix Gasbarra, (Hamburg: Rowohlt, 1963), p. 139.

62. For the fullest account of Brecht's time in America, see James K. Lyon, *Bertolt Brecht in America* (Princeton: Princeton University Press, 1980). See also Alexander Stephan, *Communazis: FBI Surveillance of German Emigré Writers* (New Haven: Yale University Press, 2000).

63. Helene Weigel Archive (henceforth HWA), 161. Stated in a letter from Herr Heymann, of the Culture and Education Department of the SED, to Kurt Bork, of Amt für Kunst.

64. HWA, 379 [Institut der deutschen Verwaltung für Volksbildung].

65. *Journals,* p. 401.

66. Berlau *et al.,* eds., *Theaterarbeit,* p. 8.

67. Brecht succinctly defines his position on socialist realism in a note written in 1954, Bertolt Brecht Archive (henceforth BBA), 12/27; see *Brecht on Theatre,* p. 269.

68. James K. Lyon, 'Brecht in Postwar Germany: Dissident Conformist, Cultural Icon, Literary Dictator', in *Brecht Unbound,* ed. James K. Lyon and Peter Breuer (Newark: University of Delaware Press; London: Associated Universities Press, 1995), p. 76.

69. 'Artistic Director' is not an accurate translation. In the case of Weigel, 'Managing Director' might be better but is still not quite right. For information, see 'The Managing Director and Colleague', in *Helene Weigel 100,* Brecht Yearbook 25, pp. 253–347.

70. See *Journals,* p. 424.

71. Sabine Kebir, *Helene Weigel: Abstieg in den Ruhm* (Berlin: Aufbau Verlag, 2002), pp. 246–7.

72. Olga Fedianina, in Brecht Yearbook 25, p. 285.

73. BBA, 764/37. Letter from Käthe Rülicke to Herr Heinen, 9 May 1956. I am indebted to Werner Hecht for drawing my attention

to this document. I give the German because of the letter's significance

Die Schwierigkeit, Sie bei uns zu engagieren, ist merkwürdiger Art. Brecht arbeitet mit lauter jungen Leuten, die er selbst ausgebildet hat. Dramaturgen im herkömmlichen Sinne gibt es an unserem Theater gar nicht. Unsere Dramaturgen machen Regieassistenz und umgekehrt arbeiten die Regisseure in der Dramaturgie. Diese Art Arbeit ist wahrscheinlich eine Folge von Brechts eigener Tätigkeit als Schriftsteller, Dramaturg und Regisseur.

74. Carl Weber, who worked as dramaturg and director under Brecht from 1952, confirms this in 'Brecht and the Berliner Ensemble – the Making of a Model', in Thomson and Sacks, ed., *Cambridge Companion to Brecht*, pp. 167–84, p. 173.

75. HWA, 164. Protokoll der Betriebsversammlung. Notes on a board meeting held 4.1.1956.

76. For example, Vera Böhm informed me that she had invited Weigel to her school and that her employment as an *Assistentin*, a trainee dramaturg, from 1951 to 1956 had resulted from this contact. Her first year of work for the Berliner Ensemble from 1951 to 1952 was unofficial, but her official engagement ran from 1952 to 1955. Interview with author, 6.12.1996.

77. *Ibid.*

78. Bertolt Brecht, *Briefe*, ed. Günter Glaeser, 2 vols. (Frankfurt-on-Main: Suhrkamp, 1981), 1, 658–9, no. 665, items 1 and 2. Brecht's letter dated 14.5.1951 is addressed to Paul Wandel at the Ministry for People's Education of the German Democratic Republic.

79. *Ibid.*, items 3 and 4.

80. *Ibid.*

81. Margaret Eddershaw, for example, accepts the term 'collective' uncritically, imputing to it a sense of pure 'democracy'. Brecht always placed himself at the top of the hierarchy.

82. Käthe Rülicke-Weiler, *Die Dramaturgie Brechts* (Berlin: Henschelverlag, 1966).

83. For examples see Manfred Wekwerth, *Notate: Über die Arbeit des Berliner Ensembles 1956–1966* (Frankfurt-on-Main: Suhrkamp, 1967), and *Schriften: Arbeit mit Brecht* (Berlin: Henschelverlag, 1975).

84. Information supplied by Manfred Wekwerth, who trained as dramaturg and director under Brecht from 1951 to 1956, became principal director of the Berliner Ensemble from 1956 to 1968, and Intendant from 1977 to 1990. Interview with author, 4.12.1996.

85. *Brechts Lai-Tu*, p. 226.

86. Berlau *et al.*, eds., *Theaterarbeit*, 225.

87. Information from Vera Böhm, whose initial response to working on the *Modellbücher* was that it was a *Strafarbeit*, a punishment, but later appreciated what it taught her about Brecht's directing techniques. Interview with author, 6.12.1996.

88. John Rouse, *Brecht and the West German Theatre* (Ann Arbor: University of Michigan Press, 1989), p. 61.

89. Both remarks are Carl Weber's; see Thomson and Sacks, ed., *Cambridge Companion to Brecht*, p. 173.

90. See *Briefe*, I, 603–4, no. 596. *Eulenspiegel* was never completed. The second half of the letter refers to what became *Die Tage der Commune*, which did not go through final revision by Brecht but was first produced by Benno Besson and Manfred Wekwerth in Karl Marx-Stadt, 17 November 1956.

91. HWA, 164. See also Wekwerth, *Schriften: Arbeit mit Brecht*, p. 27.

92. Wekwerth, *Schriften: Arbeit mit Brecht*, pp. 26–7. [Aber nur wenige werden sich darunter Umfang und Größe dieser Arbeit vorstellen können: Yet there are few people who will be able to imagine the extent and greatness of her work.]

93. Werner Hecht was a dramaturg at the Berliner Ensemble during the 1960s and 1970s. Interview with author, 5.12.1996.

94. In 'Dramaturgie', *Théâtre/public* 67 (1986): 33.

95. HWA, 164. Bericht über Diskussion der Dramaturgie, 19 June 1957.

96. Bertolt Brecht, *Gesammelte Werke*, ed. Elisabeth Hauptmann, 8 vols. (Frankfurt-on-Main: Suhrkamp, 1967).

97. See Hans Mayer, *Erinnerung an Brecht* (Frankfurt-on-Main: Suhrkamp, 1996), p. 102. Mayer's acquaintance with Brecht began in 1948.

98. HWA, 164. Leitung und Organisation des BE, four-page typescript.

99. Joachim Tenschert, Qu'est-ce qu'un dramaturge?, *Théâtre Populaire* 38 (1960): 41–8.

100. See Loren Kruger, *Post-Imperial Brecht: Politics and Performance, East and South* (Cambridge: Cambridge University Press, 2004), p. 137 n9.

101. Volker Braun spent his time as a 'dramaturg' (he thought the term simply a convenient excuse to hire him) writing his own plays, and found the presence of dramaturgs during experiments and rehearsals invaluable, but eventually left because he felt that he was being 'schooled' to write in a Brechtian manner. Interview with author, 4.12.1996.

102. Heiner Müller, *Théâtre/public* 67 (1986): 32.

103. Figures from Martin Esslin in Jonas et al., eds., *Dramaturgy in American Theater*, p. 25.

104. For details of dramaturgs in Russia and Eastern Europe, see *Slavic and East European Arts* 4.1 (1986).

105. Dance dramaturgs of course are expected to have a specialist knowledge of dance, and opera dramaturgs of music.

106. Jonas et al., eds., *Dramaturgy in American Theater*, p. 33.

107. Hauptmann in a letter to Weigel, 18.3.1957; and Weigel in a letter to Willett, 25.3.1957, in *Helene Weigel: Briefwechsel 1935–1971*, ed. Stefan Mahlke (Berlin: Theater der Zeit, 2000), pp. 85–6.

108. *Théâtre/public* 67 (1986): 59.

109. *Ibid.*, pp. 8–12.

6 Kenneth Tynan and the National Theatre

In October 1963 Kenneth Tynan (1927–80) became the first official Literary Manager in Britain. Widely perceived as the most brilliant theatre critic since Shaw, he relinquished the post he had held at the *Observer* for nine years and entered the newly created National Theatre (NT), where he remained for a decade. His tenure has interesting parallels with Lessing's, and he certainly saw his share of crisis and controversy, but unlike Lessing, Tynan has not been internationally celebrated for his rôle: he is remembered for his reviewing and his work at the NT is framed as marginal to his career as a critic. His appointment challenged traditional British management structures assigning artistic and managerial responsibility to actor-managers, and in post Tynan provided a model of literary management that continues to be appropriated and refashioned by theatre companies throughout the United Kingdom. Yet Tynan's term as Literary Manager suffers from curious academic erasures, and the official history of the NT even appears to disclaim Tynan's power and influence while in post.[1]

One significant reason for the silences surrounding Tynan's time as Literary Manager was the invisibility of his work, much of which took place in a small office, and unlike the contributions of writers, actors, designers and directors was unfamiliar and uncomprehended. In 1998 Tynan's manuscripts became available at the British Library:[2] they reveal his functions, working relationships and prolonged internal battle for appropriate recognition of his rôle. These materials make it possible to piece together the political and logistical complexities of Tynan's work, and call for the acknowledgement of his very substantial influence at the NT during its first decade.

The founding of the National Theatre and its board

In 1949, a century after Effingham Wilson had proposed a national theatre,[3] a new bill demonstrated the first real political and financial commitment from the British government. Attlee's parliament approved the donation of £1,000,000 towards building and equipment, and agreed the Treasury should be responsible for the appointment of trustees. The National Theatre Bill generated passionate and lengthy debate, but there was broad consensus that state support for the venture was proper and that Britain's theatrical profile was poor compared to those of national theatres in continental Europe.[4] I have already discussed the singularly late British foundation of a subsidised national theatre and suggested the institutionalisation of Shakespeare and the ideological hold of commercial theatre as reasons for its delay. The difference in 1949 was the political climate of the immediate post-war years. Attlee's government of 1945–51 was the first majority Labour government, and it reflected popular radicalism largely generated by the experience of war;[5] nationalisation, legal aid and health reforms topped the domestic agenda. The notion of the all-providing state had gained currency and support since 1929 and the Great Depression had exposed myths of self-sufficiency: as Churchill phrased it, the welfare state would offer protection for all classes 'from the cradle to the grave'.[6] Though no priority, the idea of state support for a national theatre was no longer so alien.

Despite this political progress, problems of location and further sponsorship dogged material development until 1961. From 1951 to 1964 Conservative governments were preoccupied with slow economic recovery, rearmament, colonial wars and withdrawals and growing Cold War tensions. But in 1961 London County Council offered financial support, and in 1962 the South Bank was agreed as the site. The Old Vic Theatre, meanwhile, was proffered as temporary home for the NT Company. In 1946 the Old Vic had joined forces with the Shakespeare Memorial National Theatre Committee, a movement with roots in the late nineteenth century which had gained impetus from the Archer–Barker scheme published in 1907;[7] together they established a pressure group, the Joint Council of the National Theatre and the Old Vic. The Old Vic had also, in the heydays of Lilian Baylis's directorship during the 1930s and Olivier's and Ralph Richardson's joint directorship from 1944 to 1948, been perceived by many as a national theatre in all but name, and was seen by politicians and sponsors alike as a fitting temporary home for the NT Company. Accordingly, the Chancellor of the Exchequer appointed ten members of the National Theatre Board in 1962. Laurence Olivier, an NT trustee since 1958, became Director in August 1962 and *ex officio* the eleventh member of the Board. Tynan's post was established during January and February 1963, but did not include membership of the Board. When he began his work that autumn he did not envisage that his 'temporary' home, a prefabricated wooden hut near the Old Vic, would be his base for his entire tenure of office. The South Bank centre was eventually opened in 1976.

The choice of Olivier as Director was no surprise. His war work for the Ministry of Information had fostered close links with the government, and his film *Henry V*, the making of which was itself a military campaign, had enshrined him as a patriotic hero and secured him a knighthood in 1947. His domestic and international celebrity as a classical and avant-garde actor, and his experience as a director and manager, had secured his reputation in Britain as a talent beyond compare. Olivier was himself a form of national institution.

The Chancellor's selection of the Board, however, was not quite so transparent: it comprised Viscount Chandos (Chair) and Lord Wilmot, both described as Directors of Public Companies; Henry Moore, Sculptor; Sir Ashley Clarke, Retired Diplomat; Kenneth Clark, Author; William Keswick, Director and Banker; Hugh Beaumont, Theatrical Manager; Sir Douglas Logan, Principal of the University of London; Derek Salberg, Managing Director; and Freda Corbet, Chairman of the General Purposes Committee of London County Council.[8] Their exceptional individual careers were beyond question, as, in most cases, was their distinguished service[9] during the Second World War (Chandos, Wilmot and Moore had also fought in 1914–18); but though most had extensive experience as trustees of various arts foundations or were governors of the Old Vic (Chandos, Logan and Wilmot), only two, Beaumont and Salberg, had direct, long-term professional experience of day-to-day life in the theatre world. Beaumont had been the outstanding London theatre impresario of the

1940s and 1950s but belonged to a theatre world that had passed, and the authors he championed, such as Fry and Rattigan, were under vicious attack (not least by Tynan). Salberg had been Managing Director of the Alexandra Theatre in Birmingham since 1937, and those commitments were to prove so binding that he resigned from the Board after two years.[10] Keswick, a director of the Bank of England, was chosen for his financial and political acumen, Corbet for reasons of politics and funding, and Logan for impressive achievements in education; but what Kenneth Clark as a leading fine arts connoisseur and scholar, Henry Moore as a prominent artist and sculptor, or Ashley Clarke as a diplomat were expected to contribute to a national theatre is far from clear. There is more than a hint that war connections and the old boys' network played a part in their appointments, that names mattered more than practical experience of theatre. It is notable that every Board member, Olivier included, was born between 1893 and 1912. There was no one younger than 51. Tynan, born in 1927, had not served in the war, was 36 and of a different generation.

The most significant and vigorous member of the Board besides Olivier was Chandos, who did not hide his sense of proprietorship. He had given lifelong support to the project, out of a missionary belief in the supremacy of England and her drama, London providing a base for the theatre 'in the capital city of the Commonwealth and Empire';[11] and not least out of the need to 'keep undefiled the purity of the English language'.[12] Born in 1893, he was, at 70, the oldest member, had seen service as a formidable industrial executive, Conservative politician, member of Churchill's war cabinet, and Colonial Secretary (1951-4). Not unusually for the pre-1945 generations of his class, his thinking was underpinned by imperial discourses of paternal duty and patriotic loyalty. What also became apparent was that he believed in an exemplary civilising function for the NT that had more to do with a notion of ideal memorialisations of plays by his favourite authors, Shakespeare, Marlowe, Congreve and Shaw,[13] than with living theatre. First and foremost he saw himself as a representative of the government with a duty to quash any sign of political dissent.

The Board was charged with managing the NT's finances and supervising the implementation of company policy, as laid down in the *Memorandum and Articles of Association*. Board decisions were by majority vote. Their primary objective was

> to promote and assist in the advancement of education so far as such promotion and assistance shall be of charitable nature and in particular, so far as of charitable nature, to procure and increase the appreciation and understanding of the dramatic art in all its forms as a memorial to William Shakespeare.[14]

A statement defining 'education' in the context of the NT was not included, nor were parameters of 'promotion and assistance' laid down. The document sets out the Board's financial and managerial responsibilities, but there is no provision for an artistic rôle: this was to be Olivier's province.

Almost immediately the Board agreed that a subcommittee be constituted to research and make recommendations on all matters relating to repertory policy, individual actor development and touring; this was the Drama Committee, composed of four Board members: Kenneth Clark (Chair), Ashley Clarke, Beaumont and Salberg. Tynan became the fifth member when his employment began.[15] Additionally, Olivier, conscious of the burdens that would be cast on him if he remained without resident directors, insisted on his need for support, and John Dexter and William Gaskill were appointed Associate Directors.

Tynan and the idea of the dramaturg

Tynan's decision to exchange his soapbox at the *Observer* for a strange bureaucratic post with an institutional brief shocked many. He was as celebrated as a dandyish, flamboyant socialite with a love of controversy as for corruscating and incisive criticism.[16] In 1950, aged 23, he had precociously demonstrated formidable gifts with the publication of *He That Plays the King*, in which he fulminated against the state of dramatic criticism in England, denounced critics for bland frivolity, and demanded passionate intellectual judgement wedded to the cultivation of fresh responses to the art of acting.

> Criticism has taken a wrong turning into imperturbability and casualness: it has ceased to worry about communicating

excitement or scorn: it is away and somewhere else; not vitally interested. The cool, self-righteous anger of Shaw, the pungent ardour of Montague have quite vanished. Enthusiasm, even from the most erudite and magistral mouth, has become an offence against good manners, and we regard it as "a vain belief of private revelation". Like satire as Swift understood it, like ghosts in Shakespeare's sense and heroes in Dryden's, criticism has bled into weakness and deformity.[17]

By 1963, after successive appointments at various newspapers, including a stint as senior drama critic at the *New Yorker* from 1958 to 1960,[18] Tynan was overwhelmingly viewed as the critical voice of his age and an ardent supporter of the theatrical rebellion led by Arden, Osborne and Wesker. His power and influence as an analyst of plays in performance and actors at work were unmatched, Orson Welles describing him posthumously as the man who had 'the English-speaking world waiting for his next word'.[19] But Tynan had come to criticism via acting and directing, through his own experiments as an Oxford undergraduate and afterwards at the David Garrick Theatre in Lichfield. Always drawn to theatre practice, his desire for involvement in play-making processes had remained as strong as his desire to move amongst the stars he venerated.

Tynan had long been convinced that only a subsidised national theatre could save England from parochialism, ensure a broad international repertoire and create conditions for innovation and experiment. When the NT finally came to fruition, Tynan, a long-term agitator for the project, saw a chance for British theatre to liberate itself from commercial constraints on repertoire. It was also his great opportunity to be at the heart of play-making on a grand scale. His transfer back into theatre surprised only those who did not know him well.

Tynan must have spent considerable time mentally evolving a rôle for himself at the NT, for he wrote to Olivier immediately after the latter's directorship became official in August 1962. Tynan's letter is not extant, though Kathleen Tynan has summarised its contents in her biography; it apparently argued that the NT 'would need someone to recommend plays, supervise translations and commission new work'.[20] Olivier's reply, dated 21 August 1962, welcomes Tynan's idea of the position of 'Dramaturgist', which he says 'seems a decent enough translation of dramaturg',[21] accepts Tynan's self-recommendation for the post as 'an admirable one, a most welcome one and one that I'd thought of myself already',[22] and promises to forward the proposal to the Board.

Olivier's initial reaction to Tynan's suggestion had in fact been outrage.[23] Hostile to all critics but with a special enmity against Tynan,[24] Olivier would have rejected the idea outright without the intervention of his wife, Joan Plowright. She persuaded him of the advantages of Tynan's intellect applied *inside* the National Theatre, and of the potential of Tynan as an advisory resource for Olivier. She also saw the irresistible audacity of the partnership, the critical credibility that Tynan would lend the enterprise, and the protection that Tynan's presence could afford Olivier from criticism of his old-guardism.[25] Olivier, won over,[26] even expressed waggish relief that he had found a way to silence Tynan forever,[27] and thus, on 11 February 1963, at their first official meeting, the Board confirmed that Tynan was to be the NT's 'Dramaturg'.[28]

What did Tynan mean by 'dramaturg'? His major sources were Lessing, Granville Barker and Brecht. Understandably, Granville Barker's blueprint of the Literary Manager's rôle at the NT had particular influence.[29] There is no doubt that Tynan wanted the power of Barker's model, but also to extend it to include facets of Lessing's model and Brecht's practice. Tynan had certainly shown interest in the *Hamburgische Dramaturgie*.[30] He was drawn to Lessing as 'an incomparable critic',[31] by the idea of a resident theatre critic concerned with the artistic evolution of actors, plays and performance, and by the idea of refining the public's dramatic tastes, for these were amongst Tynan's own objectives.

Tynan's practical knowledge of the dramaturg was fed principally by his visits to the Berliner Ensemble in the 1950s and 1960s. For Tynan, Brecht's work was 'the most exhilarating, mind-flexing body of work in the theatre of postwar Europe',[32] and he declared himself a fascinated convert. In Berlin he watched productions, talked to Helene Weigel, and picked the minds of dramaturgs and directors about their work.[33] His interest in Brecht's dramaturgs focused on their presence in the rehearsal room as critical articulators of process and direct involvement in developing text and performance. Otherwise, he understood that Brecht's dramaturgs translated and adapted plays, advised on repertoire, wrote promotional literature and programme material, documented plays using various media, and led community workshops on Brecht's plays. Tynan was also intrigued by Brecht's only theoretical work to incorporate and explore the 'ideal' Marxist dramaturg, *The Messingkauf Dialogues*. Among his manuscripts is a typescript of a rough translation which may be his own work.[34] He thought *The Messingkauf Dialogues* sufficiently important to feature in his criticism,[35] and participated in the 'Brecht Forum' debate at the London Academy of Music and Dramatic Art in 1965, where members of the Berliner Ensemble performed sections of it. On travels to Germany and Czechoslovakia Tynan was as struck by the continental ubiquity of dramaturgs as opposed to their absence in Britain.[36] His initial sense of himself as Literary Manager, and indeed of the institution of the NT itself, was as something totally alien to British theatre culture, representing 'a triumph of continental theory'[37] over British reluctance to interrogate cherished theatrical traditions. But while Tynan drew information about dramaturgs from sources abroad, he had to invent and evolve his own rôle as the NT developed.[38]

In the year before the official opening of the NT, on 27 October 1963, the Board and Drama Committee convened regularly and formulated structural requirements for its operation. A running preoccupation at their meetings was the 'all important'[39] matter of who to appoint as head of Press and Public Relations: both committees saw that the specific agenda of the NT as the legitimate place and occasion of national representation made desirable an official spokesman to mediate between the theatre and its public, but no suitable candidate came to mind. The Board agreed that such a person must be dedicated, highly experienced and '*persona grata* in Fleet Street'.[40] Olivier suggested that the functions of press and public relations should be separated: as he saw it the function of the public relations official involved representing the policy of the Board in person and on paper, and required someone to write impressive copy on the work of the NT.

Press work, reasoned Olivier, was day-to-day routine demanding less exceptional skills; and he argued that since Tynan had already accepted an appointment as Dramaturg, and clearly had the capacity to perform a public function, he should also be Head of Public Relations.[41] Thus, Tynan's brief was extended to include public relations and the title of Dramaturg dropped.

The shift in terminology gave a clear signal of the Board's construction of Tynan's rôle. His dramaturgical functions were seen as easily subsumed in a public relations brief and thereby marginalised. It is doubtful that any Board member understood or had any detailed knowledge of the broad artistic territory that Tynan coveted and *thought* he had signalled through his use of 'dramaturg', for minutes reveal the Drama Committee understood only two functions of the dramaturg: reading plays and visiting significant productions abroad.[42] The combined executive's incomprehension of the scale of these functions alone suggests cursory attention to Tynan's strategic artistic utility; indeed, though the Board wanted the kudos of Tynan's involvement, their construction of it was depressingly superficial. Chandos later admitted that Tynan's appointment had been security against Olivier's establishment credentials; Tynan would be the 'Anti-Fuddy-Duddy'[43] element in the formula – little more than a frontman. In the first instance the Board agreed that Tynan should be engaged 'on a full-time contract from the early autumn of 1963 for one year and, thereafter, at three months' notice on either side'.[44] This meant that even Tynan's rôle as official representative was not constructed as an integral element of the NT's long-term administrative policy; as far as the Board was concerned, Tynan's employment was short-term expediency. Since the Board could not agree on the title 'Head of Public Relations', the matter was devolved to Tynan himself.[45] Undeterred, he chose the title 'Literary Manager' and in so doing saluted Granville Barker and again declared his artistic interests.

The British press reacted with clamorous perplexity. Tynan was to grow used to this, and during his ten-year stint he gave numerous interviews, explaining a rôle that was, in the main, thought 'heavy with mystery'[46] and 'one of those odd appointments that the British manage to make in their more inspired moments' – a statement revealing a depressing and typical lack of knowledge about continental traditions of dramaturgy.[47]

Tynan in post

On the eve of his inauguration as Literary Manager, Tynan saw no conflict between his identity as a critic and his decision to become a 'bureaucrat'[48] inside the NT. There was 'no frontier irrevocably crossed'.[49] It was, rather, a moment to indulge ideals and celebrate a historic new compact between critic and artist:

> It is the commercial theatre that sets up barriers between
> critic and artist, because in a theatre dependent on box-office
> takings, the critic may determine whether the artist thrives or
> starves. But in a non-commercial theatre, where profit and loss
> are not the first considerations, where actors and directors have
> security of employment, the relationship radically changes
> [and] critic and artist can work together in the common pursuit
> of perfection.[50]

Tynan had reached these conclusions from knowledge of continental models of theatre, specifically Brecht, and imagined the easy transplantation of practice. But his exemplars were products of communist states with entirely different political and economic structures, and of cultures that had long conceived of criticism as an inherent part of practice. Tynan took no account of the entrenched cultural construct of 'genius' in Britain, worked on the assumption that his critical presence would be unproblematical, and either underestimated antagonism to the theorisation of process or believed he could effect a sudden transformation in attitudes. His thinking was unrealistic. Despite the lack of any British precedent, Tynan foresaw little difficulty in his intended creative collaborations with writers, actors and directors. As for profit and loss, they were not Tynan's first considerations, but they certainly mattered to the Board.

According to Tynan state subsidy was an antidote to the antiintellectualism of commercial theatre: it would foster conditions for experimentation, allow the development of a working ethos amongst an ensemble of actors and offer a democratised theatre to audiences and theatre professionals alike:

> Subsidy is the missing link, the third force which can occupy and colonise the great intermediate area between minority theatre based on private whim and majority theatre based on private profits. This is precisely the area that the National Theatre exists to inhabit and develop; and our hope is that it will be the first, not of the few, but of the many – the beginning of a chain reaction that will set up a national grid of subsidised theatres in London and in every provincial centre.[51]

Theatre, he argued, was a civic right, an 'amenity'[52] for its people, comparable to a museum or art gallery in providing artistic edification. The potential for innovative and politically challenging work at the NT was far greater than had ever existed; it was simply a matter of educating others to understand this:

> It has to do with re-education: slowly and patiently, we have to set about re-educating actors, directors, playwrights and audiences alike ... to explain to people that *this* theatre belongs to them, and is not in any way stirred by the need or desire to show a profit ... we are not selling a product, we are providing a service.[53]

Committed to an ambitious notion of re-education, Tynan was heady with the optimism of the early 1960s and did not consider that Britain's cultural history hardly inclined audiences to be receptive to these ideas. In Germany, Schiller's notion of the theatre as a moral institution had evolved into a sophisticated social expectation and acceptance of drama as a pedagogical instrument, and Tynan imagined a nation that similarly longed for his Enlightenment programme.

The reality was otherwise, and the major problem that dogged Tynan throughout his tenure surfaced very rapidly: a much heavier and more time-consuming administrative workload than he or anyone else had anticipated. In December 1963, less than three months after starting work, Tynan complained to Stephen Arlen, the Administrative Director, about the volume of work and the dizzying proliferation of functions he and his assistant Rozina Adler were expected to perform. Tynan was already so horrified by the mismatch between his assistant's rates of pay and hours of work that he was paying her a considerable extra sum out of his own pocket:

> I feel under-privileged. I also feel under-staffed. As you know, at the moment the NT is paying Rozina 10 [pounds] per week for her NT activities, which means that she is employed on a part-time basis. This was certainly the original idea because when I started working for the NT it did not occur to me that there would be such a volume of work for her to perform. As things have worked out, I am subsidizing the NT, Rozina is working full-time (and overtime) for the NT and I am paying nearly half her salary. Not only does she handle the complex and arduous business of acknowledging scripts, registering them, and distributing them to readers, she also does a large amount of research in connection with programmes and publications, she organises my travelling arrangements, arranges for translation of foreign texts, keeps me in touch with authors' agents and many other things as well as the ordinary business of handling correspondence and memos.
>
> As we look across the corridor to the press department, we become slightly bitter. There are three people in one department. When, we wonder, shall we have equal rights?[54]

Tynan ended his memo stressing that Rozina was 'strained beyond endurance'[55] and requested the appointment of a junior secretary to help with the most burdensome correspondence, script distribution and collection. His request was not granted.

The following year Tynan wrote a detailed letter to Olivier and the two senior managers outlining the range of functions that he and Rozina were expected to fulfil:

> To: Sir Laurence
> Mr Arlen
> Mr Rowbottom   1 December 1964
>
> I am afraid that the literary department is simply not equipped to cope with the volume of work that is being

funnelled through it. At present we (i.e. Rozina and myself)
are handling:

(a) Collection, distribution and return of plays required for reading by the directors and assistant directors (at the moment
90 books are in circulation and every day brings requests for
several more).

(b) Acknowledgement, distribution and return of scripts submitted for consideration (up to 20 a week).

(c) Research for programmes, involving the tracking down, col-
lecting and return of prints, photographs, background books,
etc.; also compilation of programme texts and supervision of
reprints.

(d) Travelling to see plays, meet authors and directors, deliver
speeches, take part in debates, in London and abroad.

(e) Taping TV and radio interviews for national and international consumption; also giving interviews to critics and
journalists, both local and foreign (average: about five interviews a week).

(f) Acting as spokesman for the NT in answering appeals
addressed to the Director, and sending messages on its behalf
to other theatrical organisations.

(g) Working with playwrights and translators on scripts.

(h) Editing and part-writing NT publications (i.e. books of
RECRUITING OFFICER and OTHELLO).

(i) Reading and reporting on plays old and new. Commissioning
new plays.

(j) Attending Board, Drama and Building Committee meetings,
and representing the NT on the Commonwealth Arts
Festival Committee, the Arts Council Drama Panel and
the Arts Council Theatre Enquiry.

(k) Writing articles for the NT for publication in foreign maga-
zines and newspapers.

(l) Collating cast list material and supervising reprints.

(m) Preventing the *wrong* plays from being chosen – as far as
possible.

> This is frankly too much for myself and one secretary
> to handle. We badly need extra help, in the form of a
> shorthand typist who can also run errands. Unless this is
> forthcoming, we are going to get swamped.[56]

Tynan does not sequence his tasks as might be expected, playreading
and selection of repertoire appearing in ninth and last place respectively. The first three functions, as Tynan had noted in his letter
the previous year, were the most onerous and Rozina Adler was
doing the lion's share of this work; but the remaining ten functions
fell to Tynan entirely. Tynan also omitted three areas of his work:
formal rehearsal notes delivered to the director after significant
run-throughs, and correspondence and negotiation with the Lord
Chamberlain's office on all matters of censorship, were both a regular
part of his remit; and he wrote elsewhere of his function as company
historian,[57] by which he meant the documentation of the process of an
individual performance from page to stage. Evidently Tynan not only
already felt 'swamped' by proliferating tasks, but was also persuaded
that he effectively embodied something akin to an administrative
clearing house for the NT: work was 'funnelled' through his department. All these functions were broadly covered by the joint notions of
dramaturg and official representative, but whereas Brecht had engi-
neered a team of dramaturgs, each fulfilling a limited number of
specialist functions within a highly efficient system, Tynan had one
assistant and was expected to fulfil a brief in a theatre which could
understand neither his vision nor his need for organised support.
Increasingly he was forced to juggle an impossibly disparate and
demanding array of functions, a situation which became ever more
constraining and prevented him from executing tasks to the level of
sophistication he wanted.

Tynan as educator

It is difficult to penetrate Tynan's thinking on his rôle as educator of
the NT Company and its audiences since many of the allusions he
made to it in lectures and interviews are opaque and contradictory, and
even his understanding of the NT's function is less than clear.

Good repertory theatres fall into two main categories. One is the kind that is founded by a great director or playwright with a novel and often revolutionary approach to dramatic art. He creates a style for his own special purpose. Examples of this process would include Stanislavsky's Moscow Art Theatre, Bertolt Brecht's Berliner Ensemble and Joan Littlewood's Theatre Workshop. The other category consists of theatres with a broader, less personal *raison d'être*: whose function – more basic though not more valuable – is simply to present to the public the widest selection of good plays from all periods and places. In this group you can place the Schiller Theatre in West Berlin; the Royal Dramatic Theatre in Stockholm; and the National Theatre in the Waterloo Road.[58]

Tynan defines the NT against models of explicitly socialist theatre, and despite its manifestly political project of establishing a national repertoire he seems to depoliticise the second category. This may reflect the founding rhetoric of the NT propounded by its Board, but in practice Tynan increasingly conflated the categories, and though he cited the Schiller Theatre and the Royal Dramatic Theatre as immediate models, he was far more interested in the example of Brecht.

In the early years of his tenure he believed that state subsidy would foster the qualities he so admired in continental theatres:[59] conditions of greater experimentalism; a working ethos rooted in an ensemble of actors; and the opportunity to develop plays on the cutting edge. These were the qualities that excited him intellectually and in which he wanted significant participation. Tynan's belief that subsidy alone would generate a new spirit of iconoclasm and an ensemble of politically motivated actors and directors working towards Brechtian goals was, to say the least, romantic. When Tynan 'stumbled across' what he saw as the conservatism of the NT Company and its audiences, he confused his own interest in political avant-garde experimentalism with the purpose of the institution; nevertheless his discovery that his ideals were not shared within and without the Company left him undaunted. In fact it determined him on a path to become a 're-educator'.

We also fret over our immediate task, which is to assemble the best available actors and put them into a snow-balling repertoire of the best available plays, ancient and modern, comic and tragic, native and foreign. But we have also stumbled across an additional problem. It has to do with re-education; slowly and patiently, we have to set about re-educating actors, directors, playwrights and audiences alike. You would be surprised how hard it is, in a society where "theatre" means "theatre for private profit", to explain to people that *this* theatre actually belongs to them, and is not in any way stirred by the need or desire to show a profit ... We would rather have a first-rate work playing to less than capacity than a third-rate one filling the house. Instead of fearing criticism, we can learn from it without rancour, since we do not depend – as commercial theatre must – on rave reviews.[60]

Precisely what kind of internal 're-education' Tynan had in mind (the 'we' is ingenuous) is never elucidated, nor did he explain how it might be implemented, but his use of the word is significant given its denotation of forcible and ideologically directed alteration of political beliefs or social behaviour.[61] His description of the NT as a place free from the burden of commercial success is incompatible with the pressure to demonstrate that the theatre has popular appeal, and he clearly conceived of the NT Company as explicitly didactic, as the Berliner Ensemble was. Though Tynan had Dexter's and Gaskill's political sympathy, he certainly did not comprehend that his notion of re-education demanded economic, organisational and ideological infrastructure for the systematic implementation of such an ambitious and time-consuming retraining programme. Realistically, even if he had understood theoretically that such a programme was necessary, he could not, with his limited practical experience, have headed it; and in practice Tynan seemed to believe that he could bring about change through the force of his reputation and personality alone.

Tynan's most obvious educative rôle was planning the repertoire, a task which Olivier delegated to him from the start, and he led weekly formal discussions in his office with Olivier, Dexter and Gaskill. Many more informal discussions took place between individuals, and it was not long before the Drama Committee was dissolved because it functioned merely as a bureaucratic rubber-stamp before decisions were forwarded to the Board for discussion and approval. Though not a Board member himself, Tynan made recommendations in person, and throughout the first three years attended a monthly Board meeting. He could be outvoted by Olivier and the associate directors, and was so on a number of occasions – Olivier lists sixteen[62] – but these were exceptions, not the rule. Of the thirty-eight plays staged in the first three years, only three proceeded without Tynan's blessing, and the majority were his choices.

Despite the pressures of his myriad functions, Tynan's first three years demonstrate his attempts to make his mark as a critical and conceptual presence. Within the institutional structure Tynan had three principal channels of communication and action: contact with the Board; with Olivier in person; and with writers, actors and the associate and guest directors. He sought to create a repertoire that reflected Granville Barker's ideas of a broad spectrum of national and international drama, and programmed according to four categories: classic revivals, recent plays worthy of revival, new plays, and plays from abroad. Where possible he also tried to develop an agenda that reflected his own political ideals, and in this Brecht was again foremost in his mind:

> I have swung over to another viewpoint ... I became aware that
> art, ethics, politics, and economics were inseparable from each
> other; I realised that theatre was a branch of sociology as well as a
> means of self-expression. From men like Bertolt Brecht and
> Arthur Miller I learned that all drama was, in the widest sense
> of a wide word, political; and that no theatre could sanely
> flourish unless there was an umbilical connection between what
> was happening on the stage and what was happening in the
> world.[63]

Accordingly, one of Tynan's first priorities was the promotion of the Berliner Ensemble, who had not played in England since 1955.

Undaunted by the Cold War, Tynan negotiated the performances of four major Berliner Ensemble productions in 1965,[64] as well as conceiving and negotiating the translation of *Mother Courage and Her Children* for performance by the NT Company in the same year. Determined to provide a diet of contemporary continental responses to classical and new plays, he arranged for a visit from the French group Le Théâtre du Nouveau Monde, who performed Molière's *L'Ecole des femmes* and a new play called *Klondyke*, and brought over a version of *Hamlet* directed by Franco Zeffirelli. Tynan considered the inclusion of Shakespeare 'a necessity, though not in bulk',[65] as he did not want to overlap with the RSC. Shakespeare, however, was still Tynan's most represented playwright with nine company and visiting productions in the first three years, but his plans for Shakespeare offered an experimental or educative aspect that qualitatively distinguished the NT from the emergent tradition at Stratford: he persuaded Zeffirelli to direct *Much Ado About Nothing*, brought in the Bristol Old Vic Company for *Love's Labour's Lost* and *Henry V*, and instigated performances of *Antony and Cleopatra* and *Troilus and Cressida* by the National Youth Theatre. Besides Brecht, Tynan's selection of foreign playwrights featured Ibsen, Chekhov, Feydeau, Frisch, Miller, Ostrovsky, Sophocles and Strindberg, while British playwrights included Arden, Brighouse, Congreve, Coward, Farquhar, Marston, O'Casey, Osborne, Pinero, Shaffer, Shakespeare and Shaw.

One of Tynan's missions was to reach a wider audience by commissioning new plays with alternative subject matters or by finding ways of popularising classical drama. He admired Brecht's classical adaptations for their twentieth-century recontextualisations of political and social issues, and invited Robert Graves to revise the text of *Much Ado About Nothing* with the objective of sweeping away 'the dry cobwebs of text so that full understanding of the words isn't confined to academics'.[66] To spice the package even more he brought in Zeffirelli to direct, and the production was a success. Tynan used the ploy again, asking Keith Johnstone to adapt *Philoctetes* and Emlyn Williams *The Master Builder*, and commissioning John Osborne to write *A Bond Honoured*, based on Lope de

Vega's *La Fianza Satisfecha*. Tynan was quite clear about the significance of the new play:

> A year or so ago, I noticed that out of more than two dozen plays running in the West End, only three had been written before 1950. This is the kind of fantastic imbalance that the National Theatre exists to correct.[67]

His real passion manifested itself in the search for new plays which offered an experimental edge or a political challenge to the status quo. He could be wily in testing out an unusual proposal, and argued a case for a one-night-only showing of Adrienne Kennedy's *Scene Three, Act One*, based on John Lennon's books and directed by Victor Spinetti; but such experiments allowed Tynan to expose audiences to work that would not necessarily be expected from the NT. New plays also satisfied Tynan's desire for creative involvement, especially in helping the writer to shape text and the director to interpret it. His advisory rôle on Shaffer's *The Royal Hunt of the Sun* and *Black Comedy* was extensive; indeed, the latter play came about through Tynan's enthusiasm to develop an idea that Shaffer told him about one day, and he was welcomed by Dexter as an active critic and sounding-board during the conception, drafting and staging processes. Furthermore, his critical supervision of Arden's and Dexter's devised *Armstrong's Last Goodnight* was vital to the success of the play.

The first sign of trouble for Tynan came with his battle for the production of Franz Wedekind's *Spring Awakening* in 1964, which foreshadowed a pattern of rising tensions between himself and the Board, particularly Chandos. Tynan had anticipated difficulties with the Censor due to the play's explicit treatment of adolescent sexuality, but argued for its critical reputation on the Continent and called into account the praise it had received when staged for two nights at the Royal Court the previous year.[68] Lord Cobbold, the Censor, recommended cuts and was set to approve the play, but the Board, led by Chandos, made a unanimous decision to ban the play on grounds of taste and did so without consulting Olivier. Moreover, the Board voted to monitor repertoire suggestions and decisions much more closely, the beginning of attempts to stifle what Chandos viewed as Tynan's waywardness. Olivier managed to negotiate an undertaking to be consulted in the future, but it was an ominous sign of the Board's willingness to be dominated by their Chairman, of their distrust of Olivier's and Tynan's judgement, and their preparedness to make drastic artistic interventions. While Tynan asserted the function of the NT as an explicit debating chamber for social and political issues, the Board implicitly understood the interests of the people to reside in those of the government of the day. Understandably, their politics were informed by the dominant consensus, which like many of his generation Tynan found increasing cause to attack.

As educator of the public, one of the tasks Tynan allotted himself was the demystification of theatre-making processes. Borrowing from Brecht, he concentrated on developing programmes and publications that explained techniques of play-making and acting and provided contextual information about the productions. Audiences accustomed to receiving simple cast lists in West End theatres now had the chance to read about a play's performance history, a critique of the subject matter, or a writer or director's interpretation of a specific play or rôle. In this way Tynan could enable audiences to think critically about text and performance. Reviewers were impressed and immediately saw the value of providing information, especially in cases where play and playwright were not English. J.J. Finegan of the *Evening Herald* was filled with admiration for Tynan's programme for *Juno and the Paycock* (1966) and recommended it to his readers for its concise and illuminating content.[69] Before Tynan British programmes on the continental model were very rare, but most companies and theatres now follow his example with little understanding of their debt.

Through the publisher Rupert Hart-Davis Tynan also published two books, on the NT's productions of Farquhar's *The Recruiting Officer*[70] and on Shakespeare's *Othello*.[71] For both Tynan wrote a 'Rehearsal Logbook', short essays on aspects of the rehearsal process. For *The Recruiting Officer* he concentrated on Gaskill's working methods and selected moments of discovery for the actors; but for *Othello* he wrote an essay, 'Olivier: The Actor and the Moor', and charted Olivier's journey through the play. Both reveal Tynan's knowledge of Brecht's *Theaterarbeit* and *Modellbücher*, with their inclusion of original text, production photographs, reviews, historical notes and director's comments; but the book of *The Recruiting Officer* was not what Tynan claimed in his introduction.

> [W]hat this book contains is all you need (about almost all there is) to know about the National Theatre's highly successful production of Farquhar's *The Recruiting Officer* ...
> This is not meant to be a souvenir volume. Rather, it is a blue-print; a permanent record of a theatrical event in all its aspects; a detailed, illustrated account of a production that did for an English classic the kind of service a National Theatre exists to provide – that of cleaning away the accretions of dust and over-painting with which time has disfigured the text, and bringing out the colours and forms of the original in all their pristine vivacity. In other words, this book is a sort of guided tour; and if it proves helpful to theatre workers, students of drama or anyone who wants to know how a particular group of actors tackled the problems of a particular play, it will have served its purpose.[72]

Tynan's rehearsal logbook is short (five pages), sketchy and erratic, and shows all the signs of an author with too much else to do. The frequent omission of scenes indicates that it was simply not possible for Tynan to spend five weeks in the rehearsal room (and in fact a good deal less time was spent there). Only fourteen of the 144 pages contain critical pieces on context or process; the rest is play text interspersed with production photographs. It was certainly a start, the only British example of its kind, but far less ambitious than Tynan had intended; where Brecht had several dramaturgs working full-time to produce publications, Tynan was alone. Despite agreement with the Board that he would edit rehearsal logbooks to accompany as many productions as possible,[73] Tynan only produced two. As for the magazine that he proposed to edit regularly from July 1964,[74] not even the sample copy appeared. He simply did not have time for the painstaking compilation of books and was reluctantly forced to abandon the function.[75]

Tynan's concept of himself as an educator of the public was rooted in paradox: he was a representative of the political status quo in his institutional and cultural position, yet his main interest increasingly lay in challenging the status quo through new plays. Whilst he initially approached his obligation to represent a spectrum of world drama with energy and enthusiasm, it was a side of his work that he also described as one of the 'dull but basic jobs, which are essentially educational'.[76] The re-education of the public and the NT Company that Tynan craved seems to have appealed to and invigorated him far more strongly, but it became more and more difficult for him to pursue his political ideals.

The Tynan–Olivier partnership

Tynan's working relationship with Laurence Olivier (1907–89) was complex. Behind the scenes Olivier relied on Tynan's theatrical judgement and breadth of literary knowledge not just to plan the repertoire but to formulate ideas about directing concepts, visiting companies and casting. Tynan acted as mentor to Olivier, filling gaps in his knowledge of theatre history, and, predictably, immediately took Olivier to see the Berliner Ensemble. He acted as Olivier's researcher and consultant, and tried to stretch his views on his own acting career, successfully persuading him to play Othello, a part he had always shunned. Olivier listened intently to Tynan in the knowledge that he had a matchless 'theatrical brain'[77] working for him, but it was not an easy partnership. Tynan had worshipped Olivier's acting prowess for as long as he could remember, but next to his Literary Manager Olivier often felt intellectually inferior. Tynan phrased it diplomatically:

> We complemented each other because he has all the practical skills that an actor and director could have, and I presumably have the theoretical knowledge: where he was strong I was weak, and vice versa. He almost to a fault protests that he isn't an intellectual, and I almost to a fault protest that I'm not a participant.[78]

Tynan's function as 'ideas man'[79] extended to making critical assessments of the company's evolution and identifying areas of weakness.

Tynan's 'Reflections on Year One' noted: the difficulty of creating a permanent ensemble and suggested that guest performers became a permanent policy strategy; the need to find money for in-house publications; the idea of reduced seat prices for experimental productions; a list of the errors Tynan felt he had made in casting and in selecting directors; and a list of gaps in the company's acting strengths.[80] His points about guest performers and money for publications were accepted by Olivier and the Board. The remaining points were discussed but not acted on, but Tynan was raising important issues and activating debate.

Olivier knew his own limitations, particularly that he was not 'a safe judge' of dramatic literature, and understood how to deploy Tynan's skills to best advantage.[81] Olivier approached matters as an actor, privileging an acting rôle above text; Tynan provided the counterbalance, arguing for the pre-eminence of the play and writer. This suited Olivier. He was not particularly interested in new writers, which increasingly frustrated Tynan, who felt that Olivier had an artistic duty to show interest in contemporary drama and should support him as he supported Olivier. After three years, and just after Olivier had fobbed off an appointment with two new writers,[82] Tynan wrote a furious letter:

> Part of the reason for my presence in this organisation is to look after our writers – to persuade them that we are interested in new work, that we care about experiment; this is a hard pretence to make when one looks at our record. In three years we haven't had a single top-level (*your* level) discussion with a single new author. We have dealt only with established names. Unless we treat writers with genuine seriousness and respect, they are simply going to lose interest in us. We may well have to face the unpalatable fact that modern theatre can very well do without us, but it can't do without them.[83]

Olivier did not share Tynan's desire for contentious political plays and evasiveness on the issue was his main tactic of defence. He recognised Tynan's knack for talent-spotting, but later confessed to 'feelings of acute embarrassment when faced with anything which remotely smacks of propaganda'.[84] He could not overcome his prejudice against documentary plays or his distaste for any play that engaged with contemporary politics. This was an extraordinary (and revealing) admission from the star and director of *Henry V*, a film about a successful invasion of France premièred on D-Day, and though Tynan fought effectively against it in the early years, there is no question that Olivier's unwavering conservatism reduced his room for manoeuvre. Tynan compromised, realising that he could only try to force Olivier's hand when he thought he had a play or project of exceptional merit, but after the furore over Rolf Hochhuth's play *Soldiers* in 1967, Olivier quietly blocked any new play that was overtly anti-establishment. Tynan was forced to water down his political agenda. At the end of his tenure he wrote that latterly 'My policy of having no policy was partly tailored to the limitations (and strengths) of Larry's temperament – pragmatic, empirical, wary of grand designs and distant goals.'[85]

Tynan and Olivier's partnership was one of mutual dependence, and while Olivier was Tynan's champion he was also his silencer, for without Olivier's support Tynan had no power base. As far as Olivier was concerned, Tynan was vital to the success both of the NT and of his own directorship, but Olivier hid from the Board the extent of his dependence on Tynan as architect of the repertoire and company consultant, and Tynan's significant contribution to the artistic running of the theatre remained 'invisible'. Olivier, preoccupied with his acting or directing, did not have the same agenda as Tynan, nor did he ever bring his weight to bear on the matter of Tynan's workload. In some ways it was useful for Olivier to hold Tynan in check, preventing him from expending his energies in artistic areas that Olivier thought unprofitable. Though Tynan described his relationship with Olivier in humorous terms, calling himself 'a navigator not a pilot'[86] and a 'back-seat driver at the National Theatre',[87] his very metaphors suggest that he was all too conscious of the power he was accorded yet prevented from officially claiming, and as far as the Board was concerned Tynan had cosmetic uses but was essentially an expendable commodity.

Tynan and the politics of the rehearsal room

Tynan's endeavours to forge himself a rôle as an articulator of process and to become a production consultant, like his educational ambitions, enjoyed initial success but ran into increasing problems. His assumption that both critic and director would share a common aim, as he knew was the case at the Berliner Ensemble, proved naïve, for whereas Brecht had instituted a collaborative training programme for the entire artistic company, insisting that directors trained their faculties as critics and that critics underwent training in directing, Tynan expected to enter the artistic process with automatic acceptance as a necessary part of it. Brecht's practice had evolved according to the principles of a specific theory of drama developed over three decades. For him, the critical eye functioned as a means of supervising the dialectical relationship between theory, text and performance. Brecht had realised his artistic objectives within the vast machinery of the highly efficient administration that he controlled. Though Tynan had visited the Berliner Ensemble he was ignorant of its organisational structures, and had not analysed the details of its company training policy. A patchily informed convert, he failed to appreciate the very particular conditions that Brecht had created for himself, and wrongly presumed on the strength of his journalistic reputation for his evangelising mission. He also underestimated the difficulties of creating a committed ensemble identity: British actors had little experience of ensemble work, and well-known actors in particular tended to view a binding three- or four-year contract as unwarrantably restrictive.

Resident directors Dexter and Gaskill were strong advocates of Brecht, fresh from the political school of the Royal Court. Brecht's influence on them had been both political and aesthetic, but the presence of a critic in the rehearsal room was a new idea. Dexter was eager to collaborate; Gaskill 'suspicious' from the start, seeing no place for Tynan in the rehearsal process.[88] Gaskill also disapproved of Tynan's significant rôle in casting, which he thought swayed by desire for 'big stars': Tynan, as he saw it, was straying into the director's territory.[89]

In the first three years Tynan's collaborations with Dexter were happy. His participation in the inception, writing and development of Peter Shaffer's *Black Comedy* (1965) was the model of working practice for which he had been striving. Shaffer had outlined an idea for a play centred on the light–dark convention of theatre, which Tynan immediately championed to Olivier and won his support to develop. During the writing and rehearsal process Tynan worked closely with Shaffer, advising on structure, editing drafts and helping Dexter to find the dramaturgical shape of the play. For Tynan the production was a high point, and in the programme he wrote that it was 'A home-grown addition to the play catalogues, and the kind of risk that only a permanent company could have taken'.[90] The latter was an exaggeration, but Tynan was proud of his achievements.

After the first three years Tynan's workload prevented him from spending much time in the rehearsal room. Furthermore, the political furore over Rolf Hochhuth's *Soldiers* in 1967 cast a shadow over Tynan's judgement of new plays and Olivier blocked all subsequent attempts to pursue anything that posed the slightest risk. Tynan's relationship with Dexter had proved unique, for, perhaps with the exception of Jonathan Miller, he was not accepted as a legitimate critical presence by Gaskill or incoming guest directors. Miller prized Tynan's 'curiously practical' sense of what made a play work when the production was in difficulty,[91] though his formulation implies that he felt Tynan did not belong in the rehearsal room. Even Dexter's position was riven with contradiction, and Tynan, disillusioned, withdrew from extensive collaboration. His critical function became confined to attendance at run-throughs and the delivery of formal rehearsal notes to the director.[92] Dexter tried to lure Tynan back into a working partnership during his preparation for Molière's *The Misanthrope* in 1972, but was adamant about certain conditions of the partnership:

> I would prefer your attendance at rehearsals to be on a *regular* basis,
> I would like the company to feel your presence not as a critic but as
> an active participant. I know you find the day to day details of
> rehearsals tedious, but your sudden arrival at a late stage
> produces nothing but panic, dissention [*sic*] and hostility which
> the director must then work hard to counteract if your usually
> valid suggestions are to be put into operation ... So please, try and

make a weekly visit and in the first week *MORE* ... I remember 'Black Comedy', 'Recruiting Officer', 'Othello' and other occasions when you were part of the creation not just a gadfly, stinging in the latter hot days of work. Sorry to go on at this length, but the play and I need your help, but it must be as an involved worker.[93]

This is a bleak summation of Tynan's position as critic, and signals a failure on his part to experiment with strategies that would have lessened the need for such disruptive last-minute interventions. Tynan, Dexter argued, was analogous to a harbinger of doom, a person 'who arrives only in crisis wearing a Chamberlain crisis face', but (as with Lessing) it was the actors who objected to the criticism, even if it was 'usually valid'.[94] No doubt Tynan lacked diplomacy, and could have saved his comments for the director alone, but Dexter clearly sanctioned Tynan's addresses to the cast. If this was Tynan's notion of 're-education', it was viewed as wholly destructive; but Dexter's insistence that Tynan's criticism is legitimated only by his presence in rehearsal on a regular basis is also questionable. Tynan's first concern was not legitimation from actors, but from the audience, of which he considered himself a representative member. Dexter paradoxically both did and did not want Tynan's critique: he did not want his 'presence as a critic', which he constructed as inherently negative and 'other' to the play-making process, but would accept 'suggestions' provided that they came from an 'active participant' or an 'involved worker'. Like the actors, Dexter was ultimately uneasy with critical confrontation, and Tynan's style of intervention only compounded that uneasiness. Dexter wrote to assuage Tynan's fears that he was viewed as 'an intruder'[95] in the rehearsal process, but Tynan had long given up on the possibility of creating an institutional culture that did not regard practice and criticism as mutually exclusive.

Guest director George Devine's clash with Tynan in March and April 1964 over Beckett's *Play* sharply illustrated Tynan's constant balancing act between the interests of the NT management, the directors and the audience. Tynan wrote a series of formal letters to Devine, explaining his concern at the turn rehearsals had taken since Beckett's arrival and intervention. He expressed disquiet over the monotonous delivery of lines, inaudibility and lack of clear exposition. In Tynan's view audience reception was being entirely overlooked and the point of theatre obscured; but Tynan was also acting in his capacity as what he termed the organisation's 'early warning system'[96] and foreseeing the ramifications of failure for only the second experimental piece at the NT:

> If it fails to get over with maximum impact, it may jeopardise our future plans for experiment and put a weapon into the hands of those people (already quite numerous) who think the National Theatre, like the Proms, should stick to the popular classics and not cater for minority tastes. It may even provoke the more conservative members of the N. T. Board to start interfering in the choice of plays – which would be disastrous![97]

Devine was incensed, and, failing to understand Tynan's agenda as resident critic for the NT and his obligations to the Board, leapt to the conclusion that Tynan's concerns about failure were motivated by cowardly fears for his self-image.[98] I cite Tynan's response in full because it highlights Devine's demonising territorial construction of him and makes explicit the suspicion with which he was generally regarded.

> Dear George:
>
> You call me 'impertinent': there speaks the advocate of a director's theatre. (And 'presumptuous' – another word you apply to me – confirms this.)
>
> You profess yourself 'shocked' by the idea that one's obligation to an author need not extend beyond a general loyalty to his script: there speaks the advocate of a *writer's* theatre. Like you I would hate the NT to become a museum: but the best way to build theatrical museums is to regard every syllable of every stage direction as holy writ.
>
> I believe in neither a director's nor a writer's theatre, but a theatre of intelligent *audiences*. I count myself a member of an intelligent audience, and I wrote to you as such. That you should disagree with me I can understand, but that you should resent my expressing my opinions is something that frankly amazes me. I thought we had outgrown the idea of theatre as a mystic rite

born of secret communion between author, director, actors and an empty auditorium. The 'dramatic purpose' you mention involves, for me, communication and contact with a live audience: and a live audience is something of which Beckett, by his own honest admission, has little personal knowledge. So far from wanting to 'turn the play into literature', I was proposing that we should liberate it from the author's (to me) rather confined view of its dramatic responsibilities.

And of course I want the play to 'come off' – for the whole of the minority to whom it is addressed. If you recall, my main worry was that it would reach only part of that minority. Perhaps I was wrong, but I don't regret having worried.[99]

Devine's concerns are purely artistic and focused inward; Tynan's position requires him to be Janus-faced, looking both inside the institution and beyond it, focused on the artistic merits of productions but in the context of the NT's obligations to public accessibility and accountability. For Devine, Tynan is the deadly enemy of art, not its critical guardian, and he constructs Tynan's legitimate opinions as a hostile assault on the integrity of his work as a director. Tynan was attempting to instil in Devine's thinking a critical consciousness of the audience, and given Devine's justification of exclusively privileging the author, was right to do so; but Devine's retreat into accusation reveals his inability to grant anyone the right to challenge his directorial authority. Olivier, who could have mediated for Tynan, took Devine's side instead and admonished his Literary Manager for a lack of diplomacy, instructing Tynan to route future criticism via him, Olivier's way of stymieing the matter once and for all.[100] Tynan seemed to be damned if he said anything and damned if he did not, and the whole episode underlines Tynan's continual battle to juggle creative, institutional and public interests.

The crisis: Hochhuth's *Soldiers*

The realisation that his hopes for the transformation of practice were falling on stony ground increasingly led Tynan to focus ideas for re-education on the public, and specifically on repertoire. Meanwhile, his desire for a more radical agenda and greater artistic control began to manifest themselves in his search for fulfilment outside the confines of the NT, and from June 1966 he was holding discussions and making plans for an erotic revue, *Oh! Calcutta!*, which eventually opened in 1969. Tynan's passion for the project, essentially a cabaret featuring much nudity, only served to refuel the notoriety he had generated the previous year by saying 'fuck' on BBC radio.[101] Both episodes strengthened Chandos's conviction that Tynan was a loose cannon, a dangerous liability to the integrity of the NT, and the crisis that blew up around Tynan's campaign to stage *Soldiers* can be seen as the climactic conjunction of territorial conflicts between himself and the Board that had been gaining momentum from the outset. The explosion itself was inevitable, *Soldiers* simply providing the touch-paper.

Hochhuth, as much *agent provocateur* as writer, had caused violent controversy with his first documentary play *The Representative*, performed in Berlin in 1963. His second play, *Soldiers*, also a documentary drama, centred on Winston Churchill and explored the moral dilemma of saturation bombing during World War Two. Hochhuth suggested that Churchill had ordered the assassination of the Polish leader-in-exile, General Sikorski, to protect his alliance with Stalin, and had shrugged off the mass-murder of Polish officers. The author claimed that secret testimonies deposited in a Swiss bank verified his story, but argued that witnesses had only given their statements on the proviso that documents would be kept secure for fifty years. Tynan saw the play's politically inflammatory potential and entered negotiations with Hochhuth at once.

Tynan's decision to promote *Soldiers* was a means of highlighting his vision of the NT as a debating house, and a deliberate attempt to force a political showdown with the Board. Anticipating hostility, Tynan began to prepare a defence of Hochhuth's hypothesis by consulting prominent politicians and historians. In January 1967, a few days before the Board's first major discussion of the play, he wrote to Olivier explaining that he believed *Soldiers* could rescue the NT from its political and artistic complacency:

> I'm worried. Nothing really specific: just a general feeling that we're losing our lead, that we are no longer making the running,

that what the NT does has become a matter of public acceptance rather than public excitement. At a time when – I Cassandra-like keep saying – audiences even for *good* theatre are dwindling all over Europe, we are doing nothing to remind them that the theatre is an independent force at the heart of the country's life – a sleeping tiger that can and should be roused whenever the national (or international) conscience needs nudging.

We have no MARAT-SADE; we have no Us. Meanwhile, Barrault has gained the respect of Gaullist France by staging LES PARAVENTS, in which the French army is reviled for its Algerian atrocities; the Royal Dramatic Theatre in Stockholm is playing to full houses with O WHAT A LOVELY PEACE!, a show that bitterly arraigns its country's politicians for their cowardly neutrality in World War II; and a millennium or so ago a Greek playwright derided his own country's heroes for their wanton devastation of Troy.

Hochhuth may not be Euripides and SOLDIERS may not be THE TROJAN WOMEN, but it is in the same tradition and in this country that tradition is in our hands. Subsidy gives us the chance – denied to movies and TV – of taking a line of our own, with no commercial pressures and without the neutralising necessity of being 'impartial'. In a way, I think Hochhuth is the test of our maturity – the test of our willingness to take a central position in the limelight of public affairs. If the play goes on under our banner, we shall be a genuinely national theatre, and, even as the stink-bombs fly, I shall be very proud of us.[102]

Once more Tynan's paradoxical construction of the NT as an institution that should be striving for 'independence' lay behind his words. The artistic credentials of the play were already secondary to interest in the political cause of presenting *Soldiers* at the NT to symbolise democracy and freedom of speech:

> I don't know whether this is a great *play*: but I think it's one of the most extraordinary things that has happened to the British theatre in my lifetime. For once, the theatre will occupy its true place – at the very heart of public life.[103]

The Board met and expressed grave doubts over *Soldiers*; Tynan wrote a memorandum airily predicting that Chandos would resign if the play went ahead, and, astonishingly, expressing confidence in his expendability as Chairman. He aligned any decision by the Board to suppress the play as akin to the policies of 'totalitarian' regimes,[104] and advocated that the NT should behave like a broadsheet newspaper presented with an article by a respectable writer that conflicted with editorial policy: 'print the piece, with a note to the effect that the opinions it expresses are not necessarily those of the editor'.[105] The violent tenor of Tynan's rhetoric, with its radical polemic and revolutionary overtones, leeched his argument of rational substance while escalating the stakes; his deliberate sensationalising of the affair was not the language of the committee, nor a civic language of loyal opposition which encouraged a reasoned discussion of the issues, but cant. Tynan the supposed radical was himself manifesting distinct signs of authoritarianism.

Tynan seemed unable to appreciate that Chandos's view that the NT should purvey the dominant political ideology of the day was reasonable, nor could he see that the real issues extended far beyond Chandos and the Board to a cultural resistance to revisiting and rewriting the recent past, itself to do with Britain's post-imperial status and the ideological memorialisation of World War Two. If Chandos wanted to preserve historical readings of Britain's moral supremacy and Churchill's heroic leadership, it was because, like the government and the majority of the populace, he still believed in both. Furthermore, if most members of the Board had served in the war, Chandos had served in Churchill's war cabinet and felt personally compromised by the defamation of Churchill's character barely a year after his funeral. Tynan anticipated but grossly underestimated Chandos's opposition, and was politically inept in assuming that he could so blatantly hold the Board to ransom.

From Chandos's point of view the NT's artistic decisions could not be separated from allegiance to the people constituting the nation, whom the NT was constitutionally established to serve, and whose suffering and victory in the Second World War *Soldiers* explicitly devalued and implicitly insulted. As one who had never seen active service, and whose personal flamboyance even in the austerity years might seem to jeer at the sacrifices made by others for the safety of all, Tynan could make no claim on Chandos's respect, and the shrill and heady rhetoric Tynan adopted would have seemed at best wilful posturing and at worst a base ingratitude akin to treason. It was not for the NT to encourage political dissent, Chandos argued; artistic decisions had to be subject to political scrutiny (which as Chair he regarded as his responsibility) for the NT to be legitimately representative of the nation. At the decisive Board meeting in April 1967 his views were recorded.

> Lord Chandos pointed out that the Chairman and members of the National Theatre Board were appointed by the Government. The National Theatre was admittedly and rightly autonomous, but it could not escape responsibility for matters rather wider that those of immediate artistic concern. His own position was one of great delicacy, but that was entirely irrelevant. Once a theatre staged a play which was purported to be a 'documentary', the 'theatre of fact', it then became concerned with more than literary and artistic matters – it became concerned with the truth.[106]

In other words, Chandos believed that artistic decisions in the NT were not the Director's territory. He effectively equated Olivier's status as Director with that of political puppet. Olivier, drawn into the battle to defend his territory more than the play, and briefed by Tynan, argued that artistic powers should be separate from the Board's broad management rôle.[107] The Board withdrew in camera excluding Tynan, and persuaded by Chandos's arguments voted against the production of Soldiers. A statement was issued to the following effect:

> Sir Winston Churchill and Lord Cherwell were grossly maligned and they [the Board] considered that the play was unsuitable for production at the National Theatre. The Director expressed himself at being unhappy with this decision.[108]

Olivier insisted on the inclusion of his dissent, but the Board won. Criticism came from all quarters of the press and intellectual élite.

Olivier had been exposed as powerless, and Chandos believed he had prevented the Director from exerting 'a form of dictatorship in the arts'.[109] Now Chandos was playing the tyrant.

Tynan kept up a furious campaign via *The Times*, arguing that repertoire and casting decisions should be the remit of the artistic directorate alone. He challenged the function of the Board, pointing out that equivalent institutions abroad did not have 'paternalistic boards' sitting in judgement of them.[110] Chandos replied that Tynan's continued employment at the NT and his pursuit of a campaign against its Chairman and the Board were incompatible, and Tynan's response sealed Chandos's determination to evict him as soon as possible:

> It would indeed be odd if the National Theatre were an industrial concern in which the chairman and the board were majority share-holders. Happily, it is nothing of the sort. My first loyalty is to the National Theatre, not to its board. *Pace* the chairman, the two are not necessarily identical.[111]

At this juncture Tynan did find the language of loyal opposition, and argues that he and the Board both have a loyalty to the idea of the NT itself. By using the company-board metaphor and rejecting it, Tynan is implicitly denying Chandos's construction of him as the 'enemy', as if they were rival shareholders, and is rebuking Chandos for failing to *allow* a loyal opposition. He also points to the curious homogeneity of the Board and the deafening silence of other Board members on the subject. In many respects, Tynan had scored a direct hit in claiming that Chandos and the Board were one and the same, but his clever language came too late, for he had caused an irrevocable schism between himself and the Board. Matters worsened when to Chandos's fury Tynan demonstrated that he would not be cowed, and with Olivier's support *Soldiers* opened at London's New Theatre on 12 December 1968. There were bomb threats and litigation against Hochhuth, but the play passed off smoothly; it was not hailed a masterpiece, but its performance was claimed as a victory against political interference. Tynan may be said to have won the battle, but it was a Pyrrhic victory.

In the wake of *Soldiers* Tynan's position at the NT became the subject of a bitter wrangle between Olivier and Chandos. Chandos campaigned relentlessly for Tynan's dismissal but Olivier adamantly refused to let him go.[112] When Tynan asked for leave of absence in 1968, Chandos pounced and said that leave would be granted only if Tynan's post were abolished. Again Olivier came to his defence, arguing that Tynan was responsible for much of the NT's success and going so far as to confess that the Board was unaware of the magnitude of Tynan's rôle.[113] Tynan's future value to the NT was 'considerable',[114] argued Olivier, who knew that he himself would be inestimably disadvantaged without Tynan's advice and support. Under persistent fire from Chandos, and desperate not to lose Tynan, Olivier struck a compromise and agreed that Tynan's title would be changed to Literary Consultant, and a second Literary Consultant, Derek Granger, appointed alongside him. This was both humiliation and punishment for Tynan: though his functions remained the same (Granger's background was television and he had everything to learn), the formal demotion was a symbolic reminder of the determination to erase his power. Most significantly of all, Tynan was excluded from attendance at Board meetings: henceforth Olivier would channel artistic suggestions to the Board, and Tynan was rendered an institutional exile.

Betwixt and between: 1968–1973

Tynan's only recourse for challenging his exclusion from participating in Board meetings was Olivier, and their mutual dependence was increasingly fraught. Olivier was getting old and frail, and was determined to avoid another *Soldiers* episode; his innate conservatism frustrated any attempt on Tynan's part to introduce politically charged new plays to the repertoire. Moreover, Olivier's tendency to think only of actors and rôles was diverting discussion from the repertoire. Tynan wrote to express his concern that the organisation had lost focus and was becoming too introverted.

> I suspect that we may be falling into a trap. We are tending to confuse ends and means in planning the repertoire. Let me explain what I mean.

> Of course it's vital to find enticing parts for valuable
> company members. But we are getting into the habit of placing
> this aim above that of finding the plays we ought to be doing.
> We ask ourselves: 'What can we find for X next year? – otherwise
> he'll leave us.' The implication here is that the purpose of
> keeping the company together is merely to keep the company
> together. But of course it isn't. The purpose of keeping the
> company together is to do first-rate plays, the best plays of all
> periods, the celebrated spectrum, in fact. Keeping individual
> actors happy is the means, in which we frequently lose sight of
> the end.[115]

Meanwhile, Tynan was as run ragged by playreading, developing plays,
public speaking, attending run-throughs and visiting theatres abroad as
ever. These functions had overtaken all others. The extent to which his
work was overlooked by the Board and other members of the organisation
is indicative of how successfully he was muffled. Examining a cast list in
1970, Tynan discovered that while it provided information about a range of
backstage and administrative staff, his own name did not appear. There
was no information, he pointed out to Olivier, about the person responsible for the selection of plays, nor was it clear to whom a member of the
audience might send a play to be read: 'Would it be too much to ask,
however lowly its position may be, that the literary department should get
some acknowledgement of its existence as part of the National Theatre
Staff.'[116] Tynan's isolation grew and Olivier was now the only member of
the Board with whom he spent considerable time. The silence between the
literary department and the Board intensified to such a degree that Tynan
perceived himself as a 'virtual stranger' at the NT.[117] When Chandos was
replaced as Chairman by Max Rayne in mid-1971, Olivier had the opportunity to renegotiate Tynan's position, but did not. Rayne had been given
no information either by Chandos, Olivier or by the other members of the
Board about Tynan's rôle; eventually he simply approached Tynan with
the question: 'What do you do?'[118] Tynan explained:

> I've been in on the planning of all the sixty-odd productions the
> NT has done. In addition to regular chores such as reading plays,

writing and editing programmes, writing and editing books on the company's productions, lecturing on the NT, talking about the NT on radio and TV here and abroad, commissioning and working on new plays and translations – I've acted as house-critic, attending rehearsals and working on them with directors.[119]

Given Tynan's contribution to the NT the level of his invisibility was remarkable; though there had been an official attempt at his erasure, there was also plain ignorance about his work that no doubt stemmed from the Board's collective ignorance of artistic practice. They were simply unaware of Tynan's hidden significance in the artistic running of the theatre.

In 1972 Olivier's plans to be away for several weeks brought on an identity crisis for Tynan. It had reached the point where he felt that it was only Olivier's presence that defined him at all, and only Olivier who had any real sense of all that he did.

But you [Olivier] are now going away for much longer than two weeks and I am thus left in the dark as to precisely what my function is to be during your absence. I knew what I was as Literary Manager; I know what Derek is as Literary Consultant. At present I am something betwixt and between which enables my enemies to attack me for holding a sinecure when the NT is doing well and to blame the whole of our artistic policy on me when the NT is doing badly. Would it really be so hard to get the position clarified one way or the other?[120]

Olivier claimed that Tynan was fortunate to be in post at all and that there was nothing he could (or, more likely, was prepared to) do. Tynan repeatedly demanded he be permitted to attend board meetings. He once more appealed for a 'slave girl' to assist Rozina in the office;[121] he asked for a salary review and noted that he was the only member of staff never to have had a raise. Still over-whelmed with work, Tynan's health gradually broke, and he experienced the first symptoms of the lung disease that would eventually kill him in 1980.

When Peter Hall accepted appointment, in 1972, as the next Director, he did so on the express condition that he would have sole artistic power. Tynan recognised immediately that Hall was 'far more the Man with the Plan'.[122] Very well read and with a totally different working style to Olivier, Hall argued that he did not require a Literary Consultant and planned to use his associates to 'check and criticise' him.[123] Hall was adamant as a condition of his acceptance of the job that Tynan should go,[124] and it is no accident that when Hall selected Tynan's successor he went for an unexpected choice, decidedly not someone in the public eye who could wield authority. John Russell Brown, an academic, was made an associate director and given responsibility for scripts, and he spent very little time at the NT.[125] He was certainly uncontroversial, but could not match Tynan's brilliance at discovering new plays or suggesting startling ideas for the repertoire. Brown left after a short time, and others followed who did impressive work, but it has become unspoken policy to choose figures with a low public profile.

Tynan's legacy

There can be no question about the significance of Tynan's artistic and administrative functions at the NT, nor of the impact of his rôle in theatres and companies throughout Britain. Even the most recent theatre histories, however, fail to understand his extraordinary impact as Britain's first Literary Manager. There is simply a gap. Tynan certainly worked in Olivier's shadow, but given the extensive literature about Olivier it is curious that their working relationship has not been more rigorously analysed. Much of Tynan's work was necessarily out of the public eye, but the veiling of his functions by the alteration of his title to 'consultant' and the policy of enforced isolation pursued by the Board undermined Tynan's official status and drastically decreased his visibility both inside and outside the organisation. In fact, Tynan's functions, especially those connected with the repertoire, are commonly assumed to have been undertaken by Olivier; thus George Rowell can write that

> The first ten tears of the National Theatre Company unquestionably
> bear the imprint of Laurence Olivier ... it is his reputation that
> ensured the publicity, crowded houses and controversy that the
> Company engendered.[126]

Olivier's reputation certainly provided glamour and legitimacy, but it
was Tynan who masterminded the programme and generated the
controversies. The lionisation of Olivier by critics and biographers
has turned him into a mythic figure and marked his tenure at the NT
as that of a 'one-man band'.[127] For Kathleen Tynan, it is Olivier
himself who must take the blame for his Literary Manager's lack of
public recognition, and she cast Olivier as the demon who 'horribly,
brilliantly thwarted and mutilated' Tynan's talents,[128] but her narrative ultimately serves only to mythologise Tynan as tragic victim.
Orson Welles, on the other hand, was puzzled by Olivier's autobiography, in which he saw the reduction of Tynan to a 'non-person, an
unperson'.[129]

Many of Tynan's functions were invisible by their nature, but
it should not be forgotten that many people had vested reasons to
preserve that invisibility. Tynan has received little testament to his
influence on writers and his part in helping to develop their work.
A letter from Tom Stoppard, written after the opening night of
Jumpers in 1972, gives some clue of how significant Tynan's intervention could be:

> I think I am extremely clever to have written it, but it would not
> have got there I think without your intervention. Thank you for
> taking up the running when it mattered. You'll never get the
> credit, of course, I'm glad to say.[130]

Stoppard's joke points to a fundamental problem with the recognition
of Tynan's rôle: the damage it could inflict on the writer's or director's
ego or reputation. Stoppard construes the necessity of Tynan's intervention as his failure as a writer. Likewise, Olivier kept his counsel
about the extent of Tynan's contribution because he knew it would
reduce his own stature: but the reasons for Tynan's invisibility extend
far beyond Olivier's or anyone else's self-image.

In fact, Olivier bestowed a great deal of power on Tynan, but that power lay precisely in the unofficial, undemarcated politics of their working relationship. It was Tynan's expectation of special treatment that was unrealistic. Despite the fact that there was no British precedent for his rôle as resident critic, Tynan expected the Board and Olivier to accept and support that rôle. Furthermore, in order to implement his Brechtian schema of re-educating theatre company and audience alike, Tynan needed a culture receptive to the idea that theatre could change society and a company mentality that saw the value of theorising practice. British culture provided him only with entrenched resistance to both, and as the *Soldiers* episode proved, Tynan was seduced by the idea of using the NT more as a weapon than as a tool. He should not have been surprised at territorially defensive constructions of him as 'other' by directors and actors, and to some extent by Olivier: if he felt he was 'intruding' in rehearsals, it was a mark of how unprepared he was for a reaction he should have predicted. If he was surprised by the degree to which actors and directors could view him as a threatening force, he forgot the power that he brought with him as a critical writer. At any rate, Tynan could not supply, like Brecht and Lessing, exemplary models of his own practice. He had no educative machine to support him and did not wield the power or have the institutional position to acquire one.

There was also an inherent contradiction in Tynan's position at the NT, just as there had been with Lessing's post in Germany two centuries earlier. If Tynan was employed at the NT to distinguish it from other theatres both in Britain and elsewhere, and to set new standards of dramatic excellence nationally and internationally, he was necessarily employed to think beyond the institution itself. In other words, Tynan was paid to be an institutional irritant, an outsider working on the inside; but from the beginning he pushed too much against the grain, a sign of how good he was and could have been at one aspect of a multiple job. Tynan's mistake was in conflating the degree of control British directors conventionally wielded as individuals over individual productions with the kind of control Brecht wielded in East Germany via a reputation, domination of a unique and directly funded company, and a highly trained team of dramaturgs with distinct specialisations. The dangerous and destructive figure whom the associate and guest directors feared, and whom Chandos felt it so necessary to defeat, is a chimæra generated by Tynan's misunderstandings of his own dramaturgy as much as by the contradictions inherent in his personality, his rôle and the polemics of the times. But for all that he does not and cannot at this distance deserve the silent obloquy to which he is still so unthinkingly condemned.

Notes

1. Simon Callow, ed., *The National: The Theatre and its Work 1963–1997* (London: Nick Hern Books/Royal National Theatre, 1997), p. 22. Throughout Tynan is presented as an intellectual dilettante 'who functioned neither as a manager nor as consultant'. This statement could not be further from the truth.
2. I am grateful to archivist Sally Brown for allowing me access to them shortly after their arrival in 1997.
3. See Effingham Wilson's 'Proposition for a National Theatre' reprinted in Geoffrey Whitworth, *The Making of a National Theatre* (London: Faber and Faber, 1951), pp. 28–9.
4. See Hansard, House of Commons Official Report, series 5, vol. 460 (1948–9), 21.1.1949, pp. 437–504; henceforth H. C. DEB. 5s.
5. For an excellent account of this period see Ralph Milibrand, *Parliamentary Socialism* (London: Merlin Press, 1979), pp. 272–349.
6. See Peter Clarke, *Hope and Glory: Britain 1900–1990* (Harmondsworth: Penguin, 1997), p. 216.
7. William Archer and H. G. Barker, *Scheme and Estimates for a National Theatre* (London: Duckworth and Co., 1907).
8. These descriptions are taken from the Memorandum and Articles of Association of the National Theatre Board, pp. 7–8; reference E1 TUB 1A in the National Theatre Archive, London (henceforth NTA); the board was officially incorporated on 8.2.1963.
9. Chandos served in the war cabinet and the Ministry of Production. Kenneth Clark worked for the Ministry of Information first as

director of the film division and then as controller of home publicity; as director of the National Gallery he superintended the
evacuation of the collection from London. Keswick worked as a
political adviser to Duff Cooper and served in the war cabinet
offices. Logan worked at the Ministry of Supply. Beaumont continued his theatrical enterprises in London. Moore worked as an
official war artist. Wilmot was seconded to the Ministry of
Economic Warfare. Salberg served in the Royal Corps of Signals
and latterly ENSA. Ashley Clarke remained in the Foreign
Office, but there is no detailed published information of his war
postings, nor can I find any information about Corbet's activities
at this time.

10. Derek Salberg, *My Love Affair with a Theatre* (Luton: Cortney
    Publications, 1978).
11. Chandos in H. C. DEB. 5s., pp. 443 and 448.
12. Draft speech for the House of Commons for the National Theatre
    Bill of 1949, Chan. II 41/7 VIII, 7, from the Chandos papers in the
    Churchill Archives, Cambridge (henceforth CA). The pollution of
    the English language was a favourite subject with Chandos, who
    frequently raised it at official events. A typical occasion was the
    laying of the foundation stone for the National Theatre, on 13 July
    1951, when he declared that 'The National Theatre will be a
    means of preserving the limpid waters of the English language
    from defilement in our industrial age'; Chan. II 4/17 X, 5.
13. *Commons Debates*, vol. 460, pp. 449–50.
14. Memorandum and Articles of Association of the National Theatre
    Board, p. 1, article 3.
15. NTA, B1–B5, minutes of the fourth preliminary meeting of the
    National Theatre Board, 4.12.1962, article 29/62.
16. His sartorial eccentricities had begun as an undergraduate at
    Oxford, where his purple doeskin suit and gold satin shirt became
    the stuff of legend.
17. Kenneth Tynan, *He That Plays The King* (London: Longmans,
    Green and Co., 1950), p. 22.
18. See Dominic Shellard, *Kenneth Tynan: A Life* (New Haven and
    London: Yale University Press, 2003), pp. 228–50.

19. From the unbound Tynan manuscripts (henceforth UTM) in the British Library (henceforth BL), file 41, page 19 of 32-page transcript. Orson Welles interviewed by Kathleen Tynan, 12.2.1983.

20. Kathleen Tynan, *The Life of Kenneth Tynan* (London: Methuen, 1988), p. 216.

21. BL, UTM, file 1.

22. *Ibid.*

23. Laurence Olivier, *Confessions of an Actor* (London: Orion Books, 1994), p. 259. Olivier's precise response to Tynan's letter was: 'how shall we slaughter the little bastard?'

24. Tynan had always brutally criticised Olivier's former wife, Vivien Leigh, for her inadequacies as an actress. In addition, Olivier had recently been subject to the lash of Tynan's pen for his directorship of the Chichester Festival Theatre.

25. Olivier, *Confessions of an Actor*, p. 259.

26. See the account of Tynan's appointment in Joan Littlewood, *Joan's Book* (London: Minerva, 1995), p. 295: 'I doubt whether Laurence Olivier had any idea what a dramaturg was.'

27. BL, UTM, file 1. Olivier's letter to Tynan dated 21.8.1962. Olivier's handwritten postscript reads: '*God – any*thing to get you off that *Observer*!'

28. NTA, B1–B5, minutes of the first meeting of the Council of Management of the National Theatre Board, 11.2.1963, article 17.

29. Tynan acknowledged this debt in a letter to John Mortimer, 28.5.1969. See Kathleen Tynan, ed., *Kenneth Tynan: Letters* (London: Weidenfeld and Nicolson, 1994), p. 449.

30. See Kenneth Tynan, *Tynan Right and Left* (London: Longman, 1967), p. 74.

31. *Ibid.*, p. 152.

32. *Ibid.*, p. 157.

33. One of these was Dr Manfred Wekwerth, who had trained as a dramaturg and director under Brecht. He recalls Tynan's curiosity about the functions of the dramaturg at the Berliner Ensemble and the conviction that the title Literary Manager was the closest

possible English translation of the concept of the profession. Interview with author, Berlin, 4.12.1996.

34. BL, UTM, file 1.
35. Tynan, *Tynan Right and Left*, pp. 159–60.
36. BL, UTM, file 11. Undated article by Tynan on Vaclav Havel. No source stated.
37. BL, UTM, file 109. Letter to the Editor from Tynan, 1965? Newspaper not stated.
38. Alan Seymour, 'Theatre 1965', *London Magazine* 5.5 (August 1965): 50.
39. NTA, B1–B5, minutes of the first meeting of the Council of Management of the National Theatre, 11.2.1963, article 17/63.
40. *Ibid.*
41. *Ibid.*
42. NTA, B2–B69, minutes of the first meeting of the Drama Committee, 11.12.1962.
43. J. Elsom and N. Tomalin, *The History of the National Theatre* (London: Jonathan Cape, 1978), p. 151. Chandos's expression.
44. NTA, B1–B5, minutes of the second meeting of the Council of Management of the National Theatre, 11.3.1963, article 33/63. Tynan's salary was set at £2,750 *p.a.*
45. See NTA, B2–B69, report by the Drama Committee, 21.2.1963.
46. Seymour, 'Theatre 1965', p. 49.
47. William Foster in the *Scotsman*, 11.11.1967.
48. BL, UTM, file 109. Draft of article entitled 'The Rise and Fall of the Political Innocent' published in the *Observer*, 25.8.1963.
49. *Ibid.*
50. *Ibid.*
51. See 'The National Theatre: A Speech to the Royal Society of Arts' (1964), in Kenneth Tynan, *A View of the English Stage* (London: Davis-Poynter, 1975), pp. 357–8.
52. *Ibid.*, p. 355.
53. *Ibid.*, p. 361.
54. BL, UTM, file 1. Letter dated 18.12.1963.
55. *Ibid.*

56. BL, UTM, file 1. The third addressee was George Rowbottom, General Manager. See also Tynan, *Letters*, pp. 312–13, but note that Kathleen Tynan makes slight editorial changes.

57. Tynan, *Letters*, p. 339. Letter from Kenneth Tynan to Peter Shaffer dated 16.2.1966. Tynan indicates that this function was discussed and agreed on when he first joined the NT.

58. Tynan, 'National Theatre', p. 362.

59. *Ibid.*, p. 361.

60. Tynan, *View of the English Stage*, p. 361.

61. Examples of usage in the *OED* include references to the re-education of the German people by the GDR after 1947 and communist Chinese techniques of re-education.

62. BL, UTM, file 2. Letter to Tynan from Olivier, 16.2.1972.

63. See the preface in Kenneth Tynan, *Curtains* (London: Longmans, 1961), p. x.

64. *The Resistible Rise of Arturo Ui* (9.8.1965); *Coriolanus* (10.8.1965); *The Threepenny Opera* (11.8.1965); *The Days of the Commune* (12.8.1965).

65. Tynan, 'National Theatre', p. 362.

66. Tynan, *Letters*, p. 303. Letter to Robert Graves, 25.8.1964.

67. Tynan, 'National Theatre', p. 362.

68. Tynan, *Letters*, pp. 309–10. Letter to Lord Cobbold, 29.10.1964.

69. J. J. Finegan, 'All about "Juno": a job well done', *Evening Herald*, 7.5.1966, p. 8.

70. Kenneth Tynan, ed., *The Recruiting Officer* (London: Rupert Hart-Davis, 1965).

71. Kenneth Tynan, ed., *Othello* (London: Rupert Hart-Davis, 1965).

72. Tynan, *Recruiting Officer*, p. 7.

73. NTA, B10–B5, minutes of the eighth meeting of the Council of Management of the National Theatre, 19.11.1963.

74. NTA, B1–B5, minutes of the sixteenth meeting of the Council of Management of the National Theatre, 13.7.1964.

75. Confirmed in John Dexter, *The Honourable Beast* (London: Nick Hern Books, 1993), p. 18.

76. Charles Marowitz, 'Talk with Tynan', *Encore* 10.44 (July/August 1963): 8.

77. Olivier, *Confessions of an Actor*, p. 347. Letter from Olivier to Chandos, 24.10.1968.
78. Roger Hudson, Catherine Itzin and Simon Trussler, 'The Critic Comes Full Circle', *Theatre Quarterly* 1.2 (April–June 1971): 37–48, 44.
79. BL, UTM, file 1. Draft of unpublished article entitled 'At the National'.
80. Tynan, *Letters*, pp. 306–8. Memorandum to Olivier, 22.10.1964.
81. BL, UTM, file 2. Letter from Olivier to Tynan, 25.10.1972.
82. Clancy Sigal and Roger Smith, who had written a treatment for a drama documentary on the Cuban missile crisis.
83. Tynan, *Letters*, p. 362. Letter to Olivier, 23.8.1966.
84. BL, UTM, file 2. Memorandum from Olivier to Tynan, 25.10.1972.
85. Kenneth Tynan, *The Diaries of Kenneth Tynan*, ed. John Lahr (London: Bloomsbury, 2001), p. 98, 5.7.1972.
86. Tynan, 'National Theatre', p. 364.
87. *Ibid.*
88. Dexter's assessment of Gaskill's attitude in Dexter, *Honourable Beast*, p. 250.
89. BL, UTM, file 21, page 1 of 11-page transcript. Gaskill interviewed by Kathleen Tynan, 6.9.1982.
90. NTA, P1, 3.
91. From an interview in 'Reputations: Kenneth Tynan', written and presented by Anthony Howard and broadcast on BBC television, 25.7.1982.
92. Tynan's notes were precise and never ran to more than three or four pages. They were restricted to textual matters, problems of audibility and delivery, and the weaknesses of specific actors. He did not proffer comments on a director's overall interpretation. There is little record of how much attention individual directors paid to these notes. Dexter used them as pointers to things he might have overlooked.
93. BL, UTM, file 2, 2–4. Letter from Dexter to Tynan, October 1972.
94. BL, UTM, file 2, 4. Letter from Dexter to Tynan, November 1972.
95. *Ibid.*
96. Marowitz, 'Talk With Tynan', p. 9.

97. Tynan, *Letters*, pp. 292–3. Letter to George Devine, 31.3.1964.

98. *Ibid.*, p. 293n5.

99. *Ibid.*, p. 294. Letter to George Devine, 10.4.1964.

100. *Ibid.*, pp. 292–4n5.

101. In a BBC Radio 3 programme broadcast at 13.00 hrs, 16.11.1965.

102. Tynan, *Letters*, p. 376. Memorandum to Olivier, 3.1.1967.

103. *Ibid.*, p. 375. Postscript of a memorandum to Olivier, 23.12.1966.

104. *Ibid.*, pp. 377–9. Memorandum to the National Theatre Board, 7.1.1967.

105. *Ibid.*, p. 377.

106. NTA, B1–B5, minutes of the thirty-eighth meeting of the Council of Management of the National Theatre, 9.1.1967.

107. BL, UTM, file 2. Draft notes for Olivier, 20.4.1967.

108. NTA, B1–B5, minutes of the fortieth meeting of the Council of Management of the National Theatre, 24.4.1967.

109. Chandos, *Times*, Letter to the Editor, 2.5.1967.

110. *Letters*, 399–400. *Times*, Letter to the Editor, 4.5.1967.

111. *Ibid.*, p. 401. *Times*, Letter to the Editor, 7.5.1967.

112. Chandos expended astonishing energy in a personal mission to remove Tynan. See CA, Chandos manuscripts, Chan II, 4/3 and 4/13.

113. Olivier, *Confessions of an Actor*, p. 345. Letter from Olivier to Chandos, 24.10.1968.

114. *Ibid.*, p. 349. Letter from Olivier to Chandos, 3.11.1968.

115. Tynan, *Letters*, p. 470. Memorandum to Olivier, 23.4.1970.

116. *Ibid.*, p. 471.

117. BL, UTM, file 2. Tynan's notes for a Board meeting at which he was called on to give an account of his functions, 1972?

118. *Ibid.*

119. *Ibid.*

120. Tynan, *Letters*, pp. 507–8. Letter to Olivier, 9.3.1972.

121. BL, UTM, file 2. Letter to Frank Dunlop, 23.1.1970.

122. *Diaries*, p. 98.

123. See Peter Hall, *Diaries*, ed. John Goodwin (London: Hamish Hamilton, 1983), p. 223.

124. *Ibid.*, p. 11.

125. Richard Beacham, 'Literary Management at the National Theatre, London: An Interview with John Russell Brown', *Theater* 10.1 (1978): 38–42.

126. George Rowell, *The Old Vic Theatre: A History* (Cambridge: Cambridge University Press, 1993), 153–4.

127. Callow, ed., *National*, p. 34.

128. Tynan, *Letters*, p. 536.

129. BL, UTM, file 41. Orson Welles interviewed by Kathleen Tynan.

130. BL, UTM, file 2. Letter to Tynan from Tom Stoppard, 20.2.1972.

7   Dramaturgy and literary management in England today

The silent revolution

Whilst Tynan's profile as Literary Manager has remained low with theatre historians, his impact on the theatre industry itself has been extraordinary. No one could have anticipated either the scale or the extent of the changes that have taken place since the 1960s, and no one could have foreseen that professional literary management would be so rapidly embraced. Two other flagship theatres followed suit first, the Royal Court employing a Literary Manager in 1979, and the Royal Shakespeare Company employing Colin Chambers in 1981.[1] The 1980s and 1990s saw a steady proliferation of appointments of both full-time and part-time literary managers, and it is unlikely that numbers have peaked, the current pattern indicating that theatres in the regions are embarking on ambitious and progressive experiments in literary management and dramaturgy. As I write there are now nine full-time Literary Managers in London, and sixteen working part-time;[2] there are eleven on full-time and four on part-time contracts in the regions. In five years the numbers of full-time posts have doubled, and the haphazard, fixed-period recruitment pattern of the 1990s has changed as more funding has become available and theatre companies have opted for longer-term investment in literary development. Most subsidised and fringe theatres both in London and in the Regions have freelance readers or literary advisers where they cannot afford other arrangements. In 1997 literary managers, dramaturgs and others involved in selecting, developing and staging new performance works held a colloquium, 'Commissioning the Future', to discuss issues connected with playreading, decision-making, present and

possible future models of literary management and resource alloca-
tion.[3] The energy and political articulacy of delegates testified to the
rapid spread of literary management strategies, and the conference
revealed the burning topicality of play selection and development
issues.

An equally important part of the changes in the national development culture is the significance of the regional new playwriting
organisations. Spread across England they include writernet,[4]
Playwrights East, Script, North West Playwrights, Playwrights
North, Yorkshire Playwrights, Pier Playwrights and South-West
Scriptwriters. These organisations, mainly established in the 1980s
and 1990s, began with a self-help ethos and are funded independently
from theatres. They play a vital rôle in the development of writers in
the early stages of their career, have been significantly boosted by new
economic investment and regional theatres now collaborate much
more effectively with them than before. The initial strategy is to
respond to all scripts with a report after which mentoring may be
offered. Many writers undergo their early apprenticeships with such
organisations, receiving their first feedback, readings, mentoring sessions and productions (if funding permits) before moving on to a
professional career. Increasingly, the new writing organisations are
taking on a substantial volume of unsolicited script-reading, and it
could be that future streamlining of literary management will mean
these organisations become even more important centres for reading
unsolicited scripts. Dramaturgs (for reasons cited later) are much
harder to track, but short-term appointments on new writing projects
all over the country have increased at a phenomenal rate since the
1980s and there are signs that this is not simply a fashionable trend.
These changes certainly point to the creation of a new administrative
tier in the theatrical hierarchy, and what has been termed 'a silent
revolution' in the management of playreading and play selection.[5] In
this respect, England has belatedly followed aspects of continental
practice. But there is also a new tier of practical workers in theatre,
who work on the development of new plays. In America they are called
dramaturgs, and without doubt England has looked to the US for its
broad models of practice in development dramaturgy.

One of the reasons that the revolution has been 'silent' in England is that it is very new and is still happening. Nonetheless, academia is out of step with the significance of the sea change; and there is also a lack of substantial professional documentation and analysis of the diverse practices of literary management and dramaturgy. In the US and in continental Europe dramaturgs and literary managers have a high profile, and in any case dramaturgy is an established subject for study and practice. Since practices in England are more recent, much information in this chapter has necessarily been gathered orally, hence the inclusion of case histories. My data has come from a survey I conducted into the work of literary managers and dramaturgs,[6] extensive interviews, discussions and correspondence with theatre practitioners, administrators and funding bodies, research at institutional and personal archives, and literature such as newsletters, theatre programmes, newspapers and pamphlets. My own work as a dramaturg specialising in the development of new writers at the Cambridge Arts Theatre in the late 1980s meant that I had an insight into the complexities of the field.

New writing

There can be no doubt that the growth of officially appointed literary managers and dramaturgs since the 1960s results principally from market demand for new plays. David Edgar argues rightly that contemporary work 'has been central to the project of the British theatre' since Osborne's *Look Back in Anger*,[7] and the boom in new play production and the upsurge in new playwriting since 1990 has led to an exponential rise in the number of literary managers and dramaturgs employed.[8] Negotiation with and development of playwrights have changed vastly too; indeed 'new play development', as it is known – the nurture and advancement of new playwrights – has in itself become a major cultural industry and in this English practices have been influenced enormously by those in the US.[9]

The contemporary demand for new plays is qualitatively different from such demand for other cultural goods in its insistence on the representation of diverse experiences, politics and aesthetics: it is set against England's post-war, post-imperial identity crisis, and as the received idea of homogeneous English nationhood has dissolved into a consciousness of different constituencies and interests, so many different (often 'minority') dramatic voices have finally been allowed on stage to challenge dominant narratives and traditional styles. In the last forty years a slow acceptance of multiculturalism and colonial decline, the self-examination enforced by England's relation to European integration and global economies, and the end of the Cold War have fostered desire for and receptivity to an unprecedented richness of international experience and influence, particularly in theatre. The end of formal censorship by the Lord Chamberlain in 1968, the further building of regional repertory theatres,[10] and the extraordinary development of the fringe theatre and small studio spaces in the 1960s and 1970s (ideal for new, experimental work) have permitted the explosion and accommodation of topical new plays.[11] The left-wing ethos of challenging the mainstream of the 1960s, combined with new ideas on education outreach, signified an interest in wooing (and therefore researching) audiences previously alienated by mainstream theatre. The specific political and/or aesthetic aims of many companies required the structured conceptualisation of artistic policy and the adoption of a distinctive creative identity, so that a new reflectiveness on the processes of theatre-making and on the relationship between product and spectator has become a central preoccupation; market forces of the 1980s also helped to force companies to consider how to target consumers. In consequence, dramaturgical functions related to creative self-reflectivity and in-house criticism, audience development, reading and developing new plays, and specialist literary and language skills have proliferated.

The boom in theatre companies and the diversity of creative experiment since the 1960s have required financial investment, and changing attitudes to subsidy and economics are also vital to the professionalisation of dramaturgs and literary managers. The foundation of the Arts Council, incorporated by Royal Charter in 1946, and of Regional Arts Boards established during the 1960s and early 1970s, signalled a significant shift in favour of at least partial state subsidy of significant theatres or work deemed of particular merit.[12] The political and artistic effects of these bodies on theatre-making in England have always been disputed, and their policies (much subject to changes of government) and wavering financial fortunes, especially in the regions, continue to impact directly on the survival or sudden death of smaller theatre companies. Subsidy is integral to the establishment of literary management departments. Predictably, those theatres perceived as having specific national rôles in relation to the dramatic canon and new writing were awarded large annual subsidies from the 1960s onwards, and were the first to employ literary managers: the National Theatre, the RSC and the Royal Court.

In the 1980s innovative theatre and new writing remained substantially underfunded and the growth in literary managers and dramaturgs was financed piecemeal; it reflected no commitment on the part of funders to their long-term integration into English theatre-making, only the resourcefulness of theatre-makers themselves in seeking to acquire targeted short-term help with certain dramaturgical functions. 'Project' funding became popular in the 1980s, and was touted by funders as a more democratic way of dispersing funds to more organisations: arguments for and against abound, but the vast majority of dramaturgs owe their employment to this type of funding, which ranges from a few weeks or months to three years. Similarly, literary managers working on the fringe, employed by smaller or touring companies without a national, sufficiently high-profile image, generally work part-time or as volunteers. Since the 1980s the opportunities for project funding have increased dramatically with short-term grants offered by the Arts Council, the Regional Arts Boards and local government; a plethora of funds awarded by charitable trusts (who often support areas perceived as neglected); the establishment of the National Heritage (early 1990s) and National Lottery funds (mid-1990s); and, last but far from least, sponsorship by corporations and charitable trusts, which continues to play a major rôle in the funding of new writing projects at theatres all over the country.

The professionalisation of dramaturgical functions

If the job title 'Literary Manager' (as well as its functions) has gained acceptance in the theatre industry, the term is not widely understood by the general public. The situation regarding dramaturgs is even more confusing and complex. 'Dramaturgs' abound in the new writing industries, and it can be difficult to determine what individual companies mean by the term. Titles are a distinctly political issue, and as a new tier of functionaries embed themselves in institutions and theatre-making processes, so the search for an accurate way to describe different divisions of labour is evident in the appearance of a new set of approved labels.

In the late 1990s individuals referring to themselves as Literary Managers worked mainly behind their desks, engaged in reading and managing the incoming flow of plays, forging relationships with writers, commissioning, advising ADs on repertoire and artistic policy, tracking new writing nationally and sometimes internationally, and minimally attending rehearsals unless problems arose. Only two Literary Managers in 1998, for example, did any significant workshopping of new plays with playwrights, the majority seeing their job as a management rôle. Similarly, in 1998 individuals calling themselves 'dramaturgs' or 'writing tutors' or 'mentors' and specialising in the area of new writing, corresponded roughly to the post-Brechtian idea of the *Entwicklungsdramaturg* (Development Dramaturg), typically committed themselves to one-to-one tutorials with writers, and had a marginal or restricted voice in rehearsals. They were without exception on short-term contracts or freelance. In the late 1990s the notion of the *Produktionsdramaturg* (Production Dramaturg) was little understood in England. Production dramaturgs are theatre practitioners who form working partnerships with directors and are generally textual specialists of some kind. They develop the 'concept' for the performance with the director in the pre-production phase, are present in rehearsal, and may also work on publicity, programme material or publication of the text. Such dramaturgs are concerned overwhelmingly with textual issues and with articulating *processes* of production. The precursor is Brecht, and an increased interest in Eastern European theatres and American practices has meant that the idea is slowly gaining ground – though production dramaturgs are much rarer in England than many assume. Traditionally, many assistant directors and staff directors have performed research tasks, but those functions tend to remain invisible because they are not officially acknowledged. Of course, not all theatre companies can afford to employ literary managers or dramaturgs and the various functions have been assumed (or not, as the case may be) by other officials, including ADs, education officers, publicity and marketing departments, (assistant) directors, managers and other administrative staff.

In 2005 the situation is very different and is still changing. In the words of playwright Steve Waters, 'a new breed of literary manager has sprung up'.[13] Since new writing has been recognised as vital to the future health of theatre culture, and as a primary means of reaching new audiences, development cultures have grown exponentially. The need for development practitioners is no longer questioned by many in the industry, though what they are called is still a matter of much debate. This 'new breed' of literary managers regard practical development skills as a vital part of their job: by this they mean the ability to develop an idea with a playwright through one-to-one sessions and workshops with actors, editing and cutting skills, and a willingness to participate in rehearsals if required. Increasingly the practical realm of the dramaturg is merging with the conventional management rôle of the literary manager. Currently the use of the word *dramaturg* by industry practitioners in England denotes a practical involvement in theatre-making either with writers or directors or both. The new breed of literary managers are also often directors, and their status is rising – many now prefer to use appellations such as Writing Director, Literary Director, Literary Associate, Director, Associate Dramaturg, Dramaturg or Associate Director to indicate their executive status and/or to differentiate themselves from what some see as an 'old-fashioned' desk-bound model of literary management.[14] When funding allows, the current trend is for theatres and new writing organisations to employ more than one dramaturgical official: one to manage the conventional functions of literary management and the other to act as a practical animateur of new writing. Functions are less clearly demarcated than hitherto, another indication of a cultural shift.

A significant landmark in the professionalisation of dramaturgical functions was the founding of the Dramaturgs' Network in 2002.[15] The Dramaturgs' Network 'is an organisation of professional dramaturgs and literary managers'. Its twin aims are 'to promote dramaturgy and the rôle of the dramaturg in British theatre and performance arts through practical means' and 'to create a nation-wide network for practising dramaturgs as a forum for support, shared ideas, knowledge and resources'.[16] The Dramaturgs Network launched their collaboration with the Directors' Guild of Great Britain in 2003, certainly a coup in promoting the idea of the production dramaturg, but it is too early to tell what effect this partnership will have. Members of the Dramaturgs' Network argue that

> It came about as a response to the changing theatre culture in England. It emerged when young professionals refused to be dismissed and began to challenge the view that "the dramaturg's job doesn't exist in England". What the Dramaturgs' Network did was simply to unite all those professionals who wanted to work as dramaturgs. It strengthened their position and amplified their voices. Through its outreach work the Network has helped to explain the work and function of a dramaturg and increased the appreciation of the job amongst theatre practitioners.[17]

The Literary Managers' Forum first convened in 2000 and has a membership of forty,[18] but interestingly it is organised and hosted annually by the Writers' Guild of Great Britain. The forum provides playwrights with the possibility of meeting literary managers, voicing their concerns and discussing pertinent issues. It is also one way of holding literary managers to account. A further symbolic signal of professionalisation is the fact that the Arts Council of England is currently actively engaged in encouraging and funding debates on literary management and dramaturgy within the profession. Discussions focus on difficulties faced, the importance of writing in the regions, the success of existing development models and ways of elevating the status of literary managers within the creative process.[19]

Dramaturgs and the politics of identity

If literary managers have traditionally been concerned with defining the identity of a company by playing a key rôle in artistic programming, the spread of development dramaturgs (also called writing

tutors and mentors) is connected with the desire to empower particular constituencies of writers, and is to do with wider political issues of
audience access and participation. Funding criteria under the Blair
government have promoted 'access', 'diversity', 'excellence', 'education' and 'economic value' as cornerstones of artistic policy, and theatres are required to demonstrate that they are working to acquire
new audiences, especially those who have traditionally been
marginalised.[20]

The Theatre Writers' Union,[21] founded in 1975 to represent
dramatists, was a key player in publicising widespread dissatisfaction
with the lack of organised reading services at theatres in the regions. In
the late 1970s and early 1980s the Arts Council of England discussed
establishing 'Regional Dramaturgs' and a 'National Script Centre' to
overcome the lack of script-reading and consultancy facilities beyond
London. But costs would have been substantial and there was lack of
will, especially given that the move to centralise script-reading could
be seen as politically counter to writers' and theatres' interests
because it created a major bureaucratic machine, threatened to disem-
power individual theatres' play selection processes and promulgated
standardisation.[22] Consequently nothing was done, and regional new
writing organisations and many new writing theatre companies grew
out of a frustration with London-centred new writing schemes and
from a sense that playwrights outside London had little access to
theatres or chance of having their plays read, let alone opportunities
for development experience. A growing post-Thatcherite political confidence in regional government has also served these initiatives,
which have found favour with Regional Arts Boards and local councils.
Thus the regions have been powerful advocates of change in the structure and practice of development.

The initial substantial spread of short-term appointments of
dramaturgs during the 1980s can be explicitly linked to regional new
writing organisations. The first organisation was North West
Playwrights, founded in 1982, which attracted national attention
through its summer festivals of new writing in the 1980s and up to
the mid-1990s, and who pioneered the short-term hire of dramaturgs
in pre-rehearsal and rehearsal periods specifically to tutor playwrights

in stagecraft and to mediate between director and playwright. The primary influence was the post-Brechtian idea of the production dramaturg, but the model found to be most useful was a new writing theatre, the O'Neill Centre, in the United States.[23] Short-term hire of 'dramaturgs' is now common practice for regional new writing organisations, and of course for many theatre companies.

In the 1990s the deployment of dramaturgs became explicitly associated with the agendas of minority politics, most obviously perhaps with ethnic minorities. The London Arts Board supported initiatives targeted at developing 'black and Asian' playwrights and at training 'black and Asian' dramaturgs as writing tutors, researchers and production dramaturgs.[24] One of the aims was to encourage trainees to consider a career in literary management, where ethnic minorities are drastically under-represented.[25] As yet it it difficult to assess the efficacy of these experiments. Writernet, the new writing organisation, has conducted limited research on the lack of development opportunities for black playwrights, but the insistence in the scheme 'Going Black Under the Skin' on 'Black Dramaturgy' as 'a distinct aesthetic', its notions of 'African consciousness' and 'Black culture', seemed to reinforce through naïve oversimplification the prejudices they sought to counter.[26]

The employment of dramaturgs is also associated with the conscious promotion of theatre by and for other minority groups such as women playwrights, the disabled, young offenders and in particular children's theatre. Red Ladder theatre company, for example, commissioned and toured issue-based plays to teenagers in communities that did not frequent theatre, and employed a part-time dramaturg to help their often young and inexperienced playwrights shape ideas into dramatic form.[27] Until recently children's theatre was marginalised (like other forms of writing for the young), but children are now a major new target audience, and Young Writers' Programmes at both London and regional theatres are major employers of dramaturgs. After a long battle for funding, Polka, the specialist children's theatre company in London, now has both a Literary Manager and a development dramaturg. These two posts are important victories and indicate a new commitment to the literary values of writing for children.

Writernet has also employed dramaturgs for mentoring projects targeted at women. The pilot scheme for inexperienced women writers asked dramaturgs/mentors to help trainee writers with their general career development and to act as script advisers, rôle models and constructive critics.[28] The results were difficult to assess, and John Deeney, reporting on the scheme, came to the conclusion that the process of mentoring was itself 'remarkably elusive' and required further research.[29] The project, nevertheless, raised interesting issues about how to train and support writers, and how female playwrights, an under-represented group on mainstream stages, might gain better access to them.[30] Writernet's research projects certainly point to the underlying desire to promote neglected constituencies of new writing, and dramaturgs, whether as writing tutors, researchers or production advisers, are increasingly employed to highlight particular political agendas.

Creative and cultural interventions: the D-word

For all the voices advocating dramaturgs, there are as many that express hostility – and with an intensity that is often puzzling. In England, and to a lesser extent the US, the dramaturg conjures up deeply entrenched cultural fears, territoriality and prejudice. It goes without saying that the involvement of a production or development dramaturg in a project inherently shifts the manner in which theatre-making processes are organised and cuts across territories that have traditionally been occupied mainly by the writer and director (and also by the actor and designer). The deep-rooted suspicion of the way in which the dramaturg is understood to insinuate himself or herself into decision-making and production processes and thereby challenge conventional power structures is often articulated as a knee-jerk prejudice against the word itself: Veltman has cited the words of 'a well-respected Literary Manager' in an article that pleads for tolerance: 'it's not even an English word and it's completely pretentious'.[31] American commentators have similar reactions to the 'ugly "turg-word"',[32] and argue that the hostility 'partly reflects America's historical anti-intellectualism',[33] a charge frequently made against English theatre.

In a chapter revealingly entitled 'The Show that needs a Dramaturg has a bad Director' the American McCabe launches a coruscating attack on this 'new phenomenon',[34] condemning dramaturgs as creatively bankrupt and destructive forces, whether acting as advocates for the playwright, adviser or researcher to the director, or offering counsel on repertoire:

> This function of the dramaturg has a certain appeal, but unfortunately it is to theatre what socialism is to economics: an interesting theory with a certain surface plausibility but no track record that suggests it actually works.
>
> The real-life hitch is that dramaturgs work for directors. The professional dramaturg is a creature of the not-for-profit resident theatre; producers who are in business to make money have by and large not seen the wisdom of hiring someone who neither writes the play, nor directs it, nor designs it, nor acts in it, nor stage manages it, nor works as a technician on it. Dramaturgs are hired by not-for-profit theatres run by artistic directors who each want an artistic staff that will work to support, not contradict, the type of theatre the artistic director wishes to pursue.[35]

McCabe happily deploys the language of Soviet dictatorship in relation to dramaturgs, and equally happily invests himself with a supreme and 'natural' authority that he claims is 'inevitably weakened if someone else is seen as the master of the play'.[36] But in underlining the ambiguity of the dramaturg's position in theatre-making processes, he also points to the major problem in Britain and America: the dramaturg's rôle is neither clearly defined nor understood in a broad cultural sense, and there are real anxieties about empowering them to make creative interventions.[37] McCabe patently feels under threat as a director. Edward Kemp, a writer and director, and perhaps England's best-known production dramaturg, identifies 'directors' paranoia' as a considerable hindrance in the development of the dramaturg's profession:

> Most directors in England are untrained, but are at the top of the pyramid in terms of the way theatre is organised. Their

paranoia is that they have no qualifications except that they have proved they can direct through doing it. Some directors want absolute control and feel that a dramaturg would undermine their authority; some directors feel that dramaturgs are akin to an intellectual police force. I have also met directors who use research to confirm what they already believe, and someone challenging them or pushing them further is difficult for them to tolerate.[38]

Kemp first started using the word *dramaturg* to avoid being categorised as a writer *or* a director when he saw himself as occupying a middle-ground between both. He was named 'production dramaturg' to Katie Mitchell for *The Mysteries* at the RSC in 1996, and had responsibility for the research and adaptation of the text and also acted as a consultant to Mitchell during production. This was the first time in the RSC's history that a production dramaturg was given such status, Kemp's name appearing immediately after Mitchell's in publicity and programme material. At the National Theatre, Kemp found that the objections to production dramaturgs were economic as well as ideological; working as a staff director on Congreve's *Way of the World* in 1995–6, he asked to be credited as dramaturg since 'everyone on the show understood that I was fulfilling a dramaturg's rôle', but was told that 'other directors might start asking for dramaturgs' and that this would create 'a pay-roll problem'. Kemp is the first to admit that it is not necessary to employ a dramaturg on every production, but contends that large shows with large casts can benefit from the involvement of someone 'who is not the writer and not the director but has both their interests at heart' and cites his experience of working with Alan Bennett and Nicholas Hytner on *The Madness of King George* (1991):

> By Alan's own admission, the play wasn't finished when it went into rehearsal; there were stages in the process when I felt that it would have helped to have someone assisting in the creation of a framework and focus for the script while Nick was coping with the many acting and technical challenges that the play presented.

If some directors are suspicious of dramaturgs and literary managers, then so are some playwrights. Steve Waters has grave reservations about the political implications of development culture.

> I notice a burgeoning culture of development and a shrinking culture of production. There's a recognition that new writing is the burning beacon and that it must be nurtured but there's an insistence on dictating *how* it is nurtured. This is classic New Labour strategy. Money is provided but it's controlled centrally through organisations like the Arts Council or the Lottery Fund, who institute labyrinthine processes of application. The Government insist on certain criteria: the buzz words are 'diversity', 'access', and 'excellence' – it means that arts organisations have to package their projects in particular ways and it becomes more about spin than substance, more about 'nurturing' than actual art. New play development is about a new cultural interventionism. It's meant to amount to rigorous, decentralised public spending, but in fact it's the opposite – it's rigorously centralised.[39]

For theatre producer Michael Kustow, the writing was already on the wall in the late 1980s when 'Management and Marketing had become the ends of public arts activity, not just its means. Social engineering, demanding perfectly justified advances in access and representation, took the place of a theory of art and a whole society.'[40] Kustow and Waters, like others, perceive the rise of literary managers and dramaturgs as little other than an unstoppable tide of Blairite bureaucrats who implement a particular New Labour pedagogy, driven by a missionary zeal for what they believe is the moral and political enlightenment of their theatre audiences. Waters is especially concerned about what he sees as a growing culture of interventionism, which endorses political correctness and economics over the artistic, but which gives the appearance of benevolent patronage.

> The writers' programmes that some theatres offer are about developing writers from scratch and they promulgate the philosophy that you don't wait for writers to emerge, you

make them – particularly playwrights from under-represented sections of society. That's akin to forcing a culture and at its worst can amount to a kind of cultural opportunism.

If certain literary managers see their interventions in the drafting process as a way of ensuring that a play goes into production in a theatre culture where 'the right to fail is no longer an option',[41] Waters is disturbed by what he sees as a paradoxical claim to the nurture of innovation.

> New play development is often inherently reactionary. If it's about making plays 'work' then it can too often result in conversations about the 'well-made play'. But Edward Bond's *Saved* and Sarah Kane's *Blasted* broke with convention and didn't 'work' – in ways that turned out to be revolutionary. Having a writing mentor can work, but perhaps the writer should be able to choose who that mentor is and it makes sense that they are an experienced writer. I am very worried by literary managers who see themselves as 'script editors'. The writer is in danger of becoming a construct of the literary manager's voice and could become homogenised.[42] The world of TV script-writing is not analogous to theatre – in that world the writer normally has very little status, and the worlds of film and television are even more hierarchical and bureaucratic. The demand for new plays is creating a formidable apparatus of dramaturgy, but the literary managers and dramaturgs themselves are not held to account and the systems are no more transparent than they were before.

Waters is inclined to the view that dramaturgs or writing mentors are best deployed in the earliest stages of a writer's career. Like playwright Peter Whelan,[43] he regards the proliferation of literary managers as a Blairite attempt to extend the influence of a political decision-making machine that creates more layers of arbitration and prescription under the guise of democratisation.

McCabe and Waters voice their concerns in a language that evokes oppressive state control of an extreme kind, but their alarm and animosity are far from unusual. For certain directors, producers and writers the dramaturg is associated with a sinister, communist invocation of a government official who is the enemy of creativity and the purveyor of state censorship.[44] These analogies are unfair and hyperbolical, but it is important to appreciate what lies behind them. There is more than one way of telling a story. In England formal theatre censorship ended only in 1968 and is a very recent memory, and in the US McCarthyism has left its scars. In both countries there are deep-rooted cultural fears of the standardisation of a figure who can infiltrate various production processes and potentially exercise ideological power. Furthermore, the status of writers and directors in theatre has, in historical terms, only recently been won, and the battles to be credited and recognised in their own right were hard-fought. Both McCabe and Waters fear the endorsement of non-specialists annexing the highly skilled territories of writing and directing, and they fear that deterioration – not enhancement – will be the result. It is interesting that Waters refers to the film and television industries as examples of worlds where dramaturgical imperatives of the 'correct' ways to structure a script have led to numerous tiers of legitimated intervention: current debates in those industries indicate unhappiness with the homogenising, unadventurous approaches of many script editors and an anxiety that their training may be too insubstantial.[45] There are very real questions about who is appointed a literary manager, how they are trained, what their own and the theatre's agendas are, why they promote the writers they do, how or whether they intervene on a production, and what they think the purpose of theatre is. Waters is not persuaded that English theatre companies always understand the wider political ramifications of the appointments they make. Similarly, the use of a production dramaturg is a sensitive matter and requires careful negotiation.

The growth of literary managers and dramaturgs intrinsically signals new divisions of labour in theatre-making: whilst Germany, Eastern Europe and Scandinavia negotiated new working methods some time ago, America and England are in different stages of transition. What is significant is both the reluctance English practitioners, in particular, show in redefining divisions of labour, and also the difficulties redefinition poses in a modern theatre culture that has two models of hierarchy: one positioning the writer at the top, and the other the director. Writers and directors have no lesser a status in countries where dramaturgs are widespread, but continental practices have conventionally estimated the visual impact of a production to be at least as important as the articulation of words. America and England have pursued a theatre more dominated by words, and the advent of dramaturgs undoubtedly indicates a challenge to orthodox play-making.

Academic and industry training

The curriculum vitae of a literary manager or dramaturg is unpredictable, but most have a background in directing, playwriting, education or theatre criticism. All respondents to my survey have degrees, the vast majority in drama, English or modern languages. All privileged the skills of textual and performance analysis. In 1998 no literary manager to whom I spoke had begun their career with the intention of becoming a literary manager; in 2005 the profession is now more visible and there are many aspirants. In the last few years literary management has also proved to be a useful training ground for artistic directors;[46] this career progression is a clear acknowledgement that textual specialism and knowledge of new writing is at least as important as directing, and a further signal that the traditional boundaries of theatre-making are breaking down – literary managers and dramaturgs are increasingly also writers or directors.

Training in the theatre arts is a vexed question in England: directing programmes are few and relatively new, and most established directors trained on the job as assistant directors. Similarly, playwriting programmes are uncommon in theatre academies and universities, but theatres and new writing organisations seek to fill the gap. It is significant, therefore, that new academic and vocational courses are beginning to emerge. London's most famous acting school, the Royal Academy of Dramatic Art, employed a full-time 'Academy Dramaturg', Lloyd Trott, for the first time in 2004, a signal of how seriously they regard the business of teaching actors to research and analyse play texts.[47] Four institutes have introduced theoretical

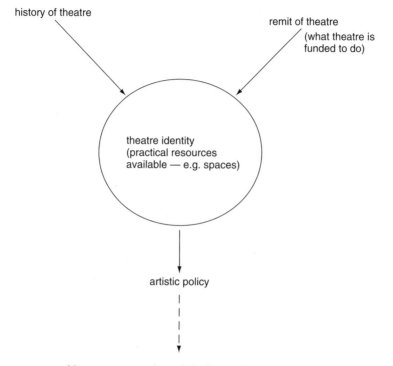

history of theatre

remit of theatre
(what theatre is
funded to do)

theatre identity
(practical resources
available — e.g. spaces)

artistic policy

Literary manager plus artistic director plus others

Value judgement on plays

Figure 7.1   Model for context of value judgements of plays: author's transcription of flipchart diagram by Graham Whybrow, Literary Manager, Royal Court Theatre, London, drawn at the 'Mentors or Censors?' Conference, Birmingham, UK, 30 January 1999.

and practical aspects of literary management and dramaturgy at MA level since 1997: the University of Birmingham and Goldsmiths' College (University of London) offer MAs in Dramaturgy, King's College (University of London) offers an MA in Text and Performance, and the Central School of Speech and Drama MA in Advanced Theatre Practice proffers an option on the theory and practice of production dramaturgy.[48] Though these degrees are still in the early stages of development, their isolation of dramaturgy and literary management as disciplines worthy of study in their own right marks the genesis of a new kind of professionalisation. Without doubt these courses raise the profile of dramaturgy: all have organised colloquia on the subject. In 1999 two major academic conferences took place: the first, provocatively titled 'Mentors or Censors?' at the University of Birmingham, sought to find an interface between practising literary managers and students of dramaturgy, identifying the functions and skills of literary managers and dramaturgs at specific companies, and testing methods of teaching certain skills in workshop conditions (see fig. 7.1); the second, in London, sought to explore territory outside the traditional textual remit of dramaturgs and to interrogate functions connected with areas such as design, fine art, puppetry and devised, site-specific or installation work.[49] If (as with creative writing) England takes a lead from university programmes in the US, where there is currently a plethora of courses in dramaturgy,[50] and if partial absorption of professional practices from Germany, Scandinavia, Holland, Croatia, Poland, the Czech Republic and Russia continues, then these disciplines are likely to gain academic and vocational momentum. That development arouses mixed feelings. Some literary managers have wondered whether theatres in England can accommodate graduates on such courses and are concerned that the standardised training and possible mass production of literary managers and dramaturgs through higher education could, if not carefully planned and monitored, result in a creative and intellectual stagnation.[51] A similar concern has been voiced in the US, where it is feared that theatres might be employing 'literary scholars rather than theatrical [directors]' and that as a result 'Theater is becoming a classroom'.[52]

If practice has boomed, theorisation is nascent. Every Literary Manager's and Dramaturg's job varies according to the project and the institution, and professionalisation in England is so recent that acknowledged models of practice have yet to evolve. Whilst aspects of Brecht's theatre practice continue to have an impact, his theory of the dramaturg has been widely misapprehended. Perhaps more troubling is the continued absence of any complete English translation of Lessing's *Hamburgische Dramaturgie*, which remains little known and less regarded by many contemporary English constructors of European theatre history. Besides Lessing and Brecht, theoretical work from continental Europe has had virtually no impact on English critical discussions. A major French interrogation of dramaturgy and literary management, inspired by Brecht and documented in the mainstream theatre journal *Théâtre/public* in 1986, occasioned no interest in England.[53] More surprisingly perhaps, Granville Barker's writings are virtually unknown in the industry. The international debate between non-text-based practitioners and academics in Holland, Denmark, Germany, France, the US, Canada and Belgium, which came of a major four-day symposium on dramaturgy in 1993, found few echoes in England at the time; though 'The New Dramaturgy',[54] a term coined at that symposium to recognise non-traditional dramaturgical functions arising from the post-1960s integration of separate performance disciplines, has begun to be discussed at events which prefer the appellation 'Alternative Dramaturgies'.[55]

Case histories

Dramaturgical activities go on at a dizzying pace in England and the rate of change is rapid. Every institutional agenda is different and individual practices vary. It would be impossible to be comprehensive. I have chosen three traditional flagship companies – the National Theatre, the Royal Court and the Royal Shakespeare Company – and a selection of major regional theatres – the Birmingham Rep, the Liverpool Everyman, the Royal Exchange in Manchester and the Stephen Joseph Theatre in Scarborough. In addition, I have covered the Theatre Writing Partnership based at Nottingham Playhouse, an unusual and highly successful new writing organisation. What is striking is the way each of these empires is booming, and the constant experimentation with new initiatives for writers and new writing. Growth is connected as much to commercial patronage as it is to subsidy. In terms of appointing, there are issues connected with age, sex, class and ethnicity. For example, the Royal Court has been progressive in the sense that it has appointed women to the position of literary manager in the past, but it seems that the National Theatre and the Royal Shakespeare Company have yet to address entrenched institutional thinking and to face issues of equal opportunities (they also have a poor record of appointing female directors and ADs).

Overall, the flagship companies tend to employ white, middle-class males – female and ethnic minority candidates soon find that they hit a glass ceiling. It is, however, beginning to look as though regional theatres will challenge the dominant patterns.

The National Theatre

The NT,[56] on London's South Bank, is dedicated to staging the best classical and modern national and international work. The NT incorporates three commercial stages: the Lyttelton and Olivier, which seat *c.* 890 and *c.* 1,150 respectively, and which opened in 1976; and the Cottesloe, a more intimate experimental space seating *c.* 400, which opened in 1977. In 1982 the NT acquired a studio space nearby for private, non-commercial usage; it was designated for training as well as project and play development, and actors are largely drawn from the NT company subject to availability. During Peter Hall's reign as Artistic Director (1973–88), which succeeded the Olivier–Tynan double act, the post of Literary Manager was effectively downgraded to 'Scripts Adviser and Associate to the NT'[57] and an academic appointed, John Russell Brown, 'a figure as far removed from Tynan or any potential Tynanism as could be conceived of'.[58] Under Richard Eyre's artistic directorship (1988–95) the post of Literary Manager was augmented and Nicholas Wright employed, followed by Giles Croft.[59] Jack Bradley joined as Scripts Adviser in 1994 and became Literary Manager in 1995 for the then AD, Richard Eyre. He has continued in post throughout Trevor Nunn's Artistic Directorship (1995–2002) and since the current AD Nicholas Hytner took over.[60] Bradley was selected primarily for his expertise in new play development, and with a view to building a stronger relationship between the work nurtured at the NT studio and the main stages.[61]

> Before me Peter Gill and John Burgess had developed a pool of new writers and I helped bring in the next generation, names like Patrick Marber, Tanika Gupta, Joe Penhall and Moira Buffini.[62]

Nunn attached far greater importance to new playwrights than Hall or Eyre at the NT, a philosophy 'underpinned by a desire to open the National's doors' and reach out to new audiences, especially the under-25s.[63] By the time Nunn left, new plays made up 60 per cent of the repertoire, indicating a very considerable shift in programming policy. Hytner has shown a similar commitment to new writing.

Bradley's department consists of a full-time Assistant Literary Manager, a full-time Scripts Assistant, and a Senior Reader employed two and a half days a week. A team of freelance readers are regularly deployed and Nicholas Drake, a Literary Associate, is closely involved with work at the studio. The NT receives about 1,500 unsolicited scripts a year, a volume that has doubled in the last decade and which includes an upsurge in submissions of musicals.

> The most important skills in my position are the capacity to assess scripts and knowledge of the theatre and new writing industries. We don't read all of everything sent to us, but the system in the department allows for 80–90% of scripts to be read fully. A proportion of those scripts are read up to four times. The NT is publicly funded and we have a responsibility to read new plays, though the system is always under review. I open everything that comes in and make a decision with the Senior Reader about what goes a stage further. It's like panning for gold: you always hope that you're going to come across something extraordinary.

Aside from reading plays and developing writers, Bradley's other functions can involve adapting or cutting a play text, writing articles for programmes (particularly for new plays), giving talks and undertaking educational outreach work. He attends rehearsals and comments as required, regarding himself as an 'outside eye'. The writers' attachment scheme at the NT has flourished, and Bradley observes that some writers choose an attachment over a commission because they might prefer to develop their play through the studio rather than work in isolation. The NT has raised the number of writers' attachments from six to twelve because of the non-delivery of studio commissions.[64]

> Bringing the writer into the theatre itself is the great strength of the attachment system. It allows the writer to connect with actors and directors in a way that a commission doesn't. There's no doubt that by being pro-active and inclusive the NT has

generated more work that is appropriate to its stages. There are certainly times when I've put a case for a particular project: for example, I was all too aware of the paucity of plays by black and Asian writers, and set up the Writers' Development Initiative: money was ear-marked and Kwame Kwei-Armah and Trevor Williams both forged their careers through the scheme.

When I started out I used to go and find mentors for the writers on attachment, but as writers have matured they act as mentor to the younger ones. Nick Drake, Lucy Davies (who is Head of the Studio) and I all share mentoring rôles. You have to protect writers and give them creative space: when I assigned Lyn Coghlan to be Tanika Gupta's mentor a few years ago I told her I didn't necessarily want to see the first three drafts. I don't show Nick [Hytner] or the Associate Directors early drafts because I don't want to air a play before it's ready.

One of the major cultural shifts in the NT is what Bradley calls the 'evolution of environment' for writers. Before his arrival dramatists invited to work in the studio rarely saw their work realised on the main stages, but there is now a movement of writers from the studio into the main house and vice versa.

I might develop a play through one-to-one discussions with the playwright, through readings, exploratory workshops or through workshop productions. I would say that I have dramaturgical skills but do not act as a dramaturg in the continental sense of a dramaturg working with a director: I think play advocacy is to be commended but is of limited value in a system which vests power in a director-led theatre. Plays need champions and directors are the best champions where a playwright is concerned. The dramaturg shouldn't be a buffer between the writer and director, and any relationship established with a writer must clearly define the limits a dramaturg has in decision-making.

A new play is workshopped in the studio before it goes to the main stage, and Bradley cites the experiments on Kwame Kwei-Armah's *Elmina's Kitchen* (2003?), in which all four possible endings were tested out; the three two-week workshops on Philip Pullman's *His Dark Materials* (2003); and the two weeks David Hare spent working with actors in the studio on *The Permanent Way* (2003).

A cultural shift is also evident in the strategic programming of new writing:

> The AD has the last word on selecting the repertoire. I don't necessarily attend Board meetings, but unlike Tynan's day the Board do not involve themselves in artistic decisions. Obviously, I do have to think about actors when I'm proposing a play, but play selection is more about having the right idea for the right moment. I think in terms of the full spectrum of colours, a selection that is interesting for classical and contemporary alike, and of course I'm obliged to honour the dramatic canon. The process of play selection is multi-faceted, something many people can't fully understand because the factors alter with the project. For example, there will always be a creative tension between the desire to present the new voice with the responsibility to nurture the emerging writer, that is, to produce more than one play by a writer.
>
> I believe strongly that new writers have to be protected: you can't just throw them to the wolves. A limited and protected run on the smallest stage, the Cottesloe, is one way to programme a new writer and that's what we did with Zinnie Harris's *Further than the Furthest Thing* (2000). In 1995 we programmed David Hare's *Skylight* mid-week because we knew we didn't have to worry about pulling in audiences and put Patrick Marber's *Dealer's Choice* on at the weekend. We've also experimented with short preview periods for new plays, taken them off for a while, and allowed the reviews to sell the play before it comes back on. Programming is connected to marketing. For *Elmina's Kitchen* we completely changed our marketing strategy and leafleted areas with high populations of blacks and Asians, like Hackney and Brixton. We couldn't rely on a good review in the *Guardian* to sell tickets to those audiences.

A second institutional shift has been the commitment to expanding the contemporary international canon; Bradley argues that the NT is less 'conservatively European and more catholic in taste' and has set up schemes such as 'Channels' and 'Intertext' to teach a new generation of writers how to translate plays, and exchange partnerships exist with Austria, France, Quebec, the Czech republic and Argentina.

> I'm of the view that plays need to be translated by playwrights; our in-house policy is to do versions rather than straight translations. I was conscious that we tended to turn to the same small group of people for translations: Martin Crimp for Marivaux, David Lan for Chekhov, and Nick Wright for Ibsen. We ran masterclasses for people embarking on it for the first time. Translating is an extremely good way of learning about play structure and offers a good income for new writers, but more than anything it is healthy to widen the pool of experienced translators.

The Royal Court

Mindful of Barker's experiments the Royal Court has maintained its status as a national house of cutting-edge new drama,[65] particularly since George Devine's Artistic Directorship from 1956 to 1965. Following the success of Osborne's *Look Back in Anger* in 1956, Devine worked strenuously to ensure that the Royal Court became identified as 'a symbolic centre of rebellion and dissent among young artists, intellectuals and theatre workers'[66] – and the capacity to generate controversy remains an integral part of the theatre's identity today. During the 1990s the Royal Court's position as an international house of new writing gained considerable prestige: under Stephen Daldry's Artistic Directorship from 1993 to 1996 the annual number of productions doubled from nine or ten to its current nineteen. Situated in Sloane Square, west of central London, the main house seats *c*. 400; the Theatre Upstairs, a small studio which seats *c*. 80, was added in 1969 and enabled the production of low-budget new plays. The Royal Court currently receives an annual public subsidy and has been completely refurbished, and it has entered a new age of commercial patronage with the Jerwood Foundation.[67]

The first officially titled Literary Manager, whose *sole* responsibilities were literary management, was Rob Ritchie, who served from 1979 to 1984; directors and playwrights had previously been designated to supervise the script-reading system and correspond with authors. In the late 1950s directors William Gaskill and John Dexter were responsible for script-reading, followed by Keith Johnstone (1965–8), Christopher Hampton (1968–70), David Hare (1969–70), Ann Jellicoe (1973–5) and Richard Crane (1978–9).[68] Ritchie's successors were Michael Hastings (1985–6) and Kate Harwood (1988–91), both playwrights, and Mel Kenyon (1991–2, now a leading agent) and Robin Hooper (1992–4).[69] The current Literary Manager, Graham Whybrow, appointed in 1994, had worked as a barrister and had taken work as a playreader to assuage a consuming passion for theatre.[70]

Whybrow sees his chief responsibilities as typical for the Literary Manager of a new writing theatre: finding and developing plays and writers for production; fostering relationships with developing writers whose work may be produced there or elsewhere; managing relationships with writers, including commissioning and developing scripts before rehearsal;[71] and giving notes to the director as required at run-throughs and premières. The Royal Court receives *c.* 3,000 plays a year and Whybrow has a part-time Literary Assistant who helps with reading, script report writing and general administration. Whybrow argues that

> Reading plays is too often dismissed as a laughably easy
> pursuit; in fact it is an extraordinarily refined skill. I train my
> assistants very carefully and select freelance readers only after
> I am satisfied that they are able to make significant inferences
> about a play's performative potential: a reader has to have the
> imagination to think about what will interest actors, what
> directors need, how an audience will react emotionally,
> intellectually and aesthetically, and has to understand dramatic
> form. I train readers empirically, and my potential freelance
> readers undergo an informal probationary period of a few

weeks: I generally give them a mixture of plays and see how
fast, responsive and analytical their assessments are – if
they are out of tune with the artistic policy of the Royal Court
then I can't rely on their judgement. At present I have five
readers, but the ideal number would be eight. Readers have to
be able to spot potential and make imaginative leaps: it's rare
for a play to arrive in perfect form – new voices are often raw
and uncompromising and literary critics might view them as
'flawed', but those are the voices that could challenge the
canon and create excitement, and the question 'What is a
play?' must always remain open. I try to select readers from
diverse backgrounds, a mixture of playwrights, directors and
script advisors who are sometimes linguists or academics –
people with a specialist knowledge. I've noted that some of my
best readers have been people who are creative in another
medium, artists or sculptors, who have an instinct for *making*
things and an intuition about a singular, emergent voice.[72] Of
course, I ask for internal readers, especially when a play is
of interest; initially I give a promising play to the Artistic
Director and to the resident playwright, but if I think the play
is one we should snap up then I send a copy to as many people
as I can internally.

Whybrow does his best to open his post every day and examine plays
carefully as they arrive. He is sceptical of the debate about processing
'unsolicited' scripts.

> I do not accept the terminology 'unsolicited'; if a theatre has
> a Literary Manager or a reading system then plays are being
> openly solicited. I would not relish a system where all the
> filtering happens through internal theatre contacts and literary
> agents – in France and Germany I think it's led to the
> deprivileging of the writer and the artistic supremacy of the
> director and it can leave new writers without any means of
> access to theatre.[73]
>
> It's my responsibility not to miss the play with a
> difference, and I carve out time to make sure that I don't.

Remarkable plays have landed on my desk and the moment
I become so pressurised that opening the post is under threat
I know it's time to reorganise my priorities. I try to build
in many safety-checks. Apart from logging each play and
checking on whether we have existing reports on the
playwright's previous work, I read the first page, and if I'm
arrested I read the first scene of a play, and should the play
be particularly compelling I read it the same night. If I'm
persuaded that there is no time to lose I can take an option on
a play before the Artistic Director has read it – it is essential to
be able to act swiftly. Plays that I do not read all the way
through are filtered through my literary assistant and are sent
out to readers. I try to return plays within a matter of weeks,
and plays which have no hope of production at the Royal
Court are usually sent back within seven days. It's a constant
struggle to manage the tide of manuscripts, but it is vital for
both the theatre and for writers that the system is efficient.
A report is filed on each play, and I also train readers and
assistants in the art of writing assessments: I want a useful
archival resource and reports which give an accurate
representation of content, form, technical requirements, and
linguistic style. Some of my predecessors wrote reports for the
writers and sent them back with the play, but I felt that I had
to concentrate on building a confidential data resource for the
theatre, and I cannot fulfil the rôle of a public service for
myriads of aspiring writers because I am in the business of
looking for plays with production potential for the Royal
Court,[74] so a simple letter is sent either rejecting, or accepting,
or asking the writer to come and discuss their work further
with me.

Whybrow organises weekly script meetings where promising
plays are discussed and encourages debate by selecting readers who
will have different views on a play as champions and critics.

If a play causes red-hot discussion it's usually a good sign. The
script meetings are inclusive events by which I mean that

everyone is engaged in searching for and discussing the plays in question: the worst thing I could do for the culture of the Royal Court is to claim that I 'discover' all the plays. These meetings also raise awareness of writers and writing, and should ideally provide a map of all that's worth talking about in the new writing world.

Script meetings are attended by Whybrow, his Literary Assistant, and generally the AD, associate directors, resident playwright, Director of the Royal Court Young People's Theatre, Literary Associate (playwright Stephen Jeffreys) and perhaps other playwrights or directors associated with the theatre. Whybrow sometimes asks other members of staff – box-office, sound, lighting, or casting staff – to read plays and attend:

> Including people who may break a consensus is an illuminating exercise. Sometimes I've removed the title page of a play and the name of the author to free up opinion-forming and remove the inhibitions readers may have about canonical or established authors. There must always be a dialectic in the discussions between the play in question and the artistic context of plays produced at the Royal Court. Value judgements on plays are made in specific historical, cultural and material circumstances which themselves relate to the identity of the theatre: I make judgements about plays *in relation to their suitability for production at the Royal Court* – if I am emphatic about this point it is because I think that many people, both inside and outside the institution of theatre, underrate the degree to which Literary Managers have to think constantly about the broader issues of forging and maintaining a theatre's identity, and the broad cultural impact of the decisions made here at the Royal Court. (see fig. 7.1, p. 217)

Programming is decided in meetings between Whybrow and AD Ian Rickson, who is ultimately responsible for the selection of plays but who relies on his Literary Manager to present powerful cases.

> I stand firmly behind the Artistic Director even if I sometimes disagree with his choice. I'd say out of nineteen plays a year

I might have a strong objection to one. My objections are not based on personal preference but on my judgement about a play within the context of the Royal Court and all that it stands or artistically – on occasion I've fought passionately for plays which, on a purely subjective basis, I've disliked. For me the three key features of programming are energy, quality and diversity. From the Artistic Director's point of view I am a Literary Manager who delivers plays and writers with no agenda other than a desire for them to reach the stage; this is important because naturally many directors find plays that they would like to direct and they can become proprietorial about a particular play or playwright, which in turn can give rise to conflict. It's the Artistic Director's prerogative to decide on a director for a play, and I am actively involved in putting forward suggestions for directors, but I do so from the perspective of matching the play and its writer with a particular director's interests and talents. Creating a culture which fosters new writing has much to do with fostering a respectful and responsive director–playwright relationship.

Whybrow is adamant that his major rôle is to create a culture that fights for, fosters and defends new writing.

The Royal Court declared itself a writers' theatre in the 1950s, and I am very conscious of the heritage of George Devine and the ethos of opening up theatre to as many voices from different backgrounds as possible and of 'the right to fail'.[75] Of course subsidy is a necessary condition for a producing theatre, but the conditions in which new writing can flourish also have to be right, so I have to make sure that the culture within the Royal Court is vibrantly receptive to new playwrights. As Literary Manager my job is to advise the Artistic Director on how to make a good set of choices; I do so by restlessly and creatively questioning what the conditions for a culture of new playwriting are, and I never presume that the prevailing conditions are satisfactory – complacency is lethal in literary management.

Since Devine's reign the writer has traditionally been the core artist at the Royal Court, and the actors, director and designer are expected to reveal the play, not use it as a vehicle for self-promotion. A new play culture, argues Whybrow, must respect the writer's legal and financial rights, and at the Royal Court the writer is consulted about the director, designer and casting, has the right to attend rehearsals, is paid for doing so and earns advance payment and a 10 per cent royalty from the box office.

Whybrow views his function as a critical presence in rehearsal as limited and does not align himself with continental production dramaturgs:

> I am expected to advise on cuts and changes to a text for
> run-throughs and previews, obviously this isn't ideal but it
> can happen. Once a show is in production my rôle can become
> more that of a fire-fighter: the 'right to fail' policy of the Royal
> Court means that there is always a risk that a playwright is
> in advance of public taste, or that critics will not respond
> imaginatively to a particular play, or that audiences might be
> thin, or that the play has not reached the point of adequate
> refinement – working on new plays is a sophisticated,
> demanding task and you have to remember that there are
> high-profile directors who regard new work as such a risk to
> their reputation that they won't take it on. I've been involved
> in my fair share of midnight fire-fighting meetings. Once or
> twice I have worked with the director to cut a play radically:
> I could sense the audience's bafflement and incomprehension
> and I could see ways of bringing out the rhythm, pace and
> clarity of the play. Happily such occasions are rare. I usually
> attend run-throughs once in the third and once in the fourth
> week, and the dress rehearsal. Clearly if there are problems
> I attend more frequently and I can be attending a play at preview
> and beyond press-night to try and gauge audience reactions.
>
> During the rehearsal stages I can act as an 'ear' for the
> playwright, I listen to what they say about the process and
> monitor their experience. I do give notes to the director, but

not in the Kenneth Tynan style of sudden-death memos which I think reeked of officialdom and authority and foreclosed on constructive dialogue. I talk informally to the director, and my critical rôle is to think about the relationship between the staging and the script; the Artistic Director can give very useful notes on directing if required. I do not act as a production dramaturg in the continental sense: my rôle is to foster the relationship between playwright and director and I worry that the Brechtian model of the dramaturg is born of defensive cultures which perceive the need for radical intervention between the writer and the director: such models are built on the idea of parent–child or teacher–pupil relationships and suggest that there are fixed sets of principles which can solve 'problems' in a play.

In Whybrow's eyes, the more successful a writer becomes, the more redundant the Literary Manager should be.

The Royal Shakespeare Company

The RSC[76] is based in Stratford-upon-Avon and owns three buildings: the Royal Shakespeare Theatre (RST),[77] which seats *c.* 1,500; the Other Place, a studio theatre built in 1974 with a seating capacity of 176; and the Swan, a thrust-stage playhouse theatre constructed in 1986 that seats *c.* 440. The artistic policy is dedicated to achieving standards of national and international excellence in staging Shakespeare and to the production of old and modern classics, as well as new plays (generally premièred at the Other Place). An ensemble company, the RSC has toured its work regionally since the 1970s, and with increasing success internationally from the 1980s.

Peter Hall, AD 1960–8, first began proceedings to formalise playreading at the RST. A formidable classical playreader himself, he was bolstered by John Barton, who acted as director, Shakespearean scholar and textual consultant, as well as adapter and moderniser of classic plays;[78] Barton was a self-taught dramaturg possessing all the critical, directorial and literary skills that Brecht recommended and who saw himself as bridging academic and theatre practice.[79] In 1960

Hall acquired the Aldwych Theatre for the RSC and transformed it into a new writing as well as a classical play venue:[80] he needed a playreader and adviser for new plays and informally asked John Holmstrom to work part-time in the last weeks of 1959; once officially AD, Hall engaged Holmstrom as full-time 'Adviser to the Company on literary and other matters' from 31 October 1960.[81] Holmstrom recalls: 'an un-magic mountain . . . a torrent of bottom-drawer scripts, in prose or verse, submitted by once- (or never-) successful British or American writers'.[82] Contractually, Holmstrom's other duties involved translations (paid *ad hoc*), necessary rewriting for RSC productions and a requirement to 'cover and report on such productions by other companies as we may require, including reports on artists, directors and designers'.[83] In practice, Holmstrom was rarely required to perform this latter function as Hall had his own ideas regarding play selection and decision making, seeking Holmstrom's advice only minimally. Holmstrom remembers attending 'a few cabinet conferences at Hall's home, where we would debate for hours and come to agreed conclusions, only to find a few days later that Peter had decided something completely different'.[84] Holmstrom had neither the institutional nor the personal power of Tynan, and in a reversal of Tynan's career pattern was seduced away from theatre to a full-time position as theatre reviewer eight months later.[85] As with Tynan, there was a consciousness that German theatre structures provided a potential model for Holmstrom, but it was not investigated and 'the term "Dramaturg" was used colloquially but not in documents'.[86] Jeremy Brooks[87] followed Holmstrom as 'Adviser on Plays', and in 1970 after Trevor Nunn took over the directorship (1968–86, co-AD with Terry Hands from 1974) Ronald Bryden was employed as 'Play Adviser'.[88] From 1977 Walter Donohue read new plays for the RSC's experimental venue at the Donmar Warehouse. Colin Chambers's appointment as 'Literary Manager' from 1981 to 1997 consciously acknowledged Tynan's example and accepted the need for a high-status literary specialist at the centre of the organisation.

My rôle as Literary Manager was evolved in the crucible of practice in the best traditions of English pragmatism – it couldn't be any other way given that this is a national culture which stigmatises intellectuals. I didn't believe, like Tynan, that you could transform a company with revolutionary ideals, and I think I was much less polemical than some people expected.[89] I was the writers' advocate and took my greatest pleasure in this function. I was of the view that the RSC needed a broad canvas and needed to encourage more women writers and more ethnic writers, but at the time, though I fought, decisions regarding new plays were usually more conservative than I liked.

As a company the RSC was conscious of public subsidy and committed to reading new plays, even if little came of it. I was in charge of reading scripts (I recall having 1,000 new plays in my office at one time), was on the planning committee for the repertoire – though decision-making often happened outside the planning committee and could be rather chaotic because it tended to depend on individual directors. I certainly tried to manage the balance of the repertoire. I managed relationships with writers, did research for individual directors if required and as relationships developed became an informal sounding board for ideas. I was involved in the editing of some texts, I attended run-throughs when possible and tried to see a new play through all its writing and production processes. I acted as a trouble shooter with plays in difficulty during rehearsal, and was regarded as a repository of the RSC's history by the press and publicity department.

During my time the pressures of economics meant that the RSC became increasingly corporate and the result was that new plays became increasingly marginalised. In the 1990s the audience came to be viewed by management as 'clients' and latterly I felt that the RSC had lost touch with its audiences and ceased to generate a dialogue with them.[90]

Simon Reade was Literary Manager from 1997 to 2001. His early decision to change the RSC's reading policy and cease processing unsolicited scripts caused considerable controversy, but he did not see it as the duty of a national house to respond to hundreds of unknown, aspirant writers a year and was quite clear that he was 'not a public service'.[91] He argued that

> a lot of writers' efforts were being wasted in the vain hope that this established, classical theatre company with its own particular, evolving new writing ethos based on commissions, would commit to a new work by a new writer, when there were many other dedicated companies whose *raison d'être* is to do just that.[92]

Paul Sirett, Reade's successor, appointed in 2001, is divided on the issue of unsolicited scripts ('officially, we don't read them'), but in any case, finds his workload extremely demanding.[93] Titled 'Dramaturg', Sirett describes the managerial responsibilities of his post as 'huge', and says that 'time-management becomes a distinct challenge when you are required to look both within and outside the organisation'. Sirett attends rehearsals selectively, acts as a representative of the RSC at specific national and international events and spends his time reading manuscripts, liaising with writers and directors and ensuring that he is 'plugged in' to developments in new writing at other theatres both at home and abroad. Correspondence alone is a vast task, and Sirett deals with thousands of inquiries from the general public. His brief also extends to the classical repertoire, and he is involved in researching and finding plays for a particular season, organising and commissioning translations,[94] researching different versions of a play and, depending on the director, may be asked to do the cuts on a script.

Sirett began his career as a playwright and came to dramaturgy through his relationship with the Theatre Royal, Stratford East (London), where five of his own plays have been produced. 'Every relationship with a writer is different', he argues, 'and with every new project, I establish what the protocol will be between myself, the writer, the director, and the producer.' New writing, he asserts, is 'essential' to the RSC, and 'enriches and informs' the classical work. Currently the company is exploring new ways of working with new material, including scripting and devising: the New Work Festival in 2004 specifically used the term *work* rather than *writing* to indicate an emphasis on looking at alternative modes of theatre-making. Process is something that the RSC is keen to share with its public, and the current AD, Michael Boyd, has opened up certain theatre-making processes to audiences. Traditionally, English theatre pratitioners have been secretive about process, so Boyd's policy change is signifi-cant.[95] Sirett is an advocate: 'we learn from the audience's response, and hopefully they learn about performance. It's a way of giving spec-tators access to theatre-making.'

Sirett is aware of the confusion surrounding the work of the dramaturg, but is very clear about its meaning where his own practice is concerned:

> I do understand the term 'dramaturg' as denoting something different from 'Literary Manager'. This is a simplistic defini-tion but I understand a Literary Manager to be someone who manages a literary department and has responsibilities to other departments, and is a person with business and budgetary acumen operating as an expert administrator as well as a literary specialist. A 'dramaturg' is a practitioner who is involved in the actual production processes and the rehearsals of a play or performance, and is practically involved in theatre-making. Ironically, I'd say that I was more of a dramaturg when I was a Literary Manager at the Soho Theatre [from 1994 to 2001], and that though I have the title of Dramaturg now I am far more of a Literary Manager! The volume of production at the RSC is so great that I can't be involved in every performance.

At the time of writing Sirett's rôle is about to change. He will specia-lise in production dramaturgy at the RSC (as well as spend more time on his own writing), and a new Literary Manager will be appointed. He thinks this division of tasks is an obvious solution and a more focused way of managing a workload that is too substantial for one person. The employment of two high-profile literary specialists certainly marks a new departure for the RSC.

Case studies: the regions

Literary management and new-writing developments in the regions are still undergoing an extraordinary and rapid revolution. In the 1990s the Birmingham Rep's researches into their audiences reflected a crisis in many regional theatres: overwhelmingly audiences were white, middle-class and over 45 (one in five was aged over 65): 'Nationwide, traditional audiences for regional theatre were literally dying out.'[96] Currently, regional theatres are undergoing a distinct renaissance and flourishing because they are winning new audiences for new writing.[97] Much of this reversal in fortunes is directly attributable to the deployment of literary managers and heavy investment in development schemes for new writers. A decentralisation of funding has given Regional Arts Boards a stronger hand in deciding how to apportion subsidy, and grass-roots new writing projects and development work have benefited substantially. In the last five years regional new play development organisations have strengthened their links with mainstream theatres, and in areas such as the Midlands and the north-west collaborations on script-reading and more strategically organised liaison with writers have led to exciting discoveries of new talent and a new confidence that plays produced in the regions can be at least as important as any play staged at a main house in London. What is very evident when discussing the situation with literary managers and dramaturgs in the regions is a sense that each one is inventing a new theatrical landscape and tapping into audiences who traditionally may not be regular theatre attenders. A new progressiveness and experimentalism in attitudes to theatre-making is being encouraged by these same literary managers, many of whom feel that the London and mainstream houses are constrained by the habitual conservatism of their audiences and critics. Ten years ago new writing in the provinces was piecemeal and ill-funded and local playwrights struggled to find access to development schemes and stages. Today regional literary managers speak of the way their work is 'transforming' theatre and 'democratising' new writing practices: it is clear that their work has only just begun and that intitiatives like the Theatre Writing Partnership (see below) offer intriguing models for the way that new writing may be serviced in the future.[98]

The Birmingham Rep

The Birmingham Rep has existed since 1913 and was the first purpose-built British repertory theatre. It was rebuilt in 1971 and its main house seats 700, while the Studio dates from 1972 and seats 140; the Studio was renamed the Door when it reopened in 1998 with a new writing policy. Ben Payne arrived as Literary Manager in 1995, and in consultation with the theatre's executive managers he has transformed the new writing culture. His title is now Associate Director and he has a full-time Literary Officer who helps him to manage a broad range of projects, plus two freelance Literary Associates who assist with the Young Writers' Scheme Transmissions. Mainly concerned with the Door, which is a platform for new work, Payne develops artistic policy, organises the programming, advises on directing and casting, directs and fund-raises for writing projects, attachments and residencies, and sees his main rôle as supporting a writer at any or at all points from development to commissioning and production (depending on need he may attend rehearsals). He aims for a minimum of four in-house productions of new plays a year. Unsolicited scripts are no longer read all year round, instead reading is centred on finding writers for the attachment programme – and there may be anywhere between two and nine writers attached to the theatre at a time. Before his tenure at the Rep, Payne worked for the new writing organisation writernet (formerly New Playwrights' Trust), and he acknowledges that his research for them on mentoring schemes for writers and on the collaborative partnerships between writers and artists from other disciplines informed aspects of his current development strategies.

> In policy terms, the theatre executive acknowledged that we needed to develop work that was diverse enough to appeal to the increasingly diverse audiences, and this, by implication, meant more new work. The writer is central to our development, and to education and outreach work in the Door. But the definition of 'writer' is flexible: we might develop work with a performance poet, for example, if we think they have an artistic energy and that this connects with the audiences we want to connect with. Writers on attachment can work on their own if they choose, but

I encourage them to work with other theatre practitioners and artists from other disciplines if appropriate.[99]

Payne is clear that the shift in his title marks a commitment to a more proactive writing policy: the term 'Literary Manager' came, in his mind, to be associated with a desk-bound individual 'operating a complicated script rejection system – it seemed a negative way of coming at new writing'. Painfully aware that 95 per cent of the scripts he read while Literary Manager were not suitable for performance at the Rep, Payne began to see that he had to invent ways of having 'more creative relationships with writers during the development of their work'.

> I think a great deal about our strategic positioning as a theatre: what sort of work are we doing and why, who is involved in the projects and productions and why. Since we wanted to explore different ways of making theatre and shift away from the well-made tradition that tends to dominate certain theatres, we needed different sorts of people from the conventional literary manager. We wanted to work with different writers from different communities. You can't just sit and wait for writers to come to the theatre, you have to create the opportunities for them to meet and work with you. It helps to develop an idea with a writer so that they aren't operating in a vacuum. The Young Writers' Programme here has been an extraordinary success: I'm seeing writers who started with us at 14 getting professional commissions. The programmes, workshops and projects we run provide a pathway for writers into theatre as well as television, film and radio.

Payne is excited by the energy of new writing in his constituency and reflects that new playhouses in London are increasingly ill-served by the narrow perspective that reviewers impose on them. His one lament is the difficulty of obtaining more money for commissions and productions. Sponsors and trust funds currently invest in development work, he argues, and he would like to see equal enthusiasm for product as there is for process.

Liverpool Everyman Theatre and the Liverpool Playhouse

Run by the same organisation since 1999, the Liverpool Merseyside Theatre Trust, the Liverpool Everyman and Liverpool Playhouse are separate buildings. The Playhouse is a Victorian proscenium-arch theatre with a capacity of 700, and the Everyman is a 1960s construction seating 450. Suzanne Bell was appointed to the permanent post of Literary Manager in 2001 in the wake of a decision by the theatres' Board of Directors, the Arts Council of England and Liverpool City Council to commit to new writing at both local and national levels.[100] Liverpool theatres had not employed a literary manager for some time, so Bell's first priority was to implement an efficient reading service.

> I receive about 500 unsolicited scripts a year. When I arrived I realised that writers had simply been sending their plays into a black hole. Local writers were frustrated and disillusioned. The volume of reading was so great that I had to employ a team of readers – I now have three professional readers who work freelance for me. I read any script that they think holds a kernel of interest. I meet the readers weekly or fortnightly, depending on what they have for me. Every play is read and responded to within eight weeks. The tide has turned now and writers are very appreciative of our support. I also set up a writers' database, which provides information on funding, commissions, career development, writing events and competitions. Over 800 people have registered.[101]

Bell thinks Liverpool is unique for the vibrancy of its writing culture, and from the first was very conscious of the city's tradition in new writing. She took her cue from the writers themselves, and has modelled her job description to suit their demands.

> When I arrived I met up with playwrights and asked them 'What makes a good Literary Manager?' I met directors and talked to the internationally acclaimed dramatists of this city: Alan Bleasdale, Willy Russell and Jimmy McGovern. What I have fashioned comes from a constant dialogue with writers. You can't walk anywhere in this city without falling over a

writer – it's brilliant! I think there was some scepticism from
established playwrights when I arrived: they asked me 'What
is a Literary Manager? What do you do?' I was an unknown.
But those same writers are now thoroughly committed to the
writing projects here and are very excited about the burning
new talents that we're staging. By the end of 2004 we will have
produced four new plays, three by local dramatists and one a
European première. We're aiming to commission four new
plays in 2005.

Bell has a background in directing on the London fringe, and assistant-
directed at the Royal Court from 1998 to 2000. She also assisted and
directed at the Royal Exchange, Manchester. She analyses scripts
'with a director's eye', and observes that it is not unusual for literary
managers to be directors.[102] Her system for decision-making about
productions is strongly influenced by her time at various theatres in
England (particularly the Royal Court's Young Writers' Scheme) and
time spent in the United States.

> The scripts that we produce are chosen through a script meeting
> process. There are nine people in the core group, but anyone in
> the building can come along, and everyone votes for the script
> they want. Often feelings run very high. When we read Laurence
> Wilson's *Urban Legend*, I was receiving text messages at seven
> in the morning from people who couldn't be at the meeting but
> wanted to register a positive vote!

The second priority for Bell was the establishment of the Young
Writers' Programme, already distinguished by launching the career
of Katie Douglas with *Fly*, which gained enthusiastic reviews and
ensured further commissions by London theatres and a residency at
the National Theatre. The Young Writers' Programme caters for
16–25-year-olds, offers fifteen places a year and is divided into three
terms. Bell runs the weekly workshops, which concentrate on the
'fundamentals of playwriting', redrafting processes, different dramatic
genres and different media, and at the end actors are invited in to give
readings of the playwrights' work. Bell is insistent that the programme

also has to introduce young playwrights to new writing cultures. In addition, she runs a writers' attachment scheme. All three writers on the scheme from 2003 have secured a production.

> It's rare for writers attachment schemes to be as successful as this, but I find that writers in Liverpool respond to challenges you set them in the most vigorous way. I try to ensure that writers have the opportunity to meet as many other professional practitioners as possible, and offer them financial support to see a broad range of new writing across the country. It has a huge impact on them and opens their eyes to another world. The writer-in-residence, Tony Green, is a local who worked incredibly hard and who went through some very tough times creatively, but he won through.
>
> In response to demand I set up New Leaf in 2004. This is a non-age-specific writers' group who meet fortnightly. The writers have greater experience and the idea is that the group helps to broaden their knowledge of new writing nationally. I want to arrange for more workshops and masterclasses for older and established writers. Theatres tend to concentrate on the very young because of the way funding works. I already run writers' masterclasses and workshops on Saturdays when professional writers and directors come in and work with our local writers, but more needs to be done and I have to set about fund-raising.[103]

Bell does not work as a production dramaturg in the Brechtian sense, but she acts as a researcher on the classical plays produced at the Liverpool Playhouse. She spends much of her time developing new drafts of plays with writers, and attends rehearsals of any developing writer's play as much as possible.

Bell is quite adamant that new writing is:

> keeping the theatre in Liverpool alive. The plays are topical, political, funny and full of energy. Tony Green's new play *The Kindness of Strangers* (2004), about asylum seekers, is absolutely in the Everyman Liverpool tradition: it delivers a hard political punch but is also an epic extravaganza. At the Every Word event,

a festival of new writing we held, we got audiences of 400 for the readings, which is staggering. Hopefully, Liverpool is rapidly on its way to becoming a new writing centre of excellence, and since it is also the European City of Culture in 2008 we have the opportunity of being on a world-wide stage. The theatre here is a political debating space. The writers feel they own the space, and the audiences are coming because they can relate to the stories being staged. My wishes for the future would be for a studio space, a designated workshop space, more in-house productions, more international work and more funding of actors to help develop a writer's work. I think there are prejudices about regional theatre, but there is a plethora of new writing productions happening outside London. These are exciting times, and I firmly believe that new writing is the way to keep theatre fresh, challenging and engaged.

The Royal Exchange Theatre, Manchester

Run by a group directorate and situated in the heart of Manchester, the Royal Exchange is a theatre-in-the-round built in 1976 that seats 750. Its studio theatre dates from 1998, has 90–100 seats, is uniquely a blue box (as opposed to a black box) and a flexible space with three movable walls and no fixed seating. The architecture, like that of Alan Ayckbourn's theatre in Scarborough, suggests a desire to develop an intimate relationship with audiences. Sarah Frankcom, Literary Manager from 1999 to 2004 and now Associate Artistic Director, runs the Literary Management Department with Jo Combes, who was appointed Associate Director in 2004. Both women direct at the theatre and argue that this is their strength when it comes to developing budding playwrights. Frankcom trained as a drama teacher, worked on Theatre-in-Education projects, and workshopped new plays at the National Theatre Studio. In particular, she learned much from established playwright Robert Holman. Since arriving at the theatre, Frankcom has sought to change the way new writing is managed and produced.

When I came the Literary Department was run in an old-fashioned style. The Literary Manager read and responded to scripts, commissioned writers and went out and about to see plays. The directorate decided that they wanted a practical, hands-on person more in the tradition of a dramaturg. I run workshops for writers and try to discover what works and doesn't work about a play. Recently we've revised our policy on script reading: we now prioritise writers from the north-west and the UK. We get 400 to 600 unsolicited scripts a year, and as many again from agents. The prioritisation is about using the resources we have effectively. A play of interest circulates amongst the Associate Directors and Artistic Directors, and if we are all keen we either commission the writer, go straight for production, or invite the writer to begin a dialogue with us and encourage their work.[104]

The Royal Exchange is committed to a strong new writing policy and aims for a high percentage of new plays in its annual programme. Frankcom is clear that the challenge of filling a 750-seat regional theatre is tough, and that strategies in Manchester are very different from those adopted in London.

We've got a lot better at getting plays into the right shape before we produce them. New plays don't arrive in a fully formed state. Increasingly we identify writers with original voices, but their theatrical experience is limited. We try to school fledgling writers in the classical and contemporary repertoires. New writing is vital for new audiences and for a new generation of theatre practitioners. If we can't make theatre relevant to the now and engage our spectators then theatre will become obsolete.

Thinking of ways to bring in new audiences is a preoccupation: a recent experiment to entice the younger audiences who attend the Studio to book for a show in the main house has been successful, but Frankcom is passionate about the importance of community partner-ships and liaison with schools. Only by going out into the community, she asserts, can there be any chance of raising the curiosity of people who do not normally go to the theatre.

We work increasingly with other agencies. For instance, we have a good relationship with the Theatre in Prisons Centre, and have done projects with young offenders and North West Playwrights.

Jo Combes trained as a director at Lamda and worked at the Orange Tree Theatre. She attended a director's course at the Royal Court, and acknowledges that the Court's 'strong social conscience for new writing' had a powerful impact on her.

I think a director's eye is crucial when you're reading a play, as you have to deal with it practically. Plus, I have the power to arrange rehearsed readings, and if there is agreement, to take a play into production at the Studio and direct it myself.

She stresses the importance of corporate sponsorship by Bruntwood in relation to the recent new writing competition at the Royal Exchange, Write no. 2, and the writers' attachment scheme. Currently four writers are on attachment: depending on their theatrical knowledge they shadow different aspects of work in the theatre and watch a play through from rehearsal to production. Combes runs 'tutorials' for these writers, where further work is developed and canonical plays are read and discussed. She has also formed a writers group from the most promising local playwrights. The cultural renaissance in Manchester, and the renewed investment and prosperity of the city, have created a strong desire in audiences to see the work of distinctive northern dramatists, Combes argues, and she is proud that the Royal Exchange continues to discover original local voices.

The Stephen Joseph Theatre

Located in the coastal town of Scarborough, in North Yorkshire, the Stephen Joseph Theatre (SJT) comprises two auditoria, the Theatre in the Round and the McCarthy, seating 404 and 160 respectively. The current building, designed by Sir Alan Ayckbourn,[105] opened in 1996, but the 'Studio Theatre Company' was originally founded at the

Library Theatre by Stephen Joseph in 1955 and subsequently moved to the Westwood Theatre.[106] Ayckbourn has been in post since 1970 and is unique in England as both an established, working playwright and AD of a theatre. Like Brecht, Ayckbourn is a renaissance man of theatre who began as an actor, became a writer and director, and has acquired a formidable technical and design knowledge of stage craftsmanship. The artistic policy states that

> The SJT will work to produce imaginative, new and entertaining theatre, overcoming usual 'customer resistance' to the untried and untested.
>
> In addition to the classics we will encourage novel, potentially commercial theatre, exploring the boundaries of what might be classed as 'popular drama'.
>
> New generations of actors, writers, directors and technicians will be helped to develop their talents, take artistic notes, and flourish.
>
> The SJT will develop and expand a touring policy.[107]

Currently there are ten to twelve productions per year and 80 per cent of the repertoire is usually new work. The SJT relies on subsidies amounting to 54 per cent of its running costs: recently funding has been awarded by the Arts Council, Yorkshire Arts, Scarborough Borough Council and North Yorkshire County Council. The post of Literary Manager has evolved since the late 1980s when Gordon Townsend, a director, took responsibility for script-reading. Conol Orton worked initially as an assistant director at the SJT from 1995 and further developed the functions of literary management, later assuming the title of Literary Manager. The current Literary Manager, Laura Harvey, was appointed in April 1999, has a full-time, open-ended contract and directs two productions a year. After completing a degree in English, she trained as a director at the Derby Playhouse, where she revitalised the studio space and developed writers, designers, directors and actors.

When Ayckbourn became AD in 1970 he rapidly noted that his workload had a detrimental effect on the time available for him to read plays.

I read for a time but couldn't keep pace and became alarmed at how few scripts I could manage to read. There needed to be someone officially designated to develop relationships with writers so that they weren't fobbed off or lost through negligence. Initially an associate director read for me and over time the position of the Literary Manager evolved. I think it is vital to extend writers the courtesy of reading their work; of course, many plays are bad and are sent back with a discouraging letter, and many are simply not right for this theatre. The plays we do tend to come through Laura – she's a filter and a judge. Writers' early plays may not be quite right but the writers themselves may be interesting and we invite them to visit the theatre, see the spaces and get a sense of the audiences. I'm looking for intelligent, entertaining plays which address the widest possible audience; I don't look for writers who write like me – there'd be no point in that at all. Theatre these days has to be an event which exploits its live qualities to the full, it's not enough to do play after play, so I'm looking for ideas which will fill a theatre, an idea which will raise people's curiosity.

Harvey's main literary and administrative functions are commissioning, programming, playreading and managing her team of playreaders. Decision-making about repertoire happens through discussion between Ayckbourn and Harvey and is approved by the Financial and General Administrators. Harvey learned much about literary management from a professional friendship with Ben Payne, Literary Manager at Birmingham Repertory Theatre, while she was working at the Derby Playhouse. She receives 500–600 plays a year.

This theatre does not develop what I call grass-roots level playwrights, by that I mean those at a basic stage of their learning curve and I refer such writers to development organisations such as North West Playwrights and Yorkshire Playwrights. I have to concentrate on plays that can be produced and this generally means I am looking at new plays by writers who are more advanced in terms of their writing career.

I do all the reading for the writers we have worked with before, for scripts which come from agents, or for those who have caught my eye. I delegate the reading of unsolicited scripts to a core team of six readers, who are all writers, actors or directors and are people whose judgement I trust. Readers must have an innate sense of theatricality. There are two major questions for them to address when reading: does the play excite them? is it workable on stage? I have come across readers who can write fantastic analytical reports based on content but who do not necessarily have imaginative vision for the theatrical potential of a piece of writing. It's not practicable to have readers' meetings because my readers are spread over a wide geographical area and the money is better spent on commissioning a playwright. I communicate with my readers by phone and we talk through each play individually so that I can tailor feedback for the writer. If a play is praised by one of my readers then of course I read it. Reading for a theatre-in-the-round is a specific skill and one which I would say I am still learning about, whereas Alan has an in-built clock for the space and knows which plays will hold.[108]

It is no accident that Ayckbourn has traditionally appointed readers and literary managers who also work as directors. He argues that

What new writers tend to lack is technical expertise, their work is often not *dramatic* in its sense of staging. I want writers to be able to talk to someone who has a head for directing. I've always wanted writers to have the chance to learn about all the colours on the theatrical palette, to think about lighting, sound, design and stage effects. A Literary Manager who sits in their room isolated from practice cannot help writers in the ways that they most require. In fact, I want everyone in the building to know as much as possible about plays in production and I always hold open read-throughs and encourage all my staff to come: the workshop need to know what they're building sets for and the box office need to know what it is they're selling.

Harvey agrees that her work as a director ensures that she actively relates to everyone in the building, from those in the workshop to the actors themselves, and 'is very much part of the community of theatre workers as opposed to a predominantly desk-bound official'. Harvey attends rehearsals of new plays as much as possible, but does not vocalise in rehearsals.

> I can't commit to full-time attendance of rehearsals when I'm not directing myself and as a director I know that I wouldn't want someone else vocalising while I'm at work. Alan designed a viewing gallery above the rehearsal space and feels strongly that writers and directors should observe rehearsal as much as possible. Any member of staff can go into the viewing gallery and everyone is encouraged to take an interest in plays in rehearsal. I talk outside the rehearsal room with the writer and director as appropriate. The more experienced the writer the less I am needed. It depends on relationships: I talked a great deal with the last writer-in-residence about their play-in-progress. Textually, the culture here is to fix as much as possible before a play goes into rehearsal. A dramaturg can be very valid if the director recognises that they need help with the early stages of the textual work, but both Alan and I are very skilled at developing and directing new work so I'd say that the post would be redundant at this theatre.[109]

Ayckbourn is clear that his Literary Manager 'preaches and develops the ethic of the theatre' and may be someone who has different views about theatre to himself but who sees the possibilities of the SJT. Ayckbourn found that running a theatre had a 'terrifically beneficial' effect on his writing, and remains acutely aware of the privileges that come with such a position.

> No one then or now questions one's artistic policy – I'm so established that no one censors my work. I can be writer, director and designer because I have a theatre at my disposal – this explains my output of fifty-seven plays. It was an accident that I took over after Stephen Joseph's death, not something I'd ever

planned. Certainly I was aware that Brecht had run a theatre and I was intrigued by his freedom to develop work without restraint, but I wasn't influenced by Brecht as a playwright.

Harvey is excited by the artistic freedom which Ayckbourn's status offers and finds it refreshing that she can 'think big', though frequently finds that her AD 'thinks bigger'. She has to find an equilibrium between promoting an inspiring identity and profile for the theatre and balancing the books, and has plays on her shelf she would like to stage but which are beyond budgetary means. She is optimistic, however, about improved channels of communication between Literary Managers and what she feels is an increasing tendency to share knowledge and pass on plays which may be producible at other theatres.

Harvey regards part of her rôle to be 'Alan's eyes for new work' and keeps a close watch on new plays in London, often travelling to see plays in person. She monitors international new work and reads plays in translation, arguing that 'You have to know what you're not programming too.' She undertakes research when required, and occasionally writes for programmes and does in-house publicity for a play. Increasingly, she finds herself acting as a creative information channel for writers whom she is keen to encourage, and makes new scripts available to stimulate and challenge their development. The education team at the SJT do community outreach work, so Harvey has a minimal educational rôle, occasionally leading a literary management or directing workshop for local colleges.

Harvey is very conscious of an over-concentration of arts funding in London.

> The need for literary management is the same in the regions as it is in London, and though things are changing, some regions are still very underserved by literary managers and it means that some good writers go elsewhere or remain undiscovered.

Harvey's post is maintained at the expense of an associate director, and Ayckbourn went against Arts Council recommendations in privileging a literary management position. Ayckbourn estimates that he spends 90 per cent of his time in the rehearsal room and takes only four weeks off at a time to write a play, having planned it in his head over a period of months. He opines that Harvey's post symbolises the ethic of placing writers at the heart of the theatre, and that she fosters a culture which he does not have sufficient time to manage himself. Ayckbourn is conscious of continuing a tradition that believes in the inclusion of the writer in theatre production.

> This, again, is the effect of Stephen Joseph's influence on me. In the 1950s the average playwright lived in the equivalent of a garret or a crofter's cottage, and was certainly not part of the fabric of a theatre's operations. A writer's experience of performance was largely first-night horror at what had been inflicted on his script. Stephen was very much part of a movement to reintroduce the writer to the theatre environment, and as a writer I am indebted to him for that. I avoid the term 'studio' space for the McCarthy theatre: I think the word is shot through with prejudicial implications which call to mind obscure, pretentious plays watched by minute audiences. I've always felt that you can't say to a writer: 'It doesn't matter if nobody comes' – you deny the whole point of theatre. I write for the McCarthy; you put a play on in the space for which it is most suitable, and you shouldn't ghettoise new playwrights and effectively curb their imaginative potential. I try to give our writers-in-residence an extended period at the theatre. Ideally I'm looking for a relationship with a writer that goes beyond doing a single play, I'm always seeking years not months from a writer. Laura is the vital and visible anchor for writers who work with us as well as for the writers we want to attract.

The Theatre Writing Partnership, East Midlands

The Theatre Writing Partnership is a scheme that is jointly funded by a group of theatres: the Nottingham Playhouse, the Derby Playhouse, the Leicester Haymarket, the Northampton Theatres and New Perspectives (a rural touring company). Esther Richardson was appointed Literary Manager to the East Midlands Region in 2001 and is based at the Nottingham Playhouse although she is responsible to all the theatres above; her title has since changed to Director of the Theatre Writing Partnership. The scheme came about through an attempt to solve a simple pragmatic problem: the sheer volume of unsolicited scripts received in the region, which were not being screened or pursued effectively. In three years the project has mush-roomed into a concern of unprecedented scale.

> Now the Theatre Writing Partnership runs a regional writers'
> programme, a young writers' programme, workshops and
> manages various grass-roots writing projects and mentoring
> schemes. We both commission and produce a lot of work. I have a
> full-time Theatre Writing Assistant, a trainee dramaturg and a
> trainee children's theatre writer. I do the project management,
> fund-raising, the artistic strategising and the producing. This is a
> major enterprise. I also direct, but not within the Theatre Writing
> Partnership. At any one time I might be liasing with up to eight
> directors. Sometimes I attend rehearsals, depending on what
> individual directors want, but time constraints mean that I can
> never attend the whole run.[110]

Richardson was an assistant to the RSC's dramaturg, Simon Reade, from 1999 to 2001, and witnessed first-hand the way that the complex politics of a large organisation can marginalise writers. She expresses her frustration with what she calls 'a self-esteem problem amongst Literary Managers', and argues that it is vital that they fight their way into executive positions so that they can exercise real power.

Inspired by the way the Theatre Writing Partnership has had such an impact on new writing, Richardson is convinced that the project is empowering the region theatrically and creating vital ports of entry for playwrights.

> I am fascinated by the huge investments being made in regional
> development work. The Theatre Writing Partnership has
> surprised everyone by its phenomenal success. I am certain that
> this is the tip of the iceberg: in ten years I think the hierarchy
> of national theatres and new writing will have been completely

redefined. The crisis in theatre criticism means that a small minority of conservative voices promote the work of a few venues and writers. This will change because theatre needs a whole new wave of writers from different bckgrounds to keep it exciting and inspirational. I really do think regional theatres have a huge part to play in the future of a lively and colourful new writing culture.

Notes

1. I refer here to the employment of a person officially designated 'Literary Manager'. Both theatres had deployed unofficial or semi-official playreaders or advisers before this time.

2. As of October 2004 full-time appointments in London: the National Theatre, the Hampstead, Polka, the Royal Court, the RSC, the Soho, Theatre Royal (Stratford East), Paines Plough, the Bush. Many of these literary managers also employ assistants. Part-time appointments are at the King's Head, Chelsea Theatre, Etcetera, the Gate, the Red Room, Mo-lan, Talawa, Clean Break, Unicorn, Croydon Warehouse, Finborough, Theatre 503, the Orange Tree, Kali, Graeae, Out of Joint. In the regions the full-time posts are at the West Yorkshire Playhouse, the Stephen Joseph Theatre, Live Theatre, Northern Stage, the Royal Exchange, Liverpool Everyman, Birmingham Rep, New Writing Partnership, Theatre Royal (Plymouth), Chichester, and Watford Palace. Some of these concerns employ other literary personnel.

3. The conference was held on 8.3.1997 at the Young Vic Theatre. See Jonathan Meth, ed., *Commissioning the Future* (London: New Playwrights Trust, 1997).

4. The New Playwrights Trust (NPT) was founded in 1985 to raise the profile and status of new writing for the theatre. In 1999 NPT became 'writernet' and its profile more information- and research-oriented in the recognition that new work is now presented by many theatre companies in England and the battle fought by many hands.

5. Ben Payne, Writers' Expo, Soho Theatre, London, 9.11.2002.

6. I gathered information from 1998 to 2004 for the purposes of this book.

7. See David Edgar, ed., *State of Play* (London: Faber and Faber, 1999), p. 4.

8. *Ibid.*, pp. 26–32, especially p. 28: 'up from the single figure percentages of the late 1980s, new work represented over 15% of the repertoire of building-based theatres between 1993 and 1997. Further its box office performance – below 50% in the late 1980s – rose to 53% in 1993–94 and thence to 57% in 1996–97, outperforming adaptations, post-war revivals, translations, classics and even Shakespeare.'

9. Ireland is following suit. See Rosy Barnes, 'The Lit Man (and Woman) Cometh', *Irish Theatre Magazine* 2.8 (spring 2001): 21–6, and 'Decoding the "D" Word', *Irish Theatre Magazine* 2.9 (summer 2001): 43–50.

10. See George Rowell and Anthony Jackson, *The Repertory Movement: A History of Regional Theatre in Britain* (Cambridge: Cambridge University Press, 1984). The authors note (p. 176) that 'The concern with the development of new drama was central to the repertory movement from its earliest discernible beginnings.'

11. See Catherine Itzin, *Stages in the Revolution* (London: Methuen, 1980).

12. For an early history see Robert Hutchison, *The Politics of the Arts Council* (London: Sinclair Browne, 1982).

13. Interview with author, 16.9.2004, Cambridge.

14. Esther Richardson, Theatre Writing Partnership, interview with author, 1.10.2004.

15. The long-established Dramaturgische Gesellschaft meets annually in Germany, as do the Literary Managers and Dramaturgs of the Americas (LMDA).

16. See www.dramaturgy.co.uk.

17. Statement collated by Hanne Slattne after consultation with members. Email to author, 4.11.2004.

18. Members are from England, Scotland and Wales.

19. Telephone interview with Alison Gagen, Theatre Officer for the West Midlands, 15.10.2004. Gagen became intrigued by the subject after learning of director Annie Castledine's very public attack, denouncing dramaturgs as unnecessary. Charles Hart is

organising the Arts Council-funded discussions for literary management and dramaturgy.

20. See Chris Smith, *Creative Britain* (London: Faber and Faber, 1998) which effectively operates as Blair's arts manifesto. Curiously, it has little to say about theatre.

21. They merged with the Writers' Guild in 1997 to form the Writers' Guild of Great Britain.

22. There is much documentation on this and a long history to which I cannot do justice here. I am grateful to Lloyd Trott for generous access to his personal archives.

23. Interview with Ian Brown, founder of North West Playwrights, 21.1.1998, Edinburgh.

24. The Talawa Theatre Company and Nitro (formerly Black Theatre Co-operative), the Oval Theatre and the Theatre Royal in East London participated in these projects, which were encouraged by Tony Craze, then Literary Director for London Arts Board. Interview 6.9.1999, London. The training of dramaturgs was organised as a shadow scheme: trainees observed professional dramaturgs at work with writers and on productions.

25. Playwright Winsome Pinnock believes that 'structural problems within the theatre itself conspire against the development of plays by black and Asian playwrights'. See Vera Gottlieb and Colin Chambers, eds., *Theatre in a Cool Climate* (Oxford: Amber Lane Press, 1999), p. 34. Pinnock is quite right. At the time of writing there is only one full-time dramaturg from an ethnic minority in England.

26. See project documentation: Tony Craze, ed., *Going Black Under the Skin* (London: New Playwrights Trust, 1997), pp. 1, 11, 13.

27. The dramaturg was playwright Noel Greig. Telephone interview, 11.4.1998.

28. See project documentation: John Deeney, ed., *The Mentoring Scheme for Women Writers* (London: New Playwrights Trust, 1996). There were six writers and six mentors, women playwrights or performance writers.

29. *Ibid.*, p. 14.

30. *Ibid.*, p. 6.

31. See Chloe Veltman, 'dramaturg. dramawot?', *NPT News* 119 (1998): 7–8, 7.

32. Jonathan Marks in Susan Jonas, Geoff Proehl and Michael Lupu, eds., *Dramaturgy in American Theater* (New York: Harcourt Brace, 1997), p. 31.

33. Robert Brustein, *ibid.*, p. 33.

34. Terry McCabe, *Mis-directing the Play* (Chicago: Ivan R. Dee, 2001), p. 65.

35. *Ibid.*, p. 70.

36. *Ibid.*, pp. 71–2.

37. A parallel debate about the legitimacy of producers to make interventions in the artistic process has been running for some time at the Arts Council of England. Interview with Alison Gagen, 15.10.2004.

38. Interview with author, 29.9.2004, London. Subsequent quotations from the same interview.

39. Interview with author, 16.9.2004, Cambridge. Subsequent quotations from the same interview.

40. Michael Kustow, *Theatre@risk* (London: Methuen, 2000), pp. 165 and 229.

41. Suzanne Bell, interview with author, 22.9.2004. I should stress that Waters has a high regard for Bell's work in Liverpool.

42. This concern has been raised in the US too, where playwright A. R. Gurney fears the 'individual voice' may be under threat by development dramaturgs. See Oscar Brockett, *The Essential Theatre*, 8th edn (New York: Harcourt Brace, 2004), p. 309.

43. Interview with author, 10.5.2004, London. Whelan: 'No doubt Blair would call it "the people's theatre".'

44. McCabe writes of production dramaturgs: 'If Trotsky had been this ineffective, Stalin would have let him live.' *Mis-directing the Play*, p. 70.

45. Interview with director, Sue Dunderdale, 29.9.2004, London.

46. Giles Croft at the Nottingham Playhouse is former Literary Manager of the NT; and Simon Reade at the Old Vic was Literary Manager for the RSC.

47. Interview with author, 29.9.2004, London.

48. The Central School of Speech and Drama began its dramaturgy option in 1997, organised by Nick Wood. David Edgar, Professor of Playwriting at the University of Birmingham from 1989 to 1999, initiated the MA in Dramaturgy in 1998. Lloyd Trott began the MA in Dramaturgy at Goldsmiths' College in 1999 and teaches on the MA at King's College. Edgar's interest in literary managers and dramaturgs came from a long-term professional curiosity as a playwright and a recognition that playreaders received little help to hone their craft. Trott has worked formally and informally as a dramaturg in new play development for over three decades. Wood's initiatives began in meetings with continental dramaturgs who had academic and professional training. The University of Glasgow runs a much respected MA in Dramaturgy and has strong connections to Scottish theatre companies for training purposes. The only undergraduate course for dramaturgs and literary managers in Britain was founded by Ian Brown at St Margaret's College, Edinburgh, in 1996.

49. 'Mentors or Censors?' was conceived and organised by David Edgar, Mary Luckhurst, Graham Whybrow (Literary Manager at the Royal Court) and Vicky Featherstone (Artistic Director of Paines Plough, a company specialising in new play development) and took place on 29–31 January 1999. See Mary Luckhurst, 'Mentors or Censors?', *NPT News* 123 (February 1999): 3–4. The second conference, 'Dramaturgy: An International Symposium', was collaboratively organised by the Central School of Speech and Drama and Total Theatre and took place at the Central School on 17–19 September 1999.

50. See Jonas *et al.*, eds., *Dramaturgs in American Theater*, p. vii.

51. Graham Whybrow at the Royal Court and Ben Jankovich, formerly at the Hampstead Theatre. Interviews with author, 12.12.1997, London, and 8.4.1997, Birmingham, respectively. In order to try and avoid the problems, the courses at St Margaret's College and Goldsmiths' College incorporate placements with theatre companies, thus giving students direct knowledge of at least one particular dramaturgical model. In America there are anxieties about the effect of so many Liberal Arts graduates implementing an unhelpful ideological hold on play selection processes.

52. See Jonas *et al.*, eds., *Dramaturgs in American Theater*, p. 79.

53. Alain Girault, ed., 'Dramaturgie', *Théâtre/public* 67 (1986).

54. The symposium document is 'Über Dramaturgie/On dramaturgy/ A propos de dramaturgie/Over dramaturgie', *Theaterschrift* 5–6 (1993).

55. Used, for example, at Writers Expo, organised by Writernet at the Soho Theatre, 9.11.2002.

56. The honorific 'royal' was granted in 1988, but has now been dropped.

57. See Peter Hall, *Diaries*, ed. John Goodwin (London: Hamish Hamilton, 1983), p. 50.

58. Simon Callow, ed., *The National Theatre: The Theatre and its Work 1963–1997* (London: Nick Hern Books/Royal National Theatre, 1997), p. 54.

59. Wright is a playwright and was co-Artistic Director (with Robert Kidd) at the Royal Court from 1975 to 1977. Croft was valued for his knowledge of the classical repertoire.

60. Hytner was initially AD designate.

61. Bradley was Literary Manager at the Soho Poly Theatre, London; he was part-time from 1989 to 1992, then full-time from 1992 to 1994, and specialised in developing new playwrights through readings, workshops and productions. Bradley began as a playwright and was increasingly asked to read and comment on others' work.

62. Telephone interview with author, 5.10.2004. Subsequent quotations are from the same interview.

63. Jack Bradley quoted in 'New Writing at the National', In Robin Butler, programme to Tom Stoppard's *The Coast of Utopia* (2002).

64. Bradley was expecting attachments to number 20 in 2005.

65. For histories of the Royal Court, see Philip Roberts, *The Royal Court Theatre 1965–1972* (Cambridge: Cambridge University Press, 1986) and *The Royal Court and the Modern Stage* (Cambridge: Cambridge University Press, 1999); and Richard Findlater, ed., *At the Royal Court: 25 Years of the English Stage Company* (Derby: Amber Lane Press, 1981). For intriguing piece-meal information on playreaders, script meetings and informal

literary management systems, 1956–1981, see Gresdna A. Doty and Billy J. Harbin, eds., *Inside the Royal Court Theatre, 1956–1981* (Baton Rouge: Louisiana State University Press, 1990).

66. Findlater, ed., *Royal Court*, p. 29.

67. Many trusts and foundations support the Royal Court, as well as sponsors, private subscribers, benefactors, and American friends. West End transfers have also helped fill the coffers.

68. Hampton was funded by the Arts Council as resident dramatist, but the Royal Court also made him superviser of scripts. He found playreading duties overwhelming: 'as resident dramatist, there was only one function I could find no time to perform: writing' (see Findlater, ed., *Royal Court*, p. 116). Hampton was allowed to employ David Hare to help with his script duties. Playwright Ann Jellicoe was the first female playreader and script superviser of prominence. Very little was paid to the superviser of scripts, but it was a way of connecting a promising playwright to the theatre and of providing a stimulating creative environment for them. Since the 1980s resident dramatists *and* Literary Managers have been employed.

69. Kenyon's appointment moved away from appointing promising playwrights as Literary Manager, recognising that literary management did not give playwrights time to develop their own work. List of unofficial and official playreaders and literary managers compiled by Graham Whybrow and Maja Zade.

70. As a reader for the Royal Court, Whybrow notably recommended plays that were turned down internally but succeeded elsewhere. Stephen Daldry, then AD, consequently employed Whybrow when the post of Literary Manager became vacant.

71. Once a director is assigned to a production, Whybrow usually works jointly in advising the writer on rewrites. This and other unattributed quotations are taken from an interview with the author, 28.1.1998, London.

72. Often the best readers were/are playwrights, and Whybrow's examination of the confidential script report archive at the Royal Court found that Edward Bond's script assessments demonstrated that he was a 'star reader' in the late 1950s and early 1960s.

John Osborne's method of rejecting a play, conversely, was always to write 'suitable for television'; see Doty and Harbin, eds., *Inside the Royal Court*, p. 89.

73. This issue is being addressed in Germany. The Baracke Theatre in Berlin found ways of outflanking orthodox channels and staging new writers; it has close contacts with Whybrow and employed his former Literary Assistant, Maja Zade, as a dramaturg in spring 1999. Royal Court playwrights, especially Mark Ravenhill and Sarah Kane, have been fashionable in Germany for some time.

74. Whybrow felt too many previous reports to writers had been politic rather than helpful, sparing the writer's blushes at the theatre's expense.

75. Legendary words, encapsulating the experimentalism of the Royal Court, attributed to Tony Richardson, who worked with George Devine. Devine felt that only through the production of new plays in a designated building would aspiring writers be drawn to the theatre and established writers spurred on to improve.

76. For comprehensive background to the RSC from the nineteenth century to 1980, see Sally Beauman, *The Royal Shakespeare Company: A History of Ten Decades* (Oxford: Oxford University Press, 1982), David Addenbrooke, *The Royal Shakespeare Company* (London: William Kimber, 1974), and Colin Chambers, *Inside the Royal Shakespeare Company* (London: Routledge, 2004).

77. The first Shakespeare Memorial Theatre at Stratford-upon-Avon was opened in 1879; the present building, opened in 1932, was renamed the Royal Shakespeare Theatre in 1961.

78. Barton still performs all these functions.

79. 'It's perfectly possible to bridge the two worlds – there's much that militates against it in English culture, of course – but I've effectively done it all my working life.' John Barton, interview with author, 6.10.1996, Trinity College, Cambridge.

80. Hall had demonstrated an eye for new writing talent as manager of the Arts Theatre, London, 1954–9, where he directed many British premières, including Beckett's *Waiting for Godot* in 1956.

81. Letter to author from John Holmstrom, 17.1.1999. He was paid £850 plus expenses *p.a.*, which he considered not ungenerous; his professional background was varied and involved playwriting, translating, reviewing, work for literary agent Peggy Ramsay, and employment as an announcer for BBC Radio 3.
82. *Ibid.*
83. *Ibid.*
84. *Ibid.*
85. He continued to read *ad hoc* before being replaced by Jeremy Brooks. *Ibid.*
86. *Ibid.*
87. Brooks was a Russian specialist and translator.
88. Bryden had taken over from Tynan as theatre critic on the *Observer* when the latter left for the NT.
89. Chambers had been a member of the Communist Party.
90. This and subsequent quotations are from an interview with the author, 14.12.1998, London.
91. *Ibid.* It is interesting that the decision not to read unsolicited scripts is contentious in England. On the Continent scripts are generally filtered through literary agents and directors before landing on dramaturgs' desks; in England, unless a theatre or company producing new plays expressly states that they do not read unsolicited scripts, it is accepted that they do. Colin Chambers felt that Reade's decision 'reinforced the idea of theatre as a private club'.
92. See Reade, 'Young Blood', *Time Out*, 3–10.9.1997, p. 139.
93. Interview with author, 28.9.2004, Stratford-upon-Avon. Subsequent quotations from the same interview.
94. Sirett commissioned fifty literal translations of plays for the Spanish season in 2004.
95. Equally significantly, Boyd trained as a director in Eastern Europe and so is familiar with dramaturgs in theatre-making.
96. See Claire Cochrane, *The Birmingham Rep: A City's Theatre 1962–2002* (Birmingham: Sir Barry Jackson Trust, 2003), p. 169.
97. See 'New Plays take centre stage at theatre awards', *Guardian*, 18.10.2004.

98. Esther Richardson, telephone interview with author, 1.10.2004.

99. Interview with author, 1.10.2004. Subsequent quotations from the same interview.

100. There was no AD at the time. The current AD, Gemma Bodinetz, was appointed in 2003.

101. Telephone interview with author, 22.9.2004. Subsequent quotations are from the same interview.

102. Bell referred to Alex Chisholm at the West Yorkshire Playhouse (Leeds) and Sarah Frankcom at the Royal Exchange (Manchester).

103. Funding for the various writing schemes is provided by the Arts Council, Five Arts Cities, North West Playwrights and BBC Northern Exposure.

104. The author interviewed Sarah Frankcom and Jo Combes by telephone on 27.9.2004. Subsequent quotations are from the same interview.

105. Ayckbourn's planning was meticulous, using all his theatrical experience to create and promote a tight-knit creative community of theatre-makers (the theatre has ninety full-time and part-time staff). He designed the observation room in the rehearsal space, and positioned his own and the Literary Manager's office as close to the rehearsal space as possible. Interview with the author, 27.1.2000, Scarborough. Subsequent quotations are from the same interview.

106. Stephen Joseph (1927–67) profoundly influenced Ayckbourn and pioneered popular 'theatre-in-the-round' in England, believing an actor's relationship with the spectator was much more direct than in proscenium-arch theatre. See Stephen Joseph, *The Story of the Playhouse in England* (London: Barrie and Rockliff, 1963); *Theatre in the Round* (London: Barrie and Rockliff, 1967); and *New Theatre Forms* (London: Isaac Pitman and Sons, 1968).

107. Artistic policy statement supplied by Literary Manager, Laura Harvey.

108. Interview with author, 27.1.2000, Scarborough. Subsequent quotations from Harvey are from the same interview.

109. Ayckbourn believes observation is critical for writers: 'The pure instrumentalists of theatre are actors and unless a writer watches

an actor intently and watches them work at their craft they will never understand that their words are simply providing a score-sheet for actors.'

110. Esther Richardson, interview with author, 1.10.2004. Subsequent quotations from the same interview.

8   Conclusion

Books written against an established academic and intellectual grain, as this one is, make possible many kinds of conclusion. If they succeed in commanding readers and forcing revaluations, they invite correction, application and enlargement by others – and I am sharply aware of how much more can be said, especially in integrating English and particular continental European theatre histories. I equally believe that the methodological framework and the historical outline I propose of English dramaturgical development since Lessing enable that further work; certainly they most clearly inform the answer I can now give to the questions with which I began more than a decade ago, as a theatre-maker in an English province observing something in process and unable to make sense of it.

The meanings of the terms *literary manager* and *dramaturg* are relative and determined by the particular cultures and institutions in which individuals operate, but the functions remain. Lessing and Brecht provide the major models, but practice in England is complicated by the fact that variants on these models have also been imported via the US. There is still powerful resistance to the theorisation of literary management and dramaturgy in England (where resistance to theory *per se* is not limited to theatre). Dramaturgical appointments on the Continent are supported by an ethos that criticism and research are an integral part of artistic creation, but in general the English dislike and resent intellectualising theatre. Although the need for greater administrative efficiency has been painfully apparent to many of those suffering the consequences of muddle and neglect, and has over time prompted the emergence of

263

increasingly specialised posts within theatres and companies, reform has been belated and until the 1960s overridden by ubiquitous commercial pressure, the dominance of (actor-)managers, and an entrenched, self-serving territoriality that construes collaboration and formal delegation as potential threat. The influence of foreign models, notably Lessing and Brecht, has been severely inhibited by partial translation of theory and misunderstanding of practice. For indigenous theorist-practitioners the situation is worse: Archer and Barker are only selectively read or considered; Tynan's literary management has been written out of history; that Ayckbourn is far more than a writer of comedies comes as a surprise to many who know his name well; and startlingly few academics or critics think even to ask about the fundamental politics of who selects plays, by what criteria, and for what purpose. There has been little attempt to understand why English theatre made official dramaturgical appointments so late in comparison to many continental countries; there is little realisation in current theatre criticism that such appointments may be important, though commentary and theorisation would provide insight to a world still largely rendered 'invisible' and would enable us to begin to understand the lessons to be drawn from the experiences of those appointed to these posts. Continental dramaturgical systems are not an automatic panacea, but do provide alternative models of analysing and organising administration and production processes.

In England a silent revolution in the professionalisation of literary management has taken place since the 1960s and is transforming theatre cultures, especially those connected with new writing. New divisions of labour are emerging and as change continues so territorial battles are likely to become more intense. Increasing numbers of dramaturgs and literary managers underline the fact that the theatre industry needed more efficient systems of finding and developing writers. The proliferation of literary managers demonstrates an impetus to privilege issues connected with playreading, play selection, writer development and artistic policy-making; as theatres engage in competitive battles over audiences for new plays or new angles on classic plays, the literary manager becomes ever more strategically important. The revolution is driven by a pervasive cultural anxiety that subsidised theatre may lose its audiences unless a ready supply of new and self-scrutinising plays can be found for theatre-going constituencies who wish to see the contemporary, post-colonial realities of England reflected on stage. This anxiety relates, in particular, to audiences of under 40 years old, and most literary managers and development dramaturgs spend a good deal of their time formulating strategies for wooing younger audiences. Beyond doubt, the primary context for the urgency of finding new plays includes a crisis of national identity informed by the loss of empire, by devolution and by an isolationist stance in relation to Europe.

The link between economics and the appointment of literary managers and dramaturgs is clear: the emergence of literary managers and dramaturgs has been enabled by a post-war state subsidy of the arts, particularly for institutions of national and regional significance. A link with the politics of the *Zeitgeist* is also clear: both literary managers and dramaturgs have flourished in the post-imperial crisis, as 'Great Britain' breaks up and the idea of a uniform, unified England erodes. Tynan's post (like Lessing's and Brecht's) was created in the consciousness of national resonance, but the increasing number of dramaturgical functionaries appointed in the last quarter of the twentieth century reflects awareness of the complex politics of group and minority identities, and of diverse theatre-making and theatre-going constituencies whose bureaucratic acknowledgement has chimed with the general post-war ethos of democratising education (and the more specific mantras of equal opportunity, multiculturalism and political correctness).

It is not yet clear whether production dramaturgs will become culturally embedded in England, as in Germany and the US, but the signs are that the English are nervous of their encroachment on territories traditionally designated to writers and directors, and that they are currently employed on short-term contracts. Development dramaturgs or writing mentors work in most new writing theatres or for development organisations, mainly on short-term or freelance contracts, and the need for them is not widely contested, though there are significant doubts about their systematic employment in some quarters. Certainly, the ever-growing deployment of dramaturgs *per se* indicates a heightened reflection on the processes of play-making and a desire to explore other ways of creating performances. All the signs are that there is a gradual shift in culture towards activity both in preproduction and in the rehearsal room; the same movement from office worker to hands-on theatre-maker that Brecht outlines in the *Messingkauf Dialogues*. The empirical approach within theatrical institutions, which has traditionally distrusted analysis and only grudgingly rated the value for practitioners of formal training above 'genius', is changing fast. At the same time, the boom in literary managers and dramaturgs points towards a greater concern for product and for matching the 'right' product with the 'right' audience. Literary managers have to think of markets more than ever before, and this is not always conducive to producing the best art. On the Continent and in the US state subsidy of theatres is on a wholly different scale, and the acculturation of dramaturgs depends as much on massive subvention as it does on further shifts in theatre-making practices. Investment in literary management and writer development requires funding over and above usual subsidy levels, and it is interesting that corporate sponsorship is playing such an important part in funding.

The main casualties of the lack of organised literary management and dramaturgy at a theatre are writers, and it could be argued that far from being under threat from the revolution in literary management, writers are being privileged. But the situation is complex. The stage is not automatically representative of its audiences, and changes in economic and cultural policy, and an era of political correctness, have led successive recent governments in England to believe that things can only be transformed through intervention and positive discrimination. State subsidy is driven more and more by politically motivated criteria, and an openly Blairite pedagogy unquestioningly underlies current structures and strategies of state-funded investment.[1] In many respects these policies have benefited certain minority constituencies. What is especially striking is that the state is implicitly acknowledging that theatre has a moral and political purpose, which cuts against traditional views of English theatre as a site of recreation as opposed to education. Non-subsidised, purely commercial theatre, which in England tends not to deploy dramaturgs, escapes the fulfilment of an educational remit, but is driven by the machinery of big business – often a great deal more dictatorial. In an age where state intervention in all educational and cultural sectors has increased, and where managers and marketing have become the instruments of implementation, it is perhaps no surprise that literary management has boomed. Whilst appointments of literary managers and dramaturgs are clearly politicised, the extreme representations of them as in some way totalitarian are worst-case scenarios and result from misunderstanding and prejudice. As with Lessing and with Brecht, there is an underlying pedagogical programme that has informed the proliferation of literary managers and dramaturgs, but it remains to be seen whether theatre-making will flourish or succumb to a new orthodoxy, and what rôle dramaturgy will (be seen to) play.

Note

1. See Jen Harvie, 'Nationalising the Creative Industries', *Contemporary Theatre Review* 13.1 (February 2003): 15–32.

Select bibliography

The bibliography is organised as follows:

Unpublished materials
  Interviews conducted by the author
  Other materials
Printed materials
  Articles, etc.
  Books
Film, video and television

Full details of collections cited as sources in 2a appear in 2b. Dedicated issues of journals cited in full appear in 2a under the name of the journal editor with a cross-reference from the journal title; similarly, project documentations, interim conference reports, etc. appear under the name of the editor or author, with a cross-reference from the name of the theatre, company, or other sponsoring institution.

Unpublished materials
Interviews conducted by the author

Alexander, Francis, 18 November 1997, 24 January 2000.
Ayckbourn, Alan, 27 January 2000.
Barton, John, 6 October 1996.
Bell, Barbara, 21 January 1998.
Bell, Suzanne, 22 September 2004.
Böhm, Vera, 6 December 1996.
Bradley, Jack, 18 November 1997, 5 October 2004.
Braun, Volker, 4 December 1996.

Brown, Ian, 21 January 1998.

Chambers, Colin, 14 December 1998.

Combes, Jo, 29 September 2004.

Craze, Tony, 6 September 1999.

Dunderdale, Sue, 29 September 2004.

Frankcom, Sarah, 27 September 2004.

Gagen, Alison, 15 October 2004.

Greig, Noel, 11 April 1998.

Harvey, Laura, 27 January 2000.

Hecht, Werner, 5 December 1996.

Jankovich, Ben, 8 April 1997.

Kemp, Edward, 29 September 2004.

Kenyon, Mel, 14 December 1999.

Maglia, Kelly, 24 January 2000.

Mulvey, Louise, 6 December 1999, 21 March 2000.

Payne, Ben, 1 October 2004.

Reade, Simon, 14 December 1998.

Richardson, Esther, 1 October 2004.

Sirett, Paul, 28 September 2004.

Trott, Lloyd, 29 September 2004.

Veltman, Chloe, 12 December 1998.

Waters, Steve, 16 September 2004.

Wekwerth, Manfred, 4 December 1996.

Whelan, Peter, 10 May 2004.

Whybrow, Graham, 12 December 1997, 28 January 1998.

Other materials

Brecht, Bertolt, note dated to 1954, in the Bertolt Brecht Archive, Berlin.

Chandos, Oliver Lyttelton, Viscount, draft speeches, notes, and other materials held in the Chandos Papers in the Churchill Archive, Cambridge.

Heymann, Herr, letter to Kurt Bork, 1 April 1949, in the Helene Weigel Archive, Berlin.

Holmstrom, John, letter to the author, 17 January 1999.

Jachmann, G., 'De Aristotelis didascaliis' (unpublished dissertation, University of Göttingen, 1909).

Memorandum and Articles of Association of the National Theatre Board, in the National Theatre Archive, London.

Notes, minutes, and other materials held in the Bertolt Brecht Archive, Berlin.

Notes, minutes, and other materials held in the Helene Weigel Archive, Berlin.

Protokoll der Betriebsversammlung. Notes on a Berliner Ensemble board meeting held on 4 January 1956, in the Helene Weigel Archive, Berlin.

Rülicke, Käthe, letter to Herr Heinen, 9 May 1956, in the Bertolt Brecht Archive, Berlin.

Stern, Tiffany, 'A History of Rehearsal in the British Professional Theatre from the Sixteenth to the Eighteenth Century' (dissertation, University of Cambridge, 1997).

Tynan, Kenneth, unbound manuscripts held as the Tynan Papers in the British Library, London.

Printed materials

Articles, etc.

Alexander, Francis, ed., The Chelsea Centre *Annual Report* (1998).

Archer, William, 'The Mausoleum of Ibsen', *Fortnightly Review* 54 (July 1893): 77–91.

Arnold, Matthew, 'The French Play in London', *Nineteenth Century* 6 (August 1879): 228–43.

Barker, Harley Granville, 'At the Moscow Art Theatre', *Seven Arts* 2 (1917): 659–61.

'Repertory Theatres', *New Quarterly* 2 (1909): 491–504.

'Two German Theatres', *Fortnightly Review* 89 (January–June 1911): 60–70.

Billington, Michael, 'Hindsight sagas', *Guardian*, 29.12.1999, G2, pp. 10–11.

'The other Marx brother', *Guardian*, 10.2.1998, G2, p. 9.

Burnand, F. C., 'Authors and Managers', *Theatre* (February–July 1879): 17.

Canaris, Volker, 'Style and the Director,' trans. Claudia Rosoux, in Hayman, ed., *German Theatre*, pp. 250–1.

Chandos, Oliver Lyttelton, Viscount, Letter to the Editor, in *The Times*, 2.5.1967.

Crawfurd, Oswald, 'The London Stage', *Fortnightly Review* 47 (April 1890): 499–516.

 'The London Stage, II. A Rejoinder', *Fortnightly Review* 47 (June 1890): 931–6.

 'The London Stage', *Fortnightly Review* 48 (August 1890): 315–316.

Craze, Tony, ed., *Going Black Under the Skin* (London: New Playwrights Trust, 1997).

Deeney, John, ed., *The Mentoring Scheme for Women Writers* (London: New Playwrights Trust, 1996).

Finegan, J. J., 'All about "Juno": a job well done', *Evening Herald*, 7.5.1966, p. 8.

Girault, Alain, ed.-in-chief, 'Dramaturgie', *Théâtre/public* 67 (January–February 1986).

Holland, Peter, 'David Garrick: 3rdly, as an Author', *Studies in Eighteenth Century Culture* 25: 39–62.

 'Theatre', in Latham and Matthews, eds., *Samuel Pepys: Companion*, pp. 431–45.

Hunt, Leigh, 'Rules for the Theatrical Critic of a Newspaper', in Archer and Lowe, eds., *Dramatic Essays*, pp. 124–7.

Irving, Henry, 'Actor-Managers II', *Nineteenth Century* 27 (June 1890): 1052–3.

Jones, H. A., 'The Actor-Manager', *Fortnightly Review* 48 (July 1890): 1–18.

Kott, Jan, 'The Dramaturg', *New Theatre Quarterly* 6.21 (February 1990): 3–4.

Luckett, Richard, 'Plays', in Latham and Matthews, eds., *Samuel Pepys: Companion*, pp. 337–42.

Luckhurst, Mary, 'Mentors or Censors?', *NPT News* 123 (February 1999): 3–4.

Marowitz, Charles, 'Talk with Tynan', *Encore* 10.44 (July/August 1963): 7–27.

McDonald, Jan, 'Shaw and the Court Theatre', in Innes, ed., *Cambridge Companion to Shaw*, pp. 261–83.

Meth, Jonathan, ed., *Commissioning the Future* (London: New Playwrights Trust, 1997).

Milhous, Judith, 'Thomas Betterton's Playwriting', *Bulletin of the New York Public Library* 77 (1974): 375–92.

Münsterer, Hans Otto, 'Recollections of Brecht in 1919 in Augsburg', in Witt, ed., *Brecht As They Knew Him*, pp. 23–31.

Piscator, Erwin, 'Über Grundlagen und Aufgaben des Proletarischen Theaters', in Piscator, *Schriften*, II, 9–12.

Reade, Simon, 'Young Blood', *Time Out*, 3–10.9.1997, p. 139.

Rees, Jasper, 'Stage Fright', *London Evening Standard*, 26.11.1999, ES, pp. 48–52.

Seymour, Alan, 'Theatre 1965', *London Magazine* 5.5 (August 1965): 49–55.

Stoker, Bram, 'Actor-Managers I', *Nineteenth Century* 27 (June 1890): 1040–51.

Tenschert, Joachim, 'Qu'est-ce qu'un dramaturge?', *Théâtre Populaire* 38 (1960): 41–8.

Tree, H. Beerbohm, 'The London Stage, I. A Reply', *Fortnightly Review* 47 (June 1890): 922–31.

 'The London Stage, II. A Stage Reply', *Fortnightly Review* 48 (July 1890): 18–21.

Tynan, Kenneth, 'The National Theatre: A Speech to the Royal Society of Arts', in Tynan, *View of the English Stage*, pp. 352–64.

 Letters to the Editor, *The Times*, 4.5.1967 and 7.5.1967.

Van Kerkhoven, Marianne, ed.-in-chief, 'Über Dramaturgie/On dramaturgy/ A propos de dramaturgie/Over dramaturgie', *Theaterschrift* 5–6 (1993).

Veltman, Chloe, 'dramaturg. dramawot?', *NPT News* 119 (1998): 7–8.

Weber Carl, 'Brecht and the Berliner Ensemble – the Making of a Model', in Thomson and Sacks, eds., *Cambridge Companion to Brecht*, pp. 167–84.

Willett, John, 'Bacon ohne Shakespeare? The problem of Mitarbeit', in Fuegi et al., eds., *Brecht, Women, Politics*, pp. 121–37.

Wilson, Effingham, 'Proposition for a National Theatre', in Whitworth, *National Theatre*, pp. 26–9.

A House for Shakespeare; a Proposition for the Consideration of the Nation (London: Mr Hurst, King William Street, Strand, 1848).

A House for Shakespeare; a Proposition for the Consideration of the Nation (London: Mr Mitchell, Red Lion Court, Fleet Street, 1848).

Wyndham, Charles, 'Actor-Managers III', *The Nineteenth Century* 27 (June 1890): 1054–8.

Books

1832 Report from the Select Committee on Dramatic Literature, in *Stage and Theatre I* (Shannon: Irish University Press, 1968) [British Parliamentary Papers].

1866 Report from the Select Committee on Theatrical Licences and Regulations, in *Stage and Theatre II* (Shannon: Irish University Press, 1970) [British Parliamentary Papers].

Addenbrooke, David, *The Royal Shakespeare Company* (London: William Kimber, 1974).

Archer, William, *About The Theatre* (London: T. Fisher Unwin, 1886).

English Dramatists of Today (London: Sampson Low, Marston, Searle and Rivington, 1882).

The Old Drama and the New (London: William Heinemann, 1923).

Play-making (1912; 4th edn, London: Chapman and Hall, 1930).

Archer, William and Barker, H. Granville, *Scheme and Estimates for a National Theatre* (London: Duckworth and Co., 1907).

Archer, William and Lowe, Robert W., eds., *Dramatic Essays* (London: Walter Scott, 1894).

Aristotle, *Poetics,* general ed. G. P. Goold, trans. and ed. Stephen Halliwell (Cambridge, MA: Harvard University Press, 1995) [Loeb Classical Library].

Aston, Elaine, *Feminist Theatre Practice: A Handbook* (London: Routledge, 1999).

Bahr, Ehrhard, ed., *Was ist Aufklärung?* (Stuttgart: Reclam, 1974).

Bancroft, Marie and Bancroft, Squire, *The Bancrofts* (London: John Murray, 1909).

Barker, Harley Granville(-), *The Exemplary Theatre* (London: Chatto and Windus, 1922).

    A National Theatre (London: Sidgwick and Jackson, 1930).

Bartram, Graham and Waine, Anthony, *Brecht in Perspective* (Harlow: Longman, 1982).

Bate, Jonathan, *Shakespearean Constitutions: Politics, Theatre, Criticism 1730–1830* (Oxford: Clarendon Press, 1989).

Beauman, Sally, *The Royal Shakespeare Company: A History of Ten Decades* (Oxford: Oxford University Press, 1982).

Beerbohm, Max, ed., *Herbert Beerbohm Tree* (London: Hutchinson and Co., 1920).

Benjamin, Walter, *Understanding Brecht*, trans. Anna Bostock (1966; London and New York: Verso, 1983).

Bentley, Eric, *The Brecht Memoir*, 2nd edn (Manchester: Carcanet, 1989).

Bentley, Gerald Eades, *The Profession of Dramatist in Shakespeare's Time 1590–1642* (Princeton: Princeton University Press, 1971).

    The Profession of Player in Shakespeare's Time (Princeton: Princeton University Press, 1984).

    Shakespeare and his Theatre (Lincoln: University of Nebraska Press, 1964).

Berlau, Ruth, Brecht, Bertolt, Hubalek, Claus, Palitzsch, Peter and Rülicke, Käthe, eds., *Theaterarbeit 6: Aufführungen des Berliner Ensemble* (Dresden: Desdner Verlag, 1952).

Bly, Mark, ed., *The Production Notebooks* (New York: Theatre Communications Group, 1996) [Theatre in Process].

Booth, Michael R., *Theatre in the Victorian Age* (Cambridge: Cambridge University Press, 1991).

Borsa, Mario, *The English Stage of Today*, trans. and ed. Selwyn Brinton (London and New York: John Lane, 1908).

Brecht, Bertolt, *Bertolt Brecht Letters 1913–1956*, trans. Ralph Manheim, ed. John Willett (London: Methuen, 1990).

    Brecht on Theatre, trans. and ed. John Willett (1964; London: Methuen, 1987).

    Brecht: Schriften zum Theater, ed. Werner Hecht (1957; 6 vols., rev. edn, Frankfurt-on-Main: Suhrkamp, 1963).

Briefe, ed. Günter Glaeser, 2 vols. (Frankfurt-on-Main: Suhrkamp, 1981).

Gesammelte Werke, ed. Elisabeth Hauptmann, 8 vols. (Frankfurt-on-Main: Suhrkamp, 1967).

Journals 1934–1955, ed. John Willett (London: Methuen, 1993).

The Messingkauf Dialogues, trans. John Willett (1965; London: Methuen, 1994).

Werke, ed. Werner Hecht, Jan Knopf, Werner Mittenzwei and Klaus-Detlef Müller, 30 vols. (Berlin: Aufbau Verlag; Frankfurt-on-Main: Suhrkamp, 1988–98).

Brockett, Oscar G., *The Essential Theatre* (1976; 6th edn, New York: Harcourt Brace, 1996).

Brook, Peter, *The Empty Space* (1968; Harmondsworth: Penguin, 1990).

Brooker, Peter, *Bertolt Brecht: Dialectics, Poetry, Politics* (London: Croom Helm, 1988).

Bunge, Hans, ed., *Brechts Lai-Tu: Erinnerungen und Notate von Ruth Berlau* (1981; 2nd edn, Darmstadt: Hermann Luchterhand, 1985).

Bunn, Alfred, *The Stage: Both Before and Behind the Curtain*, 3 vols. (London: Richard Bentley, 1840).

Burling, William J., *A Checklist of New Plays and Entertainments on the London Stage 1700–1732* (Rutherford: Fairleigh Dickinson University Press, 1993).

Byron, George Gordon, Lord, *Letters and Journals*, ed. Leslie A. Marchand, 12 vols. (London: John Murray, 1973–82).

Callow, Simon, ed., *The National: The Theatre and its Work 1963–1997* (London: Nick Hern Books/Royal National Theatre, 1997).

Cardullo, Bert, ed., *What is Dramaturgy?* (New York: Peter Lang, 1995) [American University Studies, series 26, vol. 20].

Carson, Neil, *A Companion to Henslowe's Diary* (Cambridge: Cambridge University Press, 1988).

Chambers, E. K., *William Shakespeare: A Study of Facts and Problems*, 2 vols. (Oxford: Clarendon Press, 1930).

Chothia, Jean, *English Drama of the Early Modern Period* (London and New York: Longman, 1996) [Longman Literature in English Series].

Cibber, Colley, *An Apology for the Life of Colley Cibber*, ed. B. R. S. Fone (Ann Arbor: University of Michigan Press, 1968).

Cochrane, Claire, *The Birmingham Rep* (Birmingham: Sir Barry Jackson Trust, 2003).

Cole, J. W., *The Life and Theatrical Times of Charles Kean, F. S. A.*, 2 vols. (London: Richard Bentley, 1859).

Cook, Dutton, *On the Stage*, 2 vols. (London: Sampson, Low, Marston, Searle and Rivington, 1883).

Cook, Judith, *The National Theatre* (London: Harrap, 1976).

Craig, Gordon, *Henry Irving* (London: J. M. Dent and Sons, 1930).

Davies, Thomas, *Memoirs of the Life of David Garrick*, 2 vols. (London: [n.p.] 1780).

Dexter, John, *The Honourable Beast* (London: Nick Hern Books, 1993).

Dibdin, Thomas, *The Reminiscences of Thomas Dibdin*, 2 vols. (London: Henry Colburn, 1827).

Dickson, Keith, A., *Towards Utopia: A Study of Brecht* (Oxford: Clarendon Press, 1978).

Doty, Gresdna A. and Harbin, Billy J., eds., *Inside the Royal Court Theatre, 1956–1981* (Baton Rouge: Louisiana State University Press, 1990).

Downes, John, *Roscius Anglicanus*, ed. Judith Milhous and Robert D. Hume (London: Society for Theatre Research, 1987).

Dukore, Bernard F., *Bernard Shaw, Director* (London: Allen and Unwin, 1971).

Eddershaw, Margaret, *Performing Brecht: Forty Years of British Performances* (London: Routledge, 1996).

Edgar, David, ed., *State of Play* (London: Faber and Faber, 1999).

Egan, Michael, ed., *Ibsen: The Critical Heritage* (London: Routledge and Kegan Paul, 1972).

Elsom, John, *Post-War British Theatre Criticism* (London: Routledge and Kegan Paul, 1981).

Elsom, John and Tomalin, Nicholas, *The History of the National Theatre* (London: Jonathan Cape, 1978).

Esslin, Martin, *Brecht: A Choice of Evils* (London: Eyre and Spottiswoode, 1959).

Filon, Augustin, *The English Stage*, trans. Frederic Whyte (London: John Milne; New York: Dodd, Mead and Co., 1897).

Findlater, Richard, ed., *At the Royal Court: 25 Years of the English Stage Company* (Derby: Amber Lane, 1981).

Fitzball, Edward, *Thirty-Five Years of a Dramatic Author's Life*, 2 vols. (London: T. C. Newby, 1859).

Fitzgerald, Percy, *Henry Irving. Twenty Years at the Lyceum* (London: Chapman and Hall, 1893).

Foulkes, Richard, ed., *Shakespeare and the Victorian Stage* (Cambridge: Cambridge University Press, 1986).

   British Theatre in the 1890s (Cambridge: Cambridge University Press, 1992).

Fuegi, John, *Bertolt Brecht: Chaos, According to Plan* (Cambridge: Cambridge University Press, 1987).

   Brecht and Company: Sex, Politics, and the Making of the Modern Drama (New York: Grove Press, 1994).

Fuegi, John, Bahr, Gisela and Willett, John, eds., *Brecht, Women, Politics* (Detroit: Wayne State University Press, 1983).

Garrick, David, *The Letters of David Garrick*, ed. David M. Little and George M. Kahrl, 3 vols. (Oxford: Oxford University Press, 1963).

Gaskill, William, *A Sense of direction* (London: Faber and Faber, 1988).

Gentleman, Francis *The Modish Wife ... to Which is Prefixed a Summary View of the Stage* (1775; New York: Readex Microprints, 1963).

Gottlieb, Vera and Chambers, Colin, eds., *Theatre in a Cool Climate* (Oxford: Amber Lane, 1999).

Gray, Charles Harold, *Theatrical Criticism in London to 1795* (New York: Columbia University Press, 1931).

Gray, Ronald, *Brecht the Dramatist* (Cambridge: Cambridge University Press, 1976).

Hall, Peter, *Making an Exhibition of Myself* (London: Sinclair-Stevenson, 1993).

   Peter Hall's Diaries, ed. John Goodwin (London: Hamish Hamilton, 1983).

Hanssen, Paula, *Elisabeth Hauptmann: Brecht's Silent Collaborator* (New York: Peter Lang, 1994) [New York Ottendorfer Series].

Harrold, Charles Frederick, *Carlyle and German Thought 1819–1834* (London: Archon, 1963).

Hauptmann, Elisabeth, *Julia ohne Romeo*, ed. Rosemarie Eggert and Rosemarie Hill (Berlin: Aufbau Verlag, 1977).

Hayman, Ronald, ed., *The German Theatre* (London: Oswald Wolf, 1975).

Hecht, Werner, ed., *Alles was Brecht ist*, 3rd edn (Frankfurt-on-Main: Suhrkamp, 1998).

       Brecht Chronik 1898–1956 (Frankfurt-on-Main: Suhrkamp, 1997).

Highfill, Philip, H., Burnim, Kalman A. and Langhans, Edward A., *A Biographical Dictionary of Actors, Actresses, Musicians, Dancers, Managers and other Stage Personnel in London 1660–1800*, 16 vols. (Carbondale: Southern Illinois University Press, 1973–93).

Hill, Aaron and Popple, William, *The Prompter*, ed. William W. Appleton and Kalman A. Burnim (New York: Benjamin Bloom, 1966).

Holland, Peter, *The Ornament of Action* (Cambridge: Cambridge University Press, 1979).

Hume, Robert D., *The Development of English Drama in the Late Seventeenth Century* (Oxford: Clarendon Press, 1976).

       Henry Fielding and the London Theatre 1728–1737 (Oxford: Clarendon Press, 1988).

Hume, Robert D., ed., *The London Theatre World 1660–1800* (Carbondale: Southern Illinois University Press/London and Amsterdam: Feffer and Simons, 1980).

Hunt, Leigh, *Autobiography of Leigh Hunt*, ed. Roger Ingpen, 2 vols. (London: Archibald Constable and Co., 1903).

Hutchison, Robert, *The Politics of the Arts Council* (London: Sinclair Browne, 1982).

Innes, Christopher, *Erwin Piscator's Political Theatre: The Development of Modern German Drama* (Cambridge: Cambridge University Press, 1972).

       Modern German Drama: A Study in Form (Cambridge: Cambridge University Press, 1979).

Innes, Christopher, ed., *The Cambridge Companion to George Bernard Shaw* (Cambridge: Cambridge University Press, 1998).

Itzin, Catherine, *Stages in the Revolution* (London: Methuen, 1980).

Jackson, Russell, ed., *Victorian Theatre* (London: A. and C. Black, 1989).

Johnson, John, *The Lord Chamberlain's Blue Pencil* (London: Hodder and Stoughton, 1990).

Jonas, Susan, Proehl, Geoff and Lupu, Michael, eds., *Dramaturgy in American Theater: A Source Book* (New York: Harcourt Brace, 1997).

Jones, H. A., *Renascence of the English Drama* (London and New York: Macmillan, 1895).

Joseph, Stephen, *New Theatre Forms* (London: Isaac Pitman and Sons, 1968).

   The Story of the Playhouse in England (London: Barrie and Rockliff, 1963).

   Theatre in the Round (London: Barrie and Rockliff, 1967).

Kebir, Sabine, *Ein akzeptabler Mann? Brecht und die Frauen* (Berlin: Aufbau Verlag, 1998).

   Helene Weigel: Abstieg in den Ruhm (Berlin: Aufbau Verlag, 2002).

   Ich Fragte Nicht Nach Meinem Anteil: Elisabeth Hauptmanns Arbeit mit Bertolt Brecht (Berlin: Aufbau Verlag, 1997).

Kennedy, Dennis, *Granville Barker and the Dream of Theatre* (1985; repr. with corr., Cambridge: Cambridge University Press, 1989).

Kleber, Pia and Visser, Colin, *Reinterpreting Brecht: His Influence on Contemporary Drama and Film* (Cambridge: Cambridge University Press, 1990).

Klotz, C. A., ed., *Deutsche Bibliothek der schönen Wissenschaften* (Halle, 1769).

Knopf, Jan, *Bertolt Brecht. Eine Forschungsbericht. Fragwürdiges in der Brechtforschung* (Frankfurt-on-Main: Fischer, 1974).

   Brecht-Handbuch. Lyrik, Epik, Schriften. Eine Asthetik der Widersprüche (Stuttgart: J. B. Metzler, 1984).

   Brecht-Handbuch: Theater. Eine Asthetik der Widersprüche (Stuttgart: J. B. Metzler, 1980).

Kruger, Loren, *The National Stage* (Chicago: University of Chicago Press, 1992).

   Post-Imperial Brecht: Politics and Performance, East and South (Cambridge: Cambridge University Press, 2004).

Kustow, Michael, *Theatre@risk* (London: Methuen, 2000).

Lamport, F. J., *German Classical Drama* (1990; Cambridge: Cambridge University Press, 1992).

    Lessing and the Drama (Oxford: Clarendon Press, 1981).

Latham, R. C. and Matthews, W., eds., *The Diary of Samuel Pepys*, volume x, *Companion* (London: HarperCollins, 1995).

Lennard, John and Luckhurst, Mary, *The Drama Handbook: A Guide to Reading Plays* (Oxford: Oxford University Press, 2002).

Lessing, G. E., *Hamburgische Dramaturgie*, in *Lessing's Werke*, ed. J. Petersen and W. von Olshausen, 25 vols. (Berlin: Bong and Co., 1925).

    Hamburgische Dramaturgie, ed. Klaus L. Berghahn (Stuttgart: Reklam, 1981).

    Sämtliche Schriften, ed. K. von Lachmann, 23 vols. (Berlin: Muncker, 1886–1924).

    Selected Prose Works, ed. E. Bell, trans. E. C. Beasley and Helen Zimmern (London: George Bell and Sons, 1879).

Littlewood, Joan, *Joan's Book* (London: Minerva, 1995).

Lyon, James K., *Bertolt Brecht in America* (Princeton: Princeton University Press, 1980).

MacCarthy, Desmond, *The Court Theatre 1904–1907* (London: A. H. Bullen, 1907).

Macready, William Charles, *The Diaries*, ed. William Toynbee, 2 vols. (London: Chapman and Hall, 1912).

    Reminiscences and Selections from his Diaries and Letters, ed. Frederick Pollock, 2 vols. (London: Macmillan, 1875).

Marshall, Norman, *The Producer and the Play* (1957; 2nd edn, London: MacDonald, 1962).

Martin-Harvey, John, *The Autobiography of Sir John Martin-Harvey* (London: Sampson, Low, Marston and Co., 1933).

Marx, Karl and Engels, Friedrich, *Marx-Engels-Werke*, Institut für Marxismus-Leninismus beim ZK der SED, 43 vols. (Berlin: Dietz Verlag, 1958).

Mason, A. E. W., *Sir George Alexander and the St James Theatre* (London: Macmillan, 1935).

Mayer, Hans, *Erinnerung an Brecht* (Frankfurt-on-Main: Suhrkamp, 1996).

McCabe, Terry, *Mis-directing the Play* (Chicago: Ivan R. Dee, 2001).

Melville, Lewis, *The Life and Letters of Tobias Smollett* (New York: Kennikat Press, 1966).

Mews, Siegfried, ed., *A Bertolt Brecht Reference Companion* (Westport, CT, and London: Greenwood Press, 1997).

Milhous. Judith D. and Hume, Robert D., *Producible Interpretation* (Carbondale: Southern Illinois University Press, 1985).

  A Register of English Theatrical Documents 1660–1737, 2 vols. (Carbondale: Southern Illinois University Press, 1991).

Milibrand, Ralph, *Parliamentary Socialism* (London: Merlin Press, 1979).

Mittenzwei, Werner, *Das Leben Bertolt Brecht*, 2 vols. (Berlin: Aufbau Verlag, 1986).

  Wer war Brecht (Berlin: Aufbau Verlag, 1977).

Münsterer, Hanns Otto, *The Young Brecht*, 2nd edn, trans. Tom Kuhn and Karen Leeder (London: Libris, 1992).

Nagler, A. M., *A Source Book in Theatrical History* (New York: Dover Press, 1959).

Needle, Jan and Thomson, Peter, *Brecht* (Oxford: Basil Blackwell, 1981).

Olivier, Laurence, *Confessions of an Actor* (1982; London: Orion Books, 1994).

Parsons, Mrs Clement, *Garrick and his Circle* (London: Methuen, 1906).

Paulin, Roger, *Ludwig Tieck: A Literary Biography* (Oxford: Clarendon Press, 1985).

Pavis, Patrice, *Dictionary of the Theatre* (Paris: Dunod, 1996; trans. Christine Shantz, Toronto: University of Toronto Press, 1998).

Pemberton, T. Edgar, *Sir Charles Wyndham* (London: Hutchison and Co., 1904).

Pickard-Cambridge, Arthur, *The Dramatic Festivals of Athens*, 2nd edn, rev. John Gould and D. M. Lewis (Oxford: Clarendon Press, 1988).

Piscator, Erwin, *Das Politische Theater* (1929; rev. Felix Gasbarra, Hamburg: Rowohlt, 1963).

  Schriften, ed. Ludwig Hoffmann, 2 vols. (Berlin: Henschelverlag, 1968).

[Platt, Agnes,] *Anonymous* (London: John Murray, 1936).

Purdom, C. B., *Harley Granville Barker: Man of the Theatre, Dramatist and Scholar* (Westport, CT: Greenwood Press, 1956).

Reinelt, Janelle, *After Brecht. British Epic Theatre* (Ann Arbor: University of Michigan Press, 1994).

Richards, Kenneth and Thomson, Peter, *Essays on Nineteenth-Century British Theatre* (London: Methuen, 1971).

Rilla, Paul, *Lessing und sein Zeitalter* (Berlin: Aufbau Verlag, 1981).

Roberts, Philip, *The Royal Court and the Modern Stage* (Cambridge: Cambridge University Press, 1999).

  The Royal Court Theatre 1965–1972 (Cambridge: Cambridge University Press, 1986).

Robertson, J. D., *Lessing's Dramatic Theory* (Cambridge: Cambridge University Press, 1939).

Rouse, John, *Brecht and the West German Theatre* (Ann Arbor: UMI Research Press, 1989) [Theatre and Dramatic Studies, no. 62].

Rowell, George, *The Old Vic Theatre: A History* (Cambridge: Cambridge University Press, 1993).

  The Victorian Theatre: A Survey (Oxford: Clarendon Press, 1956).

Rowell, George and Jackson, Anthony, *The Repertory Movement. A History of Regional Theatre in Britain* (Cambridge: Cambridge University Press, 1984).

Rülicke-Weiler, Käthe, *Die Dramaturgie Brechts* (Berlin: Henschelverlag, 1966).

St John, Christopher, ed., *Ellen Terry and Bernard Shaw. A Correspondence* (London: Constable and Co., 1931).

Salberg, Derek, *My Love Affair with a Theatre* (Luton: Cortney Publications, 1978).

Salmon, Eric, *Granville Barker: A Secret Life* (London: William Heinemann, 1983).

  Granville Barker and his Correspondents (Detroit: Wayne State University Press, 1986).

Schiller, Friedrich, *Der Briefwechsel zwischen Schiller und Goethe*, ed. Emil Staiger (Frankfurt-on-Main: Insel, 1966).

  Sämtliche Werke, ed. Gerhard Fricke and Herbert G. Göpfert, 5 vols. (Munich: Karl Hanser, 1980).

Schnapp, Jeffrey T., *Staging Fascism* (Stanford: Stanford University Press, 1996).

Shaw, George Bernard, *Bernard Shaw's Letters to Granville Barker*, ed. C. B. Purdom (London: Phoenix, 1956).

    Collected Letters 1874–1897, ed. Dan H. Laurence (London: Max Reinhardt, 1965).

    Major Critical Essays (1932; standard edn, London: Constable and Co., 1947).

    Our Theatres in the Nineties (1932; 3 vols., standard edn, London: Constable and Co., 1948).

Shellard, Dominic, *Kenneth Tynan: A Life* (New Haven: Yale University Press, 2003).

Senelick, Laurence, ed., *National Theatre in Northern and Eastern Europe* (Cambridge: Cambridge University Press, 1991).

Smith, Chris, *Creative Britain* (London: Faber and Faber, 1998).

Smollett, Tobias, *The Letters of Tobias Smollett*, ed. Lewis M. Knapp (Oxford: Clarendon Press, 1970).

Stafford-Clark, Max, *Letters to George: The Account of a Rehearsal* (London: Nick Hern Books, 1997).

Steinmetz, Horst, *Lessing – ein unpoetischer Dichter* (Frankfurt and Bonn: Athenäum, 1969).

Steinmetz, Horst, ed., *Schriften zur Literatur* (Stuttgart: Reklam, 1982).

Steinweg, Reiner, *Das Lehrstück. Brechts Theorie einer ästhetischen Erziehung* (Stuttgart: J. B. Metzler, 1972).

Steinweg, Reiner, ed., *Auf Anregung Bertolt Brechts: Lehrstücke mit Schülern, Arbeitern, Theaterleuten* (Frankfurt-on-Main: Suhrkamp, 1978).

    Brechts Modell der Lehrstücke. Zeugnisse, Diskussionen, Erfahrungen (Frankfurt-on-Main: Suhrkamp, 1976).

Stephens, John Russell, *The Profession of the Playwright: British Theatre 1800–1900* (Cambridge: Cambridge University Press, 1992).

Stern, Carola, *Männer lieben anders: Helene Weigel und Bertolt Brecht* (Berlin: Rowohlt, 2000).

Stern, Tiffany, *Rehearsal from Shakespeare to Sheridan* (Oxford: Oxford University Press, 2000).

Suvin, Darko, *To Brecht and Beyond: Soundings in Modern Dramaturgy* (Brighton: Harvester Press, 1984).

Taylor, George, *Players and Performances in the Victorian Theatre* (Manchester: Manchester University Press, 1989).

Taylor, John Russell, *Anger and After: A Guide to the New British Drama* (Harmondsworth: Penguin [Pelican], 1963).

    The Penguin Dictionary of the Theatre (Harmondsworth: Penguin, 1966; London: Methuen, 1967).

Thomas, David, ed., *Restoration and Georgian England 1660–1788* (Cambridge: Cambridge University Press, 1989) [Theatre in Europe: A Documentary History Series].

Thomson, Peter and Sacks, Glendyr, eds., *The Cambridge Companion to Brecht* (Cambridge: Cambridge University Press, 1994).

Trewin, John Courtenay, *The Theatre Since 1900* (London: Andrew Dakers, 1951).

Trewin, John Courtenay and Trewin, Wendy, *The Arts Theatre London 1927–1981* (London: Society for Theatre Research, 1986).

Tynan, Kathleen, *The Life of Kenneth Tynan* (London: Methuen, 1988).

Tynan, Kathleen, ed., *Kenneth Tynan: Letters* (London: Weidenfeld and Nicolson, 1994).

Tynan, Kenneth, *Curtains* (London: Longmans, 1961).

    He That Plays The King (London: Longmans, Green and Co., 1950).

    Profiles, eds. Kathleen Tynan and Ernie Eban (London: Nick Hern Books, 1989).

    Tynan Right and Left (London: Longman, 1967).

    A View of the English Stage (London: Davis-Poynter, 1975).

Tynan, Kenneth, ed., *Othello* (London: Rupert Hart-Davis, 1965).

    The Recruiting Officer (London: Rupert Hart-Davis, 1965).

Van Lennep, William, Avery, Emmet L., Scouten, Arthur H., Stone, George Winchester and Hogan, Charles Beecher, *The London Stage 1660–1800*, 11 vols. (Carbondale: Southern Illinois University Press, 1965–8).

Völker, Klaus, *Brecht*, trans. John Nowell (London: Marion Boyars, 1979).

    Brecht-Chronik (Munich: Carl Hanser, 1971).

Weigel, Hélène, *Briefwechsel 1935–1971*, ed. Stefan Mahlke (Berlin: Theater der Zeit, 2000).

Wekwerth, Manfred, *Notate: Über die Arbeit des Berliner Ensembles 1956–1966* (Frankfurt-on-Main: Suhrkamp, 1967).
  Schriften: Arbeit mit Brecht (Berlin: Henschelverlag, 1975).
White, Martin, *Renaissance Drama in Action: An Introduction to Aspects of Theatre Practice and Performance* (London and New York: Routledge, 1998).
Whitebrook, Peter, *William Archer: A Biography* (London: Methuen, 1993).
Whitworth, Geoffrey, *The Making of a National Theatre* (London: Faber and Faber, 1951).
Wilke, Judith, ed., *Hélène Weigel 100* (Madison: University of Wisconsin Press, 2000) [Brecht Yearbook 25].
Willet, John, *The Theatre of Bertolt Brecht: A Study from Eight Aspects* (1959; 3rd edn, London: Methuen, 1967).
  The Theatre of the Weimar Republic (New York and London: Holmes and Meier, 1988).
Willet, John, ed., *Brecht Then and Now, damals und heute* (Madison: University of Wisconsin Press, 1995) [Brecht Yearbook 20].
Winston, James, *Drury Lane Journal. Selections from James Winston's Diaries 1819–1827*, ed. Alfred L. Nelson and Gilbert B. Cross (London: Society of Theatre Research, 1974).
Witt, Hubert, ed., *Brecht As They Knew Him* (trans. John Peet, 1974; 3rd edn, London: Lawrence and Wishart, 1980).
Wizisla, Erdmut, ed., *1898 Bertolt Brecht 1998* (Berlin: Akademie der Künste, 1998).
Zeydel, Edwin H., *Ludwig Tieck, The German Romanticist* (Princeton: Princeton University Press, 1935).
Zimmern, Helen, *G. E. Lessing: His Life and Works* (London: Longmans, Green and Co., 1878).

Film, video and television

Die Mit-Arbeiterin – Gespräche mit Elisabeth Hauptmann, dir. Karlheinz Mund, first broadcast by Deutscher Fernsehfunk, channel 1, 3 December 1972.
Reputations: Kenneth Tynan, written and presented by Anthony Howard, first broadcast on BBC television, 25 July 1982.

Index

Ackermann, Konrad, 27
actor-managers
  nineteenth-century England, 45–9
  reaction against, 81
  wives, 54–5
actors, and Brecht, 113, 114–15
Adler, Rozina, 162–5, 188
Albrecht, H. C., 37
Alexander, Florence, 48, 54, 60
Alexander, George, 48, 54, 60
Alexandra Theatre, Birmingham, 155
Allaci, Leone, 6–7, 29–30
alternative dramaturgies, 219
Antoine, André, 68
Archer, William
  background to Blue Book, 78–88
  Blue Book, 78, 81–8
  Court Theatre, 90
  dramatic criticism, 57, 74n, 91
  experimental theatre, 69
  invention of office of literary
    manager, 78
  legacy, 264
  Lessing's influence, 24, 82–3
  rise of the playwright, 62
  support for dramaturg system, 48
  theatre reform, 68
Arden, John, 157, 169–70
Aristotle, 6–7, 29, 30–1, 34, 36, 112,
    114, 116
Arlen, Stephen, 162

Arnold, Matthew, 67–8
Arts Council, 203–4, 207–8, 213, 249
Attlee government, 153
Austria, 2, 37, 40–1
Ayckbourn, Alan, 242, 244–50, 264

Bancroft, Squire, 58, 81
Barker, Harley Granville
  background to Blue Book, 78–88
  Blue Book, 78, 81–8
  Court Theatre management, 90–2
  Exemplary Theatre, 88–98, 101
  experimental theatre, 69, 100–2
  influence on Tynan, 158, 160, 168
  invention of literary manager
    office, 78
  legacy, 2, 219, 224, 264
  Lessing's influence, 24, 82–3, 89
  literary management, 48, 78, 81–8,
    98–102
  A National Theatre, 98–102
  play selection, 93–7, 101
  and Reinhardt, 89–90, 96
  Royal Court, 224
  and Stanislavski, 89
  'Two German Theatres', 90
  Weather-Hen, 80
  withdrawal from theatre, 98
Barrault, Jean-Louis, 182
Barrie, J. M., 81
Barton, John, 4–5, 231, 259n

Bataillon, Michel, 142
Baylis, Lilian, 153
Beaumarchais, 35
Beaumont, Hugh, 154–6
Becher, R., 129
Beckett, Samuel, 178, 180
Belgium, 219
Bell, Suzanne, 239–42
Bennett, Alan, 212
Bentley, Eric, 126, 143n
Bentley, G. E., 13
Berlau, Ruth, 121, 122–3, 132–4
Berliner Ensemble
  Brecht's experiments, 95
  Brecht's organisation and training,
    128–38
  Brecht's theory of dramaturgy, 11
  Carl Weber in, 110
  didactism, 167
  foundation, 126–8
  in England, 168
  influence on Tynan, 158
  post-Brecht, 110, 138–40
Besson, Bruno, 137
Betterton, Thomas, 16
Billington, Michael, 111
Birmingham, 91, 155
Birmingham Rep, 236, 237–8, 246
Birmingham University, 217–18
Blair government, 208, 213–14, 266
Bleasdale, Alan, 239
Blue Book
  background, 78–88
  and literary management, 81–8
  play selection, 94
Bond, Edward, 214, 258n
Boucicault, Dion, 66
Boyd, Michael, 235
Bradley, A. C., 80
Bradley, Jack, 220–4, 257n
Bradshaw, Cavendish, 50
Brasch, Thomas, 140
Braun, Volker, 140, 151n

Brecht, Bertolt
  and actors, 113–15
  Arturo Ui, 122
  Berliner Ensemble
    foundation, 126–8
    organisation and training,
      128–38
    post-Brecht, 138–40
    practice of dramaturgy, 120–40
    publications, 172
    research, 135–7
  death, 138
  Deutsches Theater, 90
  Dreigroschenoper, 129
  educator, 128–38, 172
  *Furcht und Elend des Dritten
    Reiches*, 122, 126
  Galilei, 122, 126
  Die Gewehre der Frau Carrar,
    122, 129
  Herr Puntilla und sein Knecht, 129
  Die Horatier und Kuratier, 122
  identification as dramaturg, 9
  Journals, 116
  Kaukasische Kreidekreis, 129
  legacy, 2, 109–10
    dramaturg model, 9–10, 231
    Tynan, influence on, 158–9,
      165–6, 168–9, 171–2
    western reception, 109–10,
      140–3, 176, 218, 249, 267
  Lehrstücke, 122, 134
  Mann ist Mann, 121–2
  Marxism, 114–17
  Messingkauf Dialogues, 109,
    110–18, 123, 125–6, 129, 133,
    138, 141, 143, 152, 159, 266
  Modellbücher, 134, 141, 172
  Mutter Courage, 129, 169
  Notate, 132, 142,
  Piscator, Erwin, 125–6
  pre-1949 experimental
    collaborations, 89, 95, 120–6

Index

Brecht, Bertolt (cont.)
   production dramaturg, 139, 141,
      205, 209
   and Reinhardt, 89, 124–5
   A Short Organum for the Theatre,
      112
   Theaterarbeit, 134, 141–2, 172
   theory of dramaturgy, 6, 11, 110–20
   Das Verhör des Lukullus, 122, 129
Brighouse, Harold, 169
Bristol Old Vic, 169
British Museum, 79
Brome, Richard, 14
Brook, Peter, 98
Brooks, Jeremy, 232, 260n
Brown, John Russell, 189, 220
Browning, Robert, 63
Bruck, Reinhardt, 90
Brustein, Robert, 142–3
Bryden, Ronald, 232
Buffini, Moira, 220
Bunge, Hans, 132–3
Bunn, Alfred, 47, 52–3
Burgess, John, 220
Burgtheater, Vienna, 2, 41
Burnand, Francis, 63, 75n
Burri, Emil Hesse, 121
business managers, 84, 98
Byron, Lord, 50–1, 63

Calcraft, J. W., 58
Calderón de la Barca, Pedro, 39
Cambridge Arts Theatre, 202
Canada, 109–10, 219
Canaris, Volker, 9–10
Carlyle, Thomas, 7, 57, 74n
Carr, Comyns, 55, 58
cartoons, 3–4
Casson, Lewis, 92
censorship, 69, 170–1, 203, 215
Chambers, Colin, 200, 232–3, 260n
Chandos, Viscount, 154–5, 160,
      170–1, 181, 183–7, 192

Charing Cross Theatre, 76n
Chekhov, Anton, 169, 224
Cherwell, Lord, 184
Chetwood, William, 17–18
children's theatre, 209
Churchill, Winston, 153, 155, 181,
      183, 184
Cibber, Colley, 14–15
Clark, Kenneth, 154–6
Clarke, Ashley, 154–6
Cobbold, Lord, 170
Coghlan, Lyn, 222
Combes, Jo, 242, 244
Comédie Française, 49, 67
Congreve, William, 155, 169, 212
Continent. *See* Europe
Cook, Dutton, 49–50, 53
copyright, 64
Corbet, Frieda, 154–5
Court Theatre, 80, 89, 90–2
Covent Garden, 14, 45, 51, 58–9
Coward, Noël, 169
Craig, Gordon, 61
Crane, Richard, 225
Crawfurd, Oswald, 48–9
Craze, Tony, 254n
Crimp, Martin, 224
criticism, dramatic criticism, 56–8,
      129, 252
Croft, Giles, 220

Daldry, Stephen, 224
Danish Royal Theatre, 41
Davenant, William, 14, 16
David Garrick Theatre, Lichfield, 157
Davies, Lucy, 222
Davies, Thomas, 15, 18
Deeney, John, 210
Dekker, Thomas, 13
Denmark, 41, 121–2
Derby Playhouse, 245–6, 250
development dramaturgs, 201, 205
Devine, George, 178–80, 224, 229–30

288

Dexter, John, 156, 167–8, 170,
  176–8, 225
Dibdin, Thomas, 60, 76n
Dickens, Charles, 63
Diderot, Denis, 33, 35
Directors' Guild of Great Britain, 207
directors, rôle of, 83, 85–6, 92–3
Donohue, Walter, 232
Dort, Bernard, 142
Douglas, Katie, 240
D'Oyly Carte, Helen, 81
Drake, Nicholas, 221–2
Dramatic Authors' Society, 64
dramatic criticism, 19th century,
  56–8
dramaturgs
  and artistic directors, 12, 211,
    216, 246
  and audience development,
    207–10, 265
  Brecht. *See* Brecht, Bertolt
  Britain. *See* literary managers
    (Britain)
  continental theatre, 1, 202, 263
  controversies, 2–5
  cultural prejudice towards, 210–16
  definitions, 5–12, 111–12, 204–7
  development dramaturgs, 205, 209,
    214, 265
  and directors, 10, 211, 215, 222, 244
  funding of, 200–10
  history to 1800, 12–18
  identity politics, 207–10
  Lessing. *See* Lessing, Gotthold
  literary managers, 7, 8–9, 11
  New Dramaturgy, 219
  production dramaturgs, 205–6, 215
  script-reading, 208–10
  terminology, 3, 7–12, 204–7, 212,
    235, 263
  training, 216–19
Dramaturgs' Network, 206–7
Drury Lane

  in eighteenth century, 14, 15, 17
  and Byron, 50
  in-house criticism, 59
  Kean at, 59
  managers, 48, 59
  playreaders, 51, 53
  playwrights, 62
  privileges, 45
Dryden, John, 16, 157
Dudow, Slatan, 121
Duke of York's Theatre, 89

Eastern Europe, 1, 24, 140, 215
Eddershaw, Margaret, 112
Edgar, David, 202, 256n
educator rôle
  Brecht, 128–38
  Tynan, 165–73, 178
Ekhof, Konrad, 25–6, 32–4
Elizabethan Stage Society, 69
Elizabethan theatre, 13–14
Elliston, Robert, 47, 53
English Stage Society, 69
English theatre
  in eighteenth century, 14–18
  in nineteenth century
    actor-managers, 45–9
    avant-garde, 66–70
    dramatic criticism, 56–8
    in-house criticism, 59–62
    literary advisers and playreaders,
      49–56
    promotion of playwrights, 62
    research, 58
    theatre-building, 45
  anti-intellectualism, 2, 263–4
  Brechtian influence, 110, 141–3,
    176, 249
  case histories, 219–52
  children's theatre, 209
  copyright, 64
  Elizabethan theatre, 13–14
  funding, 266

English theatre (cont.)
identity politics, 207–10
Interregnum, 14, 16
literary managers. *See* literary
managers (Britain)
minority politics, 209–10
national theatre. *See* National
Theatre
new writing. *See* new writing
Parliamentary Select Committees,
64
political interventions, 210–16,
266–7
regional theatres, 207–10, 236–52
repertory theatres, 91
Restoration theatre, 14, 15
silent revolution, 200–2, 264–5
See also specific theatres
equal opportunities, 219
Essex, Lord, 50
Euripides, 91
Europe
dramaturgs, 1, 202, 263
Eastern Europe, 1, 24, 140, 215
Scandinavia, 1, 40, 109, 141, 215
theatre funding, 266
visual impact of productions, 216
Eurycles, 6
Eyre, Richard, 220

Farquhar, George, 169, 171
Fenn, Manville, 91
Feuchtwanger, Lion, 121
Feydeau, Georges, 169
Finegan, J. J., 171
Fitzball, Edward, 51–2, 59
Forman, Simon, 18
Frankcom, Sarah, 242–4
French theatre
appointment of dramaturgs, 109
avant-garde, 182
and Brecht, 142
Comédie Française, 49, 67

Dort, Bernard, 142
dramaturgy debate, 219
English nineteenth-century
adaptations, 67
influence on Germany, 28, 31–2, 35
neoclassicism, 28, 32, 67
Planchon, Roger, 142
playreading, 226
Théâtre du Nouveau Monde, 169
Théatre Français, 81
Théatre Libre, 68–9
Frisch, Max, 169
Fry, Christopher, 155
Fuegi, John, 123
Fyfe, Hamilton, 80

Gaiety Theatre, Manchester, 91–2
Galsworthy, John, 91
Garrick, David, 14–17, 78
Gaskill, William, 156, 167–8, 171,
176–8, 225
Gay, John, 122
Gemmingen, O. H. von, 37
Genet, Jean, *Les Paravents*, 182
Gentleman, Francis, 16
German theatre
in eighteenth-century context,
25, 35
and eighteenth-century French
style, 28, 31–2
Berlin *Freie Bühne*, 77n
Berliner Ensemble. *See* Berliner
Ensemble
Brecht. *See* Brecht, Bertolt
compared to English theatre,
18, 215
concepts, 162
Deutsches Theater, 90, 124–5
dramatic criticism, 56
dramaturgy debate, 219
Dresden, 38–40
Düsseldorfer Schauspielhaus, 90
employment of dramaturgs, 1, 9–10

Hamburg National Theatre, 12, 24, 26
Lessing. *See* Lessing, Gotthold
Mannheim, 38
Munich Kammerspiele, 124
playreading, 226
Reichsdramaturg, 119
and RSC, 232
Schiller Theatre, Berlin, 166
Gilbert, W. S., 62, 65
Gill, Peter, 220
Glasgow, 91–2
Goethe, J. W. von, 28, 37, 39, 56, 117
Goldoni, Carlo, 27
Gorky, Maxim, 69, 129
Gottsched, Johann Christoph, 28
Granger, Derek, 186, 188
Graves, Robert, 169
Gray, Charles Harold, 18
Green, Tony, 241
Grein, J. T., 68–9
Grillparzer, Franz, 39
Gupta, Tanika, 220, 222
Gurr, Andrew, 13

Hall, Peter, 4, 189, 220, 231–2
Hamburg National Theatre, 12, 24–9
Hampton, Christopher, 225
Hands, Terry, 232
Harcourt, C., 91
Harcourt, R. V., 91
Hare, David, 223, 225
Hare, John, 54, 81
Harris, Augustus, 48
Harris, Zinnie, 223
Harvey, Laura, 245–50
Harwood, Kate, 225
Hastings, Michael, 225
Hauptmann, Elisabeth, 121–2, 123–4, 132, 135–8, 142
Hauptmann, Gerhart, 69, 91, 131
Hazlitt, William, 57, 62
Hecht, Werner, 111, 137–9

Heine, Heinrich, 39, 82–3
Hensel, Madame, 32
Her Majesty's Theatre, 55
Hewlett, Maurice, 91
Heywood, Thomas, 13
Hochhuth, Rolf, 175, 177, 180–6
Holländer, Felix, 90
Holman, Robert, 242
Holmstrom, John, 232
Hooper, Robin, 225
Housman, A. E., 91
Hubalek, Claus, 132, 134
Hunt, Leigh, 57, 62, 71n
Huntington, Helen, 98
Hytner, Nicholas, 212, 220

Ibsen, Henrik, 69, 80, 91, 169, 224
identity politics, 207–10, 265
independent theatre clubs, 68–70
Independent Theatre Society, 68–9, 70
Interregnum, 14, 16
Ireland, 253n
Irving, Henry, 58, 60, 63, 72n, 79, 81
Italy, 27, 29

Jackson, Shannon, 6
James, Henry, 74n
Jeffreys, Stephen, 228
Jellicoe, Ann, 225
Jerwood Foundation, 225
Johnstone, Keith, 169, 225
Jones, H. A., 62, 65, 68, 81
Jones, John, 14
Jonson, Ben, 14
Jordheuil, Jean, 142
Joseph, Stephen, 245, 248, 250
Josephus, Flavius, 5, 6

Kane, Sarah, 214
Kean, Charles, 47–8, 58, 63
Kean, Edmund, 59–60
Kemble, Charles, 58
Kemp, Edward, 211–12

Kendal, Madge, 54–5
Kendal, W. H., 54
Kennedy, Adrienne, 170
Kennedy, Dennis, 88, 98
Kenney, James, 62
Kenyon, Mel, 225
Keswick, William, 154–5
Killigrew, Thomas, 16
Kinnaird, Douglas, 50
Kipling, Rudyard, 122
Kleist, Heinrich von, 39
Knigge, A. von, 37
Knopf, Jan, 112
Kott, Jan, 2
Kotzebue, August, 56
Kustow, Michael, 213
Kwei-Armah, Kwame, 222–3

Lacy, John, 15
Lamb, Charles, 57
Lamport, F. J., 36
Lan, David, 224
Lane, Dorothy, 122
Larsen, Jonathan, *Rent*, 4
Laughton, Charles, 126
Leicester Haymarket, 250
Lennon, John, 170
Lenz, J. M. R., 39, 129, 131
Lessing, Gotthold
  background, 28
  and Brecht, 112, 141, 263
  critical thinking, 9
  first official dramaturg, 2, 12, 24
  and French theatre, 28, 31–2, 35, 67
  Hamburg appointment, 12, 24–9
  Hamburgische Dramaturgie, 8, 24,
    27, 29–37, 82, 158, 218
  impact on England, 45, 56–7,
    82–3, 267
  influence on Tynan, 111, 152, 158–9
  legacy, 37–41, 218, 263
  Mina von Barnhelm, 35
  Miß Sara Sampson, 28, 35

reasons for failure, 32–7
style, 34
terminology, 6–7, 9
text and performance, 31–3
Lewes, George, 62
Lichfield, David Garrick Theatre, 157
lighting technicians, 113–14
Lincoln's Inn Fields, 14
literary advisers, nineteenth-century,
  49–56
Literary Managers and Dramaturgs of
  America, 110
literary managers (Britain)
  Anglo-American cultural
    prejudices, 2, 210–16.
  appointments, 109
  functions, 204–7
  Archer and Barker, 83–8, 98–100
  beginnings, 1, 3
  and *Blue Book*, 81–8
  case histories, 219–52
  and directors, 240
  and identity politics, 207–10, 265
  political interventions, 210–16
  professionalisation, 204–7, 264–5
  silent revolution, 200–2, 264–5
  terminology, 7, 8–9, 13, 82, 206
  training, 216–19
  Tynan. *See* Tynan, Kenneth
  See also dramaturgs
Literary Managers' Forum, 207
Littlewood, Joan, 166, 194n
Liverpool Everyman Theatre, 239–42
Liverpool Playhouse, 239–42
Liverpool Theatre, 75n, 91
Logan, Douglas, 154–5
London Arts Board, 209
Löwen, Johann Friedrich, 25–7, 30–2
Lucian, 5
Lyon, James, 128

Macready, William Charles, 47, 48,
  59, 63

Maeterlinck, Maurice, 69, 91
Manchester theatres, 91–2, 242–4
Marber, Patrick, 220, 223
Marivaux, Pierre de, 224
Marlowe, Christopher, 121, 155
Marston, John, 169
Masefield, John, 91
Mason, A. E. W., 54
McCabe, Terry, 120, 211, 214–15
McCarthy, Lillah, 90
McGovern, Jimmy, 239
Meres, Francis, 18
Mickel, Karl, 140
Miller, Arthur, 168–9
Miller, Jonathan, 177
minority politics, 209–10
Mitchell, Katie, 212
Molière, 35, 66, 169, 177
Moncrieff, W. T., 62
Montague, C. E., 157
Moore, George, 69
Moore, Henry, 154–5
Moore, Peter, 50
Morton, Thomas, 51–2, 55
Moscow, 121
Moscow Art Theatre, 166
Müller, Heiner, 9, 138, 140
Murray, Gilbert, 80, 91

National Gallery, 79
National Lottery, 204, 213
National Theatre
  Archer and Barker's campaign for,
    78–82
  Barker's *A National Theatre*,
    98–102
  Board, 154, 223
  Drama Committee, 156, 168
  and equal opportunities, 219
  foundation, 153–6
  Hochhuth's *Soldiers*, 180–6
  literary managers, 189, 212, 220–4
  national rôle, 204

Olivier–Tynan partnership, 172–5
  production dramaturgs, 212
  Tynan and rehearsal politics,
    176–80
  Tynan as educator, 165–73
  Tynan's appointment, 1, 110,
    154, 265
  Tynan's functions, 7, 85, 161–5
  Tynan's job description, 7, 186
National Youth Theatre, 169
Neher, Caspar, 121
Netherlands, 1, 109, 219
New Century Theatre, 69, 80
New Dramaturgy, 219
New Perspectives, 250
new play development, 202
New Theatre, London, 185
new writing
  Barker's promotion, 100–2
  Birmingham Rep, 237–8
  centralisation of, 213
  contemporary English theatre,
    202–4
  Liverpool theatres, 239–42
  National Theatre, 174–5, 220–4
  regional theatres, 236–52
  Royal Exchange, Manchester, 243
  Royal Shakespeare Company,
    232–5
  Stephen Joseph Theatre, 245–7
  Tynan, 174–5
Nicoll, Allardyce, 45
North West Playwrights, 208
Northampton theatres, 250
Nottingham Playhouse, 250
Nunn, Trevor, 220–1, 232

O'Casey, Sean, 169, 171
O'Neill Centre, 209
Old Vic Theatre, 153–4
Olivier, Laurence
  Hochhuth affair, 184–6
  and new writers, 174–5

Olivier, Laurence (cont.)
  NT directorship, 154–5, 159–60,
    170
  NT programmes, 177
  NT rôle, 85, 156
  Old Vic directorship, 154
  and Tynan, 157–8, 160, 167–8,
    172–5, 180–2, 185–91
Orange Tree Theatre, 244
Orton, Conol, 245
Osborne, John, 157, 169, 202,
    224, 259n
Ostrovsky, Aleksandr, 169

Palitzsch, Peter, 132, 134, 137–8
Payne, Ben, 237–8, 246
Penhall, Joe, 220
Pepys, Samuel, 18
Phelps, Samuel, 63
philosophers, and Brecht, 113–15, 119
Pinero, Arthur Wing, 62, 65–6, 81
Piscator, Erwin, 125–6
Planché, James Robinson, 58, 75n
Planchon, Roger, 142
Platt, Agnes, 56
play selection, Barker on, 93–7, 101
playreaders
  Barker on, 94–6
  Birmingham Rep, 237–8
  English nineteenth-century, 49–56
  Germany, 226
  Liverpool theatres, 239–42
  regional theatres, 208
  Royal Court, 225–8
  Royal Shakespeare Company,
    232–5
  Stephen Joseph Theatre, 245–7
playwrights
  nineteenth-century promotion, 62
  fostering, 93, 250, 266
  new writing. See new writing
  regional organisations, 201, 208–9
  and rehearsal process, 65–6

rise of avant-garde, 66–70
Theatre Writing Partnership, 250–2
translators, 224
writers' workshops, 96
Plowright, Joan, 158
Poel, William, 69, 80
Polka Theatre, 209
Portugal, 142
Prince of Wales's Theatre, 65
Princess's Theatre, London, 58
production dramaturgs, 139, 141,
    205–6, 211–12, 265
prompters, 17–18
Pseudo-Lucian, 5
Pullman, Philip, 223
Purity Campaign, 69

Rattigan, Terence, 155
Rayne, Max, 187
Reade, Simon, 233–4, 251
reading committees, 84–5, 100
Red Ladder, 209
Regional Arts Boards, 203–4, 208, 236
Regional Dramaturgs, 208
regional theatres
  case studies, 236–52
  identity politics, 207–10
rehearsal
  Brecht, 114
  and playwrights, 65–6
  Stephen Joseph Theatre, 248
  Tynan and NT politics, 176–80
Reich, Bernard, 121
Reinhardt, Max, 89–90, 96, 124–5
repertory theatres, 81, 91, 166
Restoration theatre, 14, 15
Reynolds, Frederick, 51–2
Rich, John, 14–15
Richardson, Esther, 250–2
Richardson, Ralph, 154
Rickson, Ian, 228
Ritchie, Rob, 225
Robertson, Tom, 65

Robins, Elizabeth, 91
Rosenstand-Goiske, Peter, 41
Rouse, John, 9, 134
Rowe, John, 14
Rowley, Samuel, 13
Rowley, William, 13
Royal Academy of Dramatic Art,
    98, 216
Royal Court, 119, 170, 200, 204, 219,
    224–31, 244, 258n
Royal Dramatic Theatre, Stockholm,
    166, 182
Royal Exchange Theatre, Manchester,
    242–4
Royal Shakespeare Company (RSC)
    Barton affair, 4
    and equal opportunities, 219
    literary managers, 200, 212, 231–5
    national rôle, 204
    and production dramaturgs, 212
    and Tynan, 169
Rülicke, Käthe, 132, 134, 142
Russell, Willy, 239

Salberg, Derek, 154–6
Savage, Ralph, 13
Savoy Theatre, 89
Scandinavia, 1, 40, 109, 141, 215
Schiller, Friedrich, 28, 37–40, 56, 117,
    125, 162
Schink, J. F., 37
Schlösser, Reiner, 146n
Schnitzler, Arthur, 91
Schönemann, Johann Friedrich, 27
Schreyvogel, Joseph, 41
Schröder, Friedrich Ludwig, 38
Scotland, 91, 256n
Scottish Repertory Company, 92
selection of plays, 2, 93–7, 101
Shaffer, Peter, 170, 176–7
Shakespeare Committee, 79
Shakespeare Memorial National
    Theatre Committee, 153

Shakespeare, William
    in eighteenth century, 16, 18
    in nineteenth century, 53, 58, 63,
        67, 69, 87
    actor-playwright, 13
    and Brecht, 117, 131
    and Chandos, 155
    and German theatre, 28, 32, 38, 39
    Henry V, 175
    institutionalisation, 153
    and Jonson, 14
    and National Theatre, 156, 169
    Othello, 171, 173
    Richard II, 80
    and Tynan, 169
Shaw, George Bernard
    and actor-managers' wives, 55
    and Barker, 80, 90
    and Chandos, 155
    Court Theatre, 91
    dramatic criticism, 57–8, 61
    and Lessing, 82–3
    and national theatre concept, 81
    New Drama, 69
    NT performances, 169
    playreading, 72n
    rehearsal authority, 65–6
    rise of the playwright, 62, 65
    Tynan on, 157
Sheridan, Richard Brinsley, 14
Sidney, Philip, 18
Sikorski, General, 181
Sirett, Paul, 234–5
Smollett, Tobias, 15, 17
Society of Authors, 64
Soho Theatre, 235
Solger, Karl, 39
Sophocles, 169
Sosulski, Michael, 33
Spain, 109, 142
spectators, Brechtian view, 117
Spinetti, Victor, 170
St James's Theatre, London, 54–5

Stage Society, 80
Stahl, Ernst Leopold, 90
Stalin, Joseph, 120, 181
Stanislavski, 89, 133, 166
Steele, Richard, 18
Steffin, Margarete, 121, 122
Stephen Joseph Theatre, Scarborough,
    244–50
Stephens, John Russell, 49, 64
Stoppard, Tom, 190
Strabo, 5–6
Strindberg, August, 169
Strittmatter, Erwin, 129
Sweden, 166, 182
Swift, Jonathan, 157

Taylor, Tom, 75n
Tenschert, Joachim, 139–40
Terry, Ellen, 60–1
Theatre Royal, Stratford East, 234
Theatre Workshop, 166
Theatre Writers' Union, 208
Theatre Writing Partnership, 236,
    250–2
Thomson, Lynn, 4–5
Tieck, Ludwig, 37–40, 112
Tobin, John, 71n
Tolstoy, Leo, 69
Toole, J. L., 63
Townsend, Gordon, 245
training, literary managers, 216–19
translations, 224
Tree, Herbert Beerbohm, 47, 55, 58,
    63, 66
Trotsky, Leon, 120
Trott, Lloyd, 216
Tynan, Kathleen, 157, 190
Tynan, Kenneth
    and Brecht, 158–9, 161, 165–6,
        168–9, 171–2, 176, 191
    and censorship, 165, 170
    concept of dramaturg, 156–61
    Drama Committee member, 156

educator, 165–73, 178
first official English dramaturg, 2,
    143, 152
and Granville Barker, 158, 160, 168
He That Plays the King, 156–7
and Hochhuth's *Soldiers*, 180–6
legacy, 189–92, 200–1, 264
and Lessing, 158, 178, 191
manuscripts, 152
and *Messingkauf Dialogues*,
    111, 159
and new writers, 174–5
NT appointment, 1, 110, 154, 265
NT early period, 161–5
NT job description, 163–5
NT job title, 7, 186
NT post-1968, 186–9
NT programmes, 165–73
NT publications, 171–2
NT rehearsal politics, 176–80
NT rôle, 7, 85, 160
Oh! Calcutta, 181
and Olivier, 157–8, 160, 167–8,
    172–5, 180–2, 185–91
style, 231

United States
    and Brecht, 109–10, 126
    cultural prejudices, 210–11, 215
    dramaturgs, 1, 10, 202
    dramaturgy debate, 219
    dramaturgy training, 218
    Literary Managers and Dramaturgs
        of America, 110
    litigation, 4–5
    McCarthyism, 215
    O'Neill Centre, 209
    professionalisation of dramaturgs, 109
    public attention to dramaturgs, 3
    theatre funding, 266
    Yale School of Dramaturgy,
        18n, 110
unsolicited scripts, 226, 234, 251

Vedrenne, J. E., 89, 91
Vega, Lope de, 39, 170
Veltman, Chloe, 210
Vitez, Antoine, 142
Voltaire, 34, 35

Waters, Steve, 206, 213, 215
Weber, Carl, 110, 149n
Wedekind, Franz, 170
Weigel, Helene, 127–30, 138, 158
Wekwerth, Manfred, 129, 137, 142,
    150n, 194n
Welles, Orson, 157, 190
Werbedramaturg, 133
Wesker, Arnold, 157
Whaley, Arthur, 122
Whelan, Peter, 214
Whitehead, William, 15
Whitworth, Geoffrey, 78
Whybrow, Graham, 119, 225–31
Wienerische Dramaturgie, 37
Wilde, Oscar, 57, 62

Wilkins, W., 62
Wilkinson, Spenser, 80
Willett, John, 109, 111–12, 142
Williams, Emlyn, 169
Willoughby, W., 15
Wilmot, Lord, 154
Wilson, Effingham, 79, 153
Wilson, Laurence, 240
Winkler, Theodor, 39
Winston, James, 53
women, 55–6, 210, 219, 233
Wright, Nicholas, 220, 224
Writernet, 209–10, 237, 252n
Writers' Guild of Great Britain, 207
writers' workshops, 96
writing. *See* playwrights

Yale School of Dramaturgy, 18n, 110
Yeats, W. B., 91

Zeffirrelli, Franco, 169
Zuckmayer, Carl, 124